Trust

Interdisciplinary Perspectives

Volume 5

Editor-in-Chief

Takashi Inoguchi, Tokyo Sattelite, University of Niigata Prefecture, Tokyo, Tokyo, Japan

Series Editors

Mariko Hasegawa, Graduate University for Advanced Studies, Kanagawa, Japan
Tatsuya Kameda, Department of Social Psychology, The University of Tokyo, Tokyo, Japan
John Keane, The University of Sydney, Sydney, Australia
Taiki Takahashi, Center for Experimental Research in Social Sciences, Hokkaido University, Sapporo, Hokkaido, Japan
Ezra Vogel, Department of Sociology, Harvard University, Cambridge, MA, USA

This series presents interdisciplinary publications on trust. Trust is one of those rich concepts that have various meanings, some strong, others weak, some straightforward, others subtle. For instance, tryst, a medieval English word, means, in the context of a hare-hunt, the hunter who waits at the fringe of the forest to kill hares with a stick when they are driven out by big noises made by other hunters inside the forest. On the other hand, when one says, I trust that it will be fine tomorrow, its meaning is not strong.

More conceptually, trust is known as something that can be most useful in minimizing the costs of misunderstanding and transactions when the goal is to forge bridges and enhance bonds, launch joint undertakings, or establish reciprocal relationships. Without societies based on trust, sustained prosperity is far more difficult to achieve. The concept of trust is also very useful in understanding the propensity to take initiatives, to avoid risks, to enter into or withdraw from collaborations, and to shape and share values, norms and rules.

This series examines the meaning and its probable consequences of trust or distrust in various settings from various academic disciplines, not necessarily overtly confined to that of philosophy. Specialists of geography, anthropology, biology, neuroscience, sociology, political science and philosophy can venture to pen a volume from their respective angles. The resulting books will be both enlightening and enjoyable reading. This series welcomes proposals in these broad areas all over the world.

More information about this series at http://www.springer.com/series/15199

Satoru Kimura · Yasuhide Nakamura

Poor Quality Pharmaceuticals in Global Public Health

 Springer

Satoru Kimura
Department of Reference Standards
Pharmaceutical and Device Regulatory
Science Society of Japan
Osaka, Japan

Yasuhide Nakamura
School of Nursing and Rehabilitation
Konan Women's University
Kobe, Japan

ISSN 2509-7679   ISSN 2509-7903   (electronic)
Trust
Interdisciplinary Perspectives
ISBN 978-981-15-2091-4   ISBN 978-981-15-2089-1   (eBook)
https://doi.org/10.1007/978-981-15-2089-1

This Springer imprint is published by the registered company Springer Nature Singapore Pte Ltd.
The registered company address is: 152 Beach Road, #21-01/04 Gateway East, Singapore 189721, Singapore

Preface

Development of This Book

Kimura, one of the co-authors of this book, was long engaged in clinical development and pharmacovigilance activities for pharmaceutical products at several different foreign-affiliated pharmaceutical companies. He currently conducts surveys and research on drug-related social adverse events. The association he belongs to supplies the reference standards for pharmaceutical products that are listed in the Japanese Pharmacopoeia. Kimura has a great concern about the quality of pharmaceutical products.

Nakamura, another co-author of this book, is the foremost authority on global maternal and child health, and is a specialist in the discipline of international cooperation. Nakamura supervised Kimura throughout his master's course to doctoral course.

This book is newly written on the basis of Kimura's doctoral thesis. Needless to say, a doctoral thesis is the product of tripartite cooperation with the supervisor. This book was developed by inspiration generated through discussion between Nakamura and Kimura, both of whom are commonly concerned with public health, although their specialty and experience differ.

Purpose and Significance of This Book

This book is expected to be read by not only specialists engaged in pharmaceutical administration and regulations but also researchers, practitioners, and policy-makers who are concerned with global health. As they are goods indispensable to global public health, biomedicines have nowadays spread widely over low- through to high-income countries. Securing quality for pharmaceutical products, especially generic medicines, is an essential requirement for promotion of public health. This is a critical concern and policy challenge for pharmaceutical administration and regulations in each country as well as international organizations including the World Health Organization (WHO). Nevertheless, the problem of poor quality medicines, that is the theme of this book, has not been discussed in such a high profile manner, and the threats or issues associated with the problem have rarely attracted attention of the media or attention in the field of public health. On the other hand, some specialists consider that the problem is too complicated to fully understand its core nature.

In 1985, the WHO raised questions about the quality of medicines distributed among low-income countries; the Organization pointed out challenges regarding counterfeit and substandard medicines. In 2006, i.e., 21 years after the WHO raised the questions, the international society established the International Medical Products Anti-Counterfeiting Taskforce (IMPACT) under the initiative of WHO to initiate activities to eradicate counterfeit medicines. Although the WHO initially raised the problem of counterfeit and substandard medicines, the IMPACT focused on counterfeit medicines, which may confuse readers. Several reasons existed behind this discrepancy and the authors try to clarify these reasons in this book. The IMPACT initiative defined counterfeit medicines but did not clearly define substandard medicines. This might be because the drug specification is the concept common to the world and any deviation from that is self-evident. In reality, however, it is almost impossible to distinguish counterfeit from substandard medicines. Nevertheless, the Taskforce tried to define and combat counterfeit medicines only, which further complicated the problems related to poor quality pharmaceuticals.

It would be a straightforward scenario if it could be said that criminals make counterfeit medicines, whereas substandard medicines are legitimate but attributable to immature technical skills. However, the situation, in reality, is far from simplistic and adopting this explanation of counterfeit or substandard may lead us in a wrong direction. Specialists in pharmaceutical products who were engaged in the IMPACT indicated that the following facts got intertwined with one another, which has made the problems related to counterfeit medicines develop into an international political issue: counterfeits have caused confrontation about intellectual property rights and emotional conflict between the two worlds, that is, one consisting of high-income countries and the other composed of emerging as well as middle- and low-income countries; counterfeits are mixed up with substandard medicines; developing countries have immature capacities to adequately implement pharmaceutical administration and regulations; and crackdowns on counterfeits have been driven by law enforcement agencies. This indication implies several important insights suggestive of clues to the problem of poor quality pharmaceuticals. Firstly, although counterfeit and substandard medicines are different in nature from each other, the two are internationally mixed up. Secondly, developed countries are concerned with prevention of counterfeiting branded medicines, whereas emerging and developing countries have concerns about the quality of generic medicines. Thirdly, there exist conflicts of interests and confrontation of views among the international organizations including the WHO, developed countries, emerging countries, and developing countries. It is necessary to understand each of these pieces and create a bigger picture in understanding how they interact with one another.

The theme of this book appears different depending on where stakeholders stand in the real world. This is mainly attributable to the fact that pharmaceutical products are goods widely incorporated into the global society. Many citizens in high-, middle- to low-income countries cannot live their daily lives without biomedicines. In the past, countries and regions had their native medicines, which were used to fight diseases. Nowadays, research and development, manufacture, and distribution of biomedicines have spread globally, whereas regulations on these medicines are put into the hands of state sovereignty. There is therefore the need to have a basic understanding about different aspects of pharmaceutical products in the era of globalization.

In this book, the authors define "poor quality pharmaceuticals" as those included in the two following categories, i.e., counterfeit and substandard. Whatever the cause may be, poor quality pharmaceuticals adversely affect treatment of patients as well as maintenance and improvement of public health, which has been proven by many reported cases. Poor quality pharmaceuticals were initially distributed only in low-income countries but subsequently have been disseminated even to high-income countries. The IMACPT reached a deadlock shortly, several years, after its establishment. Following the deadlock, the international framework to combat counterfeit medicines has been taken over by the Member State Mechanism, which was a successor of the IMPACT and was proposed in 2012. In low- and middle-income countries, however, no signs suggestive of progress toward resolution of the problem of poor quality pharmaceuticals have yet been noticed. Why did the IMPACT reach the deadlock and has the problem of poor quality pharmaceuticals not been resolved, despite the efforts made by the international society? To avoid any misunderstandings, the authors would consider that adequate countermeasures have not been conceived because where the problem exists cannot be identified, or the individuals concerned do not want to face up to the reality of the situation.

This book is not a current commentary about the problem of poor quality pharmaceuticals. The problem persists. This book focuses on the international move noted over a period from the establishment of IMPACT to its transition to the Member State Mechanism because this period can be regarded as a temporal chapter. The purpose of this book is to offer an interpretation of the problems of poor quality pharmaceuticals on the basis of our investigation and discuss the lessons to be learnt from the outcome of our work.

Nowadays, pharmaceutical products, especially generic medicines, are essential tools for public health in low- to high-income countries. The Alma-Ata Declaration of 1978 identified primary health care (PHC) as the key to the attainment of the goal of "Health for All". Among the eight activities listed in the PHC, essential drugs were indicated in the 8th activity. The Declaration adopted a breakthrough approach in that for the purpose of attaining the goal of Health for All, not many different types of expensive medicines but instead a list of carefully selected, simple, and affordable medicines should be prepared in accordance with the actual situation of each country. Subsequently, a variety of stakeholders, including but not limited to high-income countries which have enough capacities to develop biomedicines, low- and middle-income countries which have no choice but to rely on imported medicines, emerging countries which are interested in manufacture and export of generic medicines, giant pharmaceutical companies which develop novel medicines, manufacturing companies for generics, donor countries which promote international cooperation regarding pharmaceutical products, and international NGOs and NPOs which are active in the field of low-income countries in which pharmaceuticals are not available, all participated in the discussion about the challenges raised by poor quality pharmaceuticals and have generated heated debate.

As described above, the problem of poor quality pharmaceuticals is a global issue from the viewpoint of public health on one hand and is a political challenge involving international cooperation and situations on the other hand. Complicated international and social factors are entangled in the problem of poor quality pharmaceuticals. Many findings and opinions have so far been reported on the basis of specialty in each area such as chemical analysis, pharmaceutical regulations, crackdown on criminals, and regulations on manufacture and distribution. However, previous studies have scarcely paid attention to the complexity of this problem so as to understand it by viewing the entire picture. If this book offers any new perspectives to the previous research, then the authors consider it significant to publish this book.

Scope and Approach for This Book

This book focuses on biomedicines (modern medicines) which are used to treat diseases in human beings. Among them, the authors especially pay attention to generic medicines which are tools for public health. It is assumed that generic medicines are handled as prescription drugs from the viewpoint of pharmaceutical regulations. In this book, the term "biomedicine" refers to medicines discovered and developed on the basis of the application of the principles of the natural sciences, especially biology and biochemistry that are the outcomes of modern sciences.

The WHO has a great concern about the quality of not only biomedicines but also traditional medicines. Some readers may feel dissatisfaction with this book because it does not discuss the quality of traditional medicines. The authors consider that the quality-related issues of traditional medicines should be assessed in the culture and environment that have fostered such traditional medicines and that it would be impractical to apply the global standards to all traditional medicines available across the globe. Some of them have already become industrial products, whereas others have remained available as herbal medicines. This diversity of formulation is one of the most excellent characteristics of traditional medicines. The authors would like to discuss the quality of traditional medicines in the future, but in this book, we focus on biomedicines.

The scope of this book covers a period from 1985 at which the WHO raised questions about quality of medicines to 2009 at which a meeting of the Executive Board of WHO was held; at the meeting, criticisms against the IMPACT were leveled by low- and middle-income countries. During this quarter century, jumping on the globalization bandwagon was appraised and, cross-border movement of goods and people was rapidly accelerated. During these times of globalization, the problem of poor quality pharmaceuticals was elicited. For a period from 2006 to the present (i.e., the end of 2018), a milestone in the international framework to address the problem of poor quality pharmaceuticals occurred. This is the transition from the IMPACT to the Member State Mechanism, as described above. How the WHO handled the problem of poor quality pharmaceuticals also changed before and after the milestone. The transition to the Member State Mechanism represents a setback or a deadlock of the IMPACT. Establishment of the Member State Mechanism was based on reflection of IMPACT. The transition from the IMPACT, which was the core in international tackling activities, to the Member State Mechanism indicated renewal of the international countermeasures. This transition is symbolized by renewing the definition of poor quality pharmaceuticals. When the IMPACT was launched, the abbreviation SSFFC (substandard/spurious/falsely-labelled/falsified/counterfeit) was used. The terms used in this abbreviation are synonyms of the term "fake" and it emphasized the nature of counterfeiting through the utilization of parallelism. The renewed definition emphasizing the nature of counterfeiting drew strong backlash from low- and middle-income countries. If some Member States would be considered by others to connive at distribution of medicines which are strongly suspected to be counterfeit, then such States might lose face. Reasons behind this issue require some discussion. At the World Health Assembly in 2017, it was agreed to adopt the terminology "Substandard and Falsified (SF) medical products" to express poor quality medicines.

In Part I, we take three approaches. First of all, the authors discuss the background behind the dissemination of the phenomenon of poor quality pharmaceuticals across the world. Then, we discuss that specification and standardization specify quality and at the same time, in high-income countries, promote advancement of biomedicines which are industrial products and contribute to, through technology transfer, global spread of biomedicines. The technology transfer has enabled low- and middle-income countries to manufacture medicines. To what extent technology transfer takes root in recipient countries has a great impact on the quality of medicines to be manufactured and distributed to the recipient countries. Namely, whether or not technology transfer is successful determines a foundation for geographical expansion of poor quality pharmaceuticals.

Secondly, the authors observe that several events and tides occurring in the times of globalization, coupled with networks involving pharmaceutical products, complicated the problem of poor quality pharmaceuticals. These events include, among others, monopolizing control by high-income countries of medicines through the use of intellectual property rights; disease-related challenges to be addressed in low and middle-income countries and the WHO's policies on pharmaceutical products; the HIV/AIDS pandemic across the world; dissatisfaction of developing countries with international support given by developed countries; sudden rise of emerging countries; and tension between the developed and the emerging and developing worlds. It should be understood that the WHO was forced to search for a solution under the environment involving these interests of stakeholders.

Thirdly, when each of these events occurred, no one might expect that it had direct relations with the quality-related problems for pharmaceuticals. However, multiple events among them interacted with one another complicating these problems more and more. These events include some factors which may be accidental, e.g., emergence of HIV/AIDS.

In Part II, the authors shed light on the local situations and proceed to our discussion in contrast to Part I which focuses on globalization. Here, as a third approach, the authors compare emerging countries with Japan regarding the actual status of the market of healthcare services and access to the market. Part II presents three case studies. The first two are concerned with the actual situations in Indonesia and India, so-called emerging countries. It was found that in these countries, the market wealthy individuals access is actually separated from the market poor individuals' use. In not only emerging countries but also low- and middle-income countries, people living in poverty have the greatest need for public health. The market of healthcare services these people access is vulnerable and completely insufficient, as indicated by case reports across the world which demonstrated that prescription-only drugs can be obtained without physicians' diagnoses and prescriptions and are used for self-medication.

The final case study is based on observation of the market of health services in Japan. The quality of pharmaceuticals available in Japan is kept high and all of the Japanese citizens benefit from high-quality pharmaceutical products. In addition, it is extremely difficult for someone to smuggle counterfeit medicines into legitimate distribution channels. In Japan, even a small-scale detection of counterfeit medicines is covered by the media as a rare, serious incident. Ordinary people even do not know the terminology "counterfeit medicines". Understanding the structure and characteristics of the Japanese market of pharmaceutical products provides significant suggestions when discussing the challenges related to the market and access to the market in low- and middle-income countries. The Japanese market of healthcare services is based on the universal health insurance system in Japan. However, introduction of a universal health insurance scheme is never the same as what type of market is formed for healthcare services. Designing a market is a challenge involving a state's policy. This is one of the concerns the authors address in this book.

The greatest characteristic of the Japanese market of healthcare services is that the market is in fact a single market based on the universal health insurance system. The single market demonstrates attainment of fair access to the market. It might be true that fair access is an incentive to form the single market. In the Japanese market, several systems assure that on the supply side, generic medicines and their counterpart originators can be competitive. In other words, incentives exist for both the supply and demand sides. In addition, there is a mechanism according to which the pharmaceutical regulatory authorities in Japan adequately intervene in the market, which successfully functions to keep the quality of pharmaceuticals high. This is an effective complementary approach to the market.

The theme of this book starts with the questions raised by the WHO. It is almost impossible to exactly grasp the whole picture of the impact given by poor quality pharmaceuticals on the socioeconomics and health in the framework of global public health. What we can do is to interpret cases discovered and reported on in an attempt to develop a model with which we estimate the magnitude of such impact. In order for us to achieve meaningful outcomes, the issue to be addressed is to identify where real problems exist, at the heart of the target of our concern, or in developing our understanding about the target. In other words, we have been critically reflective in our approach. If we had tried to resolve problems by prioritizing the norms and concept of high-income countries and not taking into account the actual situations of low- and middle-income countries, then we might have fallen into a pitfall.

In Japan, the following remonstrance has existed over as long as 800 years: *Ogoreru Mono Wa Hisashikarazu* in Japanese (which means "Pride goes before a fall"). If a sense of superiority over developing countries underlies the norms of high-income countries, globalized pharmaceuticals across the world cannot be regulated. In the world, the greatest desire to access pharmaceutical products may be derived from those living in poverty in low- and middle-income countries who comprise the greatest number of population. What approach should we try so as to build a service system for pharmaceuticals which would satisfy these people? In the last part of this book, the authors would like to address this question and learn lessons from what we have discussed throughout this book.

Terms

In this book, the authors use as a rule the term "pharmaceutical". The term "medicine" is a general term in the field of medical science. The term "drug" may sometimes imply an association with drug-related crimes. On the contrary, the term "pharmaceutical" gives a strong image of finished products which are manufactured, distributed, and dispensed to patients under pharmaceutical regulations. The term "pharmaceutical" is used in combination with those such as "company", "business", or "industry" in the fields of social science and economy. The authors use "drug" and "medicine" in the phrases that are internationally well accepted.

Several different terms are conventionally used to indicate the grade of quality for pharmaceutical products, e.g., "substandard", "counterfeit", "low", "poor", and "fake". According to the authors' experience in conducting interview surveys in the field in India, the expression "low quality" was accepted with the least resistance because it gives a neutral sound. As a matter of course, individuals are proud of their native countries. No one wants to be asked about his or her native country by others using words that have a negative image. The expression "low-quality medicine" rarely implies illegality. Conversely, the terms "counterfeit" and "fake" emphasize the act of producing a fraudulent copy. This book grapples with pharmaceutical products that do not satisfy specifications whether they are illegal or legitimate, and therefore, adopts the expression "poor quality". This expression would not be contradictory to the fact that countries have their own definitions for counterfeiting.

In this book, the authors use as a rule the following expressions according to the categories of the World Bank, when describing the situations of individual countries from the viewpoint of economic growth: high-income country; middle-income country; and low-income country. Emerging countries are not always middle-income countries and we therefore use the term "emerging country" when it is more appropriate to use this term. With regard to quality and distribution of pharmaceutical products, however, the authors sometimes use the terms "developed", "emerging", and "developing" countries. In this book, these three categories are defined. The concept of public health is based on the greatest number of population belonging to a certain scope. The scope in some cases covers only a limited district in a single country, the whole state, and even a regional target of the world. The authors would like to emphasize that this book is concerned with public health covering a global scope and include the expression "global public health" in the title of this book. In light of the above-stated explanation, the authors do hope that readers understand the intention of the title of this book, consisting of the terms "poor quality", "pharmaceuticals", and "global public health".

Osaka, Japan   Satoru Kimura
Kobe, Japan   Yasuhide Nakamura

Acknowledgements

The authors have attempted to look through a small window, i.e., the quality of pharmaceutical products, to view and get into a world that is wider and far more complicated than we imagined. Without valuable advice and cooperation from our important supporters in helping us get into that world, and precious episodes about the world spoken to us by our kind collaborators, the authors' curiosity could not have brought about anything meaningful to light.

First of all, we would like to express our sincere gratitude to Mr. Kenji Toda OBE, Senior Management Director, The Health Care Science Institute Japan, and Fellow of University College London for stimulating our curiosity into a spirit of inquiry. A master's thesis and a doctoral thesis constituted the process that gave birth to this book from the spirit of inquiry. We would like to express our cordial gratitude to Prof. Nobuhide Sawamura and Prof. Masato Kawamori at the Graduate School of Human Sciences, Osaka University for their reviewing the doctoral thesis. Discussions with Prof. Chihiro Shirakawa from an anthropological point of view were very inspiring.

We are deeply grateful to the Editorial Department of Springer Nature for accepting the publication of this book, and to Mrs. Chisato Kitagawa and her associates for accepting a difficult translation job while trying to understand what the Japanese manuscript intended to communicate. Dr. Joe Fallowfield M.B.Ch.B. LLM., who for many years was involved in Drug Safety in the pharmaceutical industry, and who was the first reader of the English translated manuscript and gave us valuable advice to help us assume what impression on translated concepts non-Japanese readers may have when they read this book. The authors will be responsible for any errors and anything which could cause readers to have difficulty comprehending the context and nuance used throughout this book.

The Pharmaceutical and Medical Device Regulatory Science Society of Japan, for which KIMURA Satoru works, gave a great deal of thoughtful consideration to allow KIMURA to concentrate both on his duties and field survey research. Many co-workers, friends, especially Dr. Toshio Suwa and our family members strongly recommended and encouraged us to publish the doctoral thesis in a scientific book so as to communicate our message to the public overseas. Their boost was essential.

Finally, we would be extremely pleased if all individuals engaged in the publication of this book would pick it up sometime in the future and remember the collaborative work with us for the publication. Technical assistance, i.e., how to use Microsoft Word and how to achieve formatting at a high level, was an inevitable process when the manuscript was stepping into a book. Whenever we have this book in our hands, we will remember the relationships with all people contributing to the publication of this book and will be filled with a sense of gratitude.

June 2019   Satoru Kimura
                                                               Yasuhide Nakamura

Contents

Abbreviations

BRICS	Brazil, Russia, India, China, South Africa
CDSCO	Central Drugs Standard Control Organisation
EMA	European Medicines Agency
FDA	US. Food & Drug Administration
GMP	Good Manufacturing Practice
HIV/AIDS	Human immunodeficiency virus/Acquired immunodeficiency syndrome
IFPMA	International Federation of Pharmaceutical Manufacturers & Association
IMPACT	International Medical Products Anti-Counterfeiting Taskforce
JPMA	The Japan Pharmaceutical Manufacturers Association
MDGs	Millennium Development Goals
MHLW	Ministry of Health, Labour and Welfare
MSF	Médecins Sans Frontières
OECD	Organisation for Economic Co-operation and Development
PIC/S	Pharmaceutical Inspection Convention and Pharmaceutical Inspection Co-operation Scheme
PSI	Pharmaceutical Security of Institute
SDGs	Sustainable Development Goals
SSFFC	Substandard/spurious/falsely-labelled/falsified/counterfeit
UNICRI	United Nations Interregional Crime and Justice Research Institute
UNODC	United Nations Office on Drugs and Crime
WHO	World Health Organization
WIPO	World Intellectual Property Organization
WTO	World Trade Organization

Chapter 1
Introduction: What "Goods" Are Pharmaceuticals?

1.1 Usage of Terms

Although it is difficult to strictly determine the situations in which some of the terms used in this book should be individually employed, the authors would like to describe how we use these terms in this book, for the purpose of avoiding criticisms or misunderstanding that our usage is too subjective.

Developed countries: Countries in which there exist research-based pharmaceutical companies with adequate capabilities to develop new medicines; in which infrastructure on both the hardware and software aspects to regulate the flow from development through to use of pharmaceuticals, such as guidelines, laws, and regulations concerning pharmaceutical affairs, are established and actually function; and which participate in the International Council for Harmonization of Technical Requirements for Pharmaceuticals for Human Use (ICH).

As the members, the drug regulatory authorities of Japan, the US, EU, Switzerland, and Canada as well as pharmaceutical industrial associations in Japan, the US, and EU participate in the ICH. As the standing observers, the WHO and the International Federation of Pharmaceutical Manufacturers & Associations (IFPMA) participate in the ICH (As of October 23, 2015).

Emerging countries: Countries which are the observers of the ICH but do not have an obligation to follow the matters decided by the ICH. Those which are not as evolved as developed countries in terms of capabilities to develop new medicines and ability to raise proposals for code of practice or guidelines. Those which export generic medicines as a result of remarkable development of national pharmaceutical industries during the period of globalization, and which are represented by India, China, South Korea, Taiwan, Brazil, and Russia. As the other observers, the Asia-Pacific Economic Cooperation (APEC), the Association of Southeast Asian Nations (ASEAN), and the other regional initiatives participate in the ICH.

Developing countries: Countries which have no or insufficient capacities to meet the national needs for medicines by self-manufacturing and therefore, rely on import

© Springer Nature Singapore Pte Ltd. 2020
S. Kimura and Y. Nakamura, *Poor Quality Pharmaceuticals in Global Public Health*, Trust 5, https://doi.org/10.1007/978-981-15-2089-1_1

of medicines from emerging countries, etc. to meet them; and do not have adequate pharmaceutical regulatory capacities, testing facilities for medicines, manpower, and several other relevant factors.

Next, the authors would like to focus on the difference between "poor quality pharmaceuticals" and "the problem of poor quality pharmaceuticals." When someone says "the problem of a certain matter," we are prone to consider that everybody has a common awareness of the matter as a problem. However, whether a given event is regarded as a problem or not is determined by individual subjectivity. When we say "the problem," we have to answer the question: "For whom is it a problem?"

The "problem" of quality is highly unlikely to be common between the developed world and the emerging and developing world because what it means may be different between the two worlds. In other words, poor quality pharmaceuticals that happen to exist in the real world differ from poor quality pharmaceuticals that are recognized as problematic. In this book, the authors are careful as much as possible in using the terms depending on the situations.

1.2   Goods Contributing to Life and Health

1.2.1   Health Care and Pharmaceutical Products

No one would disagree with the argument that pharmaceutical products are goods contributing to life and health. Pharmaceuticals play substantially large roles in health care. In the times when medical practice was not separated from dispensary, not as in modern times, medical doctors by themselves invented and produced drugs.

A Japanese surgeon Seishu Hanaoka (1760–1835) is well known because by himself he developed a general anesthetic and successfully removed breast cancer under general anesthesia for the first time in the world. Needless to say, pharmaceutical products are not equal to health care. However, if pharmaceuticals should be taken away from modern medicine, healthcare professionals would lose measures to proactively treat patients and to effectively prevent infectious diseases.

Medicines requiring physicians' prescriptions were called "ethical drugs" in the past. This may not be unrelated to the fact that medicines were used on the basis of high ideals, i.e., health care, (or to the principle that medicines should be used on the basis of the high ideals of health care). At present, this term is not frequently used but instead the expression "prescription-only drugs" is generally used. This suggests that environments surrounding pharmaceutical products and our mindset have changed.

Prescriptions exist within the framework regulating legitimate medical doctors and institutions. The increased popularity of the term "prescription-only drugs" among ordinary people may serve to indicate that pharmaceuticals have been more strongly regarded as part of the legitimate infrastructure of society than as something with an ethical nature. An individual with an illness becomes a patient when he or she is incorporated into the social infrastructure.

1.2.2 Health Care and Pharmaceutical Products from the Perspective of Economists

What goods do economists consider are healthcare and pharmaceutical products? A Japanese economist Hirofumi Uzawa[1] writes as follows, "Healthcare provides services to keep citizens in good health and help them to be free from disease or injury" (Uzawa 2000).

His description indicates that pharmaceutical products are the specific goods and measures required to provide healthcare services. He continues to observe that health care needs to be provided as a rule-free of charge or at low prices, but health care is a limited resource and cannot be provided infinitely as need arises. His observation means that health care by nature is located between what it should be and what it is in reality.

For the purpose of providing health care as a rule-free of charge or at low prices, a public burden is necessary to minimize an individuals' burden. In which way or under what systems should such provision be achieved? Problems with poor quality pharmaceuticals are sometimes discussed under the concept of "market failure," although this hackneyed phrase of "market failure" does not help us to understand the real issue. We need to discuss what the market failure is and why the failure continues.

Rich countries face ever-increasing national health expenditure due to an aging society as well as advancements in medical technology and pharmaceutical products. On the other hand, one to two billion people at the bottom of society in the world cannot get out of the difficulty in accessing essential medicines, where markets for medicines in impoverished economies are formed separately from the official market of healthcare services.

1.3 Goods Controlled by the State

1.3.1 Risks of and Regulation for Pharmaceutical Products

At present, modern medicine (including pharmaceutical products) is controlled by the state under its system. Almost all things involving modern medicine, including the contents of health care, human resources providing health care, and facilities and materials (medical devices, pharmaceutical products, sanitary materials) necessary for the provision of healthcare services are controlled by the state. For pharmaceutical products, in particular, strict control is required.

The English word "pharmaceutical" is derived from the Greek word "pharmakon" having two meanings, i.e., a medicine and a poison. This indicates that due to their

---

[1] An American economist Joseph Eugene Stiglitz who was awarded the Nobel Prize for Economics in 2001 attended classes of Hirofumi Uzawa while he was a student at University of Chicago.

nature, pharmaceuticals are associated with potential risks of causing health hazard and, therefore, require strict control. The historical development of the establishment of a system to separate prescribing medicines from dispensing them also came from the potential risks of pharmaceuticals.

Many of the social problems attributable to iatrogenesis of medicine pointed out by Illich (1976)[2] are generated from interactions between social needs and potential risks related to pharmaceutical products. A typical example of them is the social drug suffering[3] represented by the thalidomide disaster. If drug-induced adverse effects, i.e., sufferings are considered as only attributable to mistakes by license holders for the pharmaceutical products concerned or by the administrative authorities, then the social context of pharmaceutical products will be missed.

One of the victims of drug-induced sufferings in Japan raised the following questions: "Don't you think that drug-induced suffering is caused by drugs?" This delivers the real intention that the usefulness and hazard of a drug are generated and amplified through human activities. Regulating pharmaceutical products is an important policy of the state. However, the notion that pharmaceutical regulations enforced by the administrative authorities are the only ways of finding solutions restricts the vision and options for problem-solving. Problems related to both iatrogenesis and quality can be resolved in the social context.

Box 1: Drug-Induced Suffering in Japan and Social Perspective

In Japan, many drug-induced sufferings occurred after the end of World War II. The predominant ones include the diphtheria immunization incident, penicillin shock incident, thalidomide incident, cold-medicines-in-ampoules incident, SMON (Subacute Myelo-Optico-Neuropathy) incident, muscle contracture incident, dialyzer induced ophthalmologic disorders incident, AIDS incident, blood product induced HCV (hepatitis C virus) infection incident, MMR (measles, mumps, and rubella) vaccine incident, sorivudine incident, human dried dura mater induced prion infection (CJD: Creutzfeldt-Jakob Disease) incident, incident of bovine pericardium induced infection with probably acid-fast bacilli, and gefitinib incident (Doi et al. 2013).

One of the major reasons why so many drug-induced sufferings occurred in Japan after World War II was because the Japanese health insurance scheme became widespread, which assured patients' access to health care and made it unnecessary for physicians to think about a patients' financial situation.

---

[2] In his book entitled "Limits to Medicine" (1976), Ivan Illich discusses clinical iatrogenesis, social iatrogenesis, and cultural iatrogenesis, all of which result from medicalisation of life.

[3] Babies with phocomelia related to thalidomide (that was sold under the brand name of Cortegan in West Germany at that time) were born in many countries across the world. In the US, thalidomide was not approved by the FDA due to the judgment of Dr. Frances Oldham Kelsey working for FDA. However, it was disclosed that thalidomide was administered to trial subjects without permission and the disclosure triggered a move leading to the birth of "informed consent.".

Pharmaceutical companies were more and more severely competitive to lock in medical doctors with their products by excessively entertaining them for favors and overabundantly providing services with them. Defective medicines,[4] together with incautious and easygoing prescriptions, expanded health damage. Collusion between the administrative authorities and the industry, and lack of sense of responsibility delayed decisions on discontinuation or recall. Consequently, health damage led to drug scandals.

People became able to quickly and easily access healthcare services, and their dependence on medicines was intensified, which caused them to strongly rely upon prescription medicine. This was more or less one of the factors contributing to the development of drug-induced sufferings. Along with the spread of healthcare services, people recognized a change in physical condition as an illness and there was a growing tendency for individuals to depend on drug therapies (e.g., the muscle contracture incident). The medical associations and medical/pharmaceutical academia did not proactively take the initiative in preventing expansion of health damage.

In the thalidomide disaster that caused health damage across the world, it was pointed out that Grünenthal, the company that developed thalidomide, emphasized that the drug was safer than the existing hypnotic barbiturate. The background of the disaster was the intensified competition among people in obtaining sleeping pills for the purpose of escaping from the trauma that covered Europe after World War II. In the UK, it was estimated that one million people routinely took some sedatives and one in every eight prescriptions was for sleeping pills (Stephens and Brynner 2001).

1.3.2 Pharmaceutical Regulations Having the Nature of Police Laws, and Importance of the Pharmacopoeia

A pharmacopoeia is a pharmaceutical regulation and was born with the aim of securing quality of medicines. Laws and regulations established concerning pharmaceutical affairs are characterized by the strong nature of police laws used to crack down

---

[4]Defective medicines mean those which are inappropriate in terms of not only chemical substances as pharmaceutical active ingredients but also indication(s), dosage and administration, and precautions. This is closely related to how carefully an applicant company is able to develop a pharmaceutical product and to the capacity of administrative authorities in reviewing submitted registration dossiers. Lung disorder that occurred as health damage caused by gefitinib in Japan in 2002 brought about lawsuits. The focal point of the trial was the appropriateness of what was stated in the package insert of gefitinib. However, it should be considered that whether or not the use of a medicine is socially appropriate is not only attributable to the information stated in package inserts but also determined by how healthcare professionals and patients are approached regarding the use of the medicine.

on shoddy goods and illegal distribution. In particular, narcotics and antipsychotics are subject to strict control and crackdown, which indicates that risks associated with pharmaceutical products may jeopardize not only individuals but also society as a whole.

In Japan, health damage caused by clioquinol affected a large number of victims in the 1960s, which is known as the SMON (Subacute Myelo-Optico-Neuropathy) incident. In one of the lawsuits filed, the Tokyo District Court's decision discussed that the legislative intent of the pharmaceutical affairs law is "to achieve the objective from the viewpoint of law enforcement, that is, prevention of risks associated with supply of poor quality drugs."

Consequently, when problems or scandals occur in relation to medicines, responsive actions taken are to intensify crackdown or strengthen penalties so as to resolve or deter such issues. The International Medical Products Anti-Counterfeiting Taskforce (IMPACT) set the intensification of crackdown as an important pillar of the strategies to combat counterfeit drugs, as discussed in Chap. 6, and this is derived from the historical background of regulations on pharmaceutical affairs.

In Japan, the Meiji Government[5] promoted its modernization policies with western medicine as one of the keys to the policies, and greatly changed the structure of therapeutic drugs. Herbal medicinal products (Kampo products) primarily consisting of crude drugs produced in the East were replaced with chemical medicinal products as well as drugs primarily derived from western plants and their pharmaceutical products.

Pharmaceutical products (western medicinal products) indispensable to western medicine were imported by trading companies specialized in pharmaceutical business. Some of them were dishonest traders. Taking advantage of the lack of knowledge about medicines and pharmacopoeias as well as the incomplete system for crackdown, shoddy goods, and fake goods were prevalent. In order to combat this situation, the Meiji Government, with the cooperation from teachers who were "Oyatoi-gaikokujin" (foreign advisors hired by the Japanese government for their specialized knowledge to assist in the modernization of Japan at the end of the Edo Era (1600–1868) and during the Meiji Era (1868–1912)) established the first version of the Japanese Pharmacopoeia (JP) in 1886 (Japanese Meiji Emperor Year 19). Shortly after that, in 1891, the second version of JP was completed by only Japanese individuals (Nihon Yakkyokuho Kofu Hyakunen Kinen Jigyo Jikko Iinkai 1987).

The second version of JP was officially announced 3 years before the promulgation of the Meiji Constitution (that is formally called "Constitution of the Empire of Japan"), which expressly demonstrates that the critical importance of access to quality medicines was recognized from early on. This is worthy of special mention.

---

[5] In Japan, the Emperor Meiji ascended the throne in 1868 at which the Meiji era started. The Meiji Government aimed at building a new state system with the Emperor as the center of the state, and changed the name of the central city of Japan from Edo to Tokyo. The Emperor moved out of Kyoto to Tokyo (Tokyo Tento in Japanese that means transfer of the national capital to Tokyo) in 1869 (Japanese Meiji Emperor Year 2). In the Meiji era, Japan deliberately promoted modernization in order to escape from colonization by western powers. From the viewpoint of world history, the Meiji era was the period of industrial revolution in Japan.

What we learn from this history is: firstly, poor quality goods and counterfeit goods were available to consumers during the period of social changes; secondly, technical standards that should be a code, such as the Pharmacopoeia, were necessary for effective crackdowns and eradication of poor quality products; and thirdly, in Japan, at that time, problem-solving capabilities to try to catch up with the Western world were developed in a short period of time.

Box 2: Contributions by "Oyatoi-gaikokujin" in Japan

The Japanese term "Oyatoi-gaikokujin" refers to foreigners who were invited and employed by the Meiji Government, and contributed to the construction of Japan as a new state. The annual records for a period between 1872 and 1885 indicated a total of 4,357 foreign advisors consisting of 1,285 academic teachers, 1,917 engineers, 704 office clerks, 235 operatives, and 516 persons in other jobs. Among those, about 800 foreigners actually fulfilled their expected duties.

They had high level of culture and knowledge, and came from the US, the UK, France, Germany, and other developed countries to Japan. They were treated very well by the Meiji Government; the Government paid round-trip travel expenses for them, built expensive houses to lend them to the foreigners free of charge, and provided extremely high monthly salaries. For some foreigners, the maximum monthly salary was comparable to that of a minister of the Japanese central government.

In response to the preferential treatment, they substantially contributed to the construction of the State of Japan, and some of them ended their lives in the country located in the remote area of the Far East. Among them, those listed below provided memorable contributions in their individual specialty fields (of course, there were other persons who achieved the same performance as those listed below).

Guido Herman Fridolin Verbeck (the father of Japanese modern architecture), Gustave Émile Boissonade de fontarabie (the basic elements of civil and criminal laws), Karl Friedrich Hermann Roesler (the originator of the Constitution), Albert Charles Du Bousquet (establishment of the army), Sir Archibald Lucius Douglas (establishment of modern navy), Henry Willard Denison (in the field of diplomacy of the Meiji Government), Thomas William Kinder (establishment of the monetary system), Alexander Allan Shand (in the field of bank management), Gottfried Wagener (in the field of industrial development), Henry Dyer (Professor of the current University of Tokyo) and many other professors at universities, David Murray (in the field of school system reform), Edward Sylvester Morse (in the field of biology), and Ernest Francisco Fenollosa (in the fields of philosophy and art).

> While thoroughly depending on the hired foreign advisors, Japan success-
> fully fostered Japanese individuals who were fully capable of making Japan
> independent in the area of technology in as short as 15 years (Umetani 2007).

The capacity of fostering capable human resources by a state itself is the very
basic element for construction of the state. The high salaries paid to the hired foreign
advisors were necessary costs that Japan had to bear to be reborn as a modern state.
These costs were covered by the value created by extremely hard work of ordinary
people. This was totally different from the way of achieving international cooperation
nowadays, although the common thing was that Japan received human aid from
various foreign countries.

1.4 Goods as Public Health

1.4.1 Sociality and Public Nature of Pharmaceutical Products

A Japanese bacteriologist Yoshio Kawakita paid special attention to the argument
made by P. Frank, who is called the father of public health, that medical doctors
consider diseases only as individual patients' issues and are almost indifferent to
types of illnesses involving the people and, therefore, the administration of a state
must protect the health of the people in the state (Kawakita 1977). In other words,
health care has two aspects; one is to treat individual patients and the other, to
intervene in the health of a larger population as a whole.

Infection is a major representative of an illness involving the people. The need for
surveillance on infectious diseases on a global scale was recognized at the International Sanitary Conference in 1897. This subsequently resulted in the establishment
of the WHO (1948). This was the starting point for recognition that pharmaceutical
products such as antibiotics to treat infectious diseases and vaccines are the goods
to achieve the stability of society.

At present, the vast majority of the development of pharmaceuticals and their
supply to markets are performed by the private sector. We need to understand the
underlying reasons why conflicts of interests regarding pharmaceuticals strongly
emerge in reality, although pharmaceuticals and their manufacturing companies are
expected to have the public's interest at the heart.

1.4.2 Constitution of WHO and Pharmaceutical Products

In 2017, there were 194 countries participating in the WHO. The WHO functions as a consultant to health administrative authorities of Member States.[6] The Constitution of the WHO defines the scope of its roles. The Constitution specifies the duties the WHO fulfills for the sake of public health across the world and recommends that health care should be promoted in order for the WHO to fulfill the duties specified. Within the Constitutions of the WHO, Chapter 1 Objective and Article 2 of Chapter 2 Functions, prescribes the objective and functions of WHO as outlined below.

Chapter 1—Objective

Article 1
The objective of the World Health Organization (hereinafter called the Organization) shall be the attainment by all peoples of the highest possible level of health.

Chapter 2—Functions

Article 2
In order to achieve its objective, the functions of the Organization shall be:

(a) To act as the directing and coordinating authority on international health work.
(Items (b) to (o) from original text are skipped)
(p) To study and report on, in cooperation with other agencies where necessary, administrative and social techniques affecting public health and medical care from preventive and curative point of view, including hospital services and social security.

The WHO is basically in the position to spread modern medicine among the Member States from the viewpoints of prevention and treatment so as to achieve its objective, i.e., the attainment by all peoples of the highest possible level of health. Since pharmaceutical products are essential means for health care, the WHO's policies on pharmaceuticals are centered on spreading and improvement of the concept of essential medicines described in the next Sect. 1.4.3.

1.4.3 Essential Medicines

As of today, there exist as many as several thousands of active pharmaceutical ingredients and as many as tens of thousands of final products including combination drugs. From the viewpoint of primary care in public health, pharmaceuticals with established efficacy and safety are selected and separated from the others. The WHO conceptualized this selection and adopted the concept as a Model List of Essential

---

[6]Comment by the person who was the ex-Deputy Secretary General of WHO during interview conducted by the author (20 March 2014 at Osaka University).

Medicines in 1975. The concept of essential medicines was positioned in the framework of public health by the Declaration of Alma-Ata adopted at the 1st International Conference on Primary Health Care in 1978.[7]

The List of Essential Medicines is intended to enable citizens of countries with unmet basic health needs to obtain necessary medicines and use them reasonably. This List is expected to provide guidance when a Member State prepares its plan on pharmaceuticals, and, therefore, decided to be prepared for each region (or country) on the basis of advice by specialists in public health, pharmacology, and management of medicines and is revised regularly by the WHO (1975).

This Model List is particularly expected to guide Member States that have difficulties in starting activities on their own to meet health needs. This Model is not merely a list of carefully selected medicines but also contains the guidelines listed below. This List is a comprehensive system of technological concept concerning pharmacotherapy.

- Guideline for formulating national policies on the essential medicines
- Criteria on which the essential medicines are selected
- Guideline for selection of dosage forms for medicinal products
- Quality assurance
- Antibacterial agents with limited indications and resistance monitoring
- Antiviral agents
- Application of the concept of essential medicines
- Essential medicines and primary health care
- Donation of pharmaceutical products
- Post-marketing survey and pharmacovigilance for pharmaceutical products
- Information and training activities on pharmaceutical products, and others.

This Model List indicates that quality assurance is extremely important for pharmaceutical products. It describes that quality is assured by performing surveillance on each process from development, manufacturing, and distribution to use. What should be prioritized is to verify that pharmaceutical products are manufactured in compliance with GMP so that they have officially approved quality.

The WHO states that the danger of procuring medicines with unknown manufacturers cannot be overemphasized. Regarding the quality assurance framework, the WHO has proposed the policies listed below, coupled with the Model List.

The objectives of the WHO's certification scheme on the Quality of Pharmaceutical Products Moving in International Commerce are: (a) to assure that the pharmaceutical product concerned is legitimately approved in the country that exports the product; (b) to assure that the manufacturing plant concerned receives regular audits and satisfies the requirements of GMP and quality control; and (c) to facilitate information exchange among the regulatory

---

[7]Item C of Article 7, the Declaration of Alma-Ata: Primary health care includes at least: education concerning prevailing health problems and the method of preventing and controlling them; promotion of food supply and proper nutrition; an adequate supply of safe water and basic sanitation; maternal and child health care, including family planning; immunization against the major infectious diseases; prevention and control of locally endemic diseases; appropriate treatment of common diseases and injuries; and provision of essential drugs.

authorities of exporting countries about the audits performed by the authorities and regulations based on their audit results. Thus, the WHO anticipates the spread of pharmaceutical products beyond borders.

In 1988, the scope of the scheme was expanded to include raw materials for medicines, in addition to final pharmaceutical products (WHO 1988). Furthermore, the Scheme additionally required the regulatory authorities of exporting countries to submit copies of all information about the officially approved products issued by the regulatory authorities of countries in which the products are manufactured. This requirement was set while taking into account the actual situations of countries with insufficient capacities to regulate pharmaceutical affairs with respect to export and import of pharmaceutical preparations.

In 1992, the Guidelines for implementation of the WHO certificate scheme were approved (WHO 1992). In the Guidelines, proposed formats for the following documents are provided: a certificate of a pharmaceutical product (product certificate), a statement of licensing status of pharmaceutical product(s), and a batch certificate of a pharmaceutical product(s).

A pharmacopoeia is a basis of pharmaceutical administration. As a matter of course, the WHO Expert Committees had an increasing interest in the issuance of an international pharmacopoeia and initiated it in 1984. The International Pharmacopoeia was published while taking into account the countries with insufficient capacities to execute pharmaceutical regulations.

As described above, the WHO has convered the value of modern pharmaceuticals on the form of essential medicines and has greatly endeavored to maintain and improve that value. However, the pharmaceutical affairs and regulations in a country cannot be separated from the country's own and unique problems; the efforts the WHO has made are not rewarded in many aspects.

1.4.4 Generic Medicines

Newly developed medicines containing newly developed compounds as active pharmaceutical ingredients are protected as originators by intellectual property rights including substance patents. Usually, after the protection period expires, third parties manufacture medicines equivalent to counterpart originators and they are called generic medicines. Attention should be paid that "**equivalent**" is not "**identical**." Companies who develop new medicines have no obligation to disclose the know-how on the new medicine to any third party since it is a corporate secret.

The test results required for official approval for generic medicines are substantially less stringent when compared with their counterpart originators, which reduces the total cost necessary for development of generics and makes generics commercially available at lower prices. Generics are, therefore, the goods that most contribute to public health since they reduce co-payments of medical expenses patients have to pay, and publicly funded healthcare expenses. In developed countries, shares of generics in national markets are consistently high.

In 2016, volume-based penetration rates of generics were 91.7% for the US, 86.3% for Germany, 76.6% for the UK, 67.6% for France, 65.3% for Spain, and 59.2% for Italy. The same figure for Japan is 59.0% and lower than those in these developed countries. For the purpose of addressing the increasing tendency in total health expenditure, the government of Japan promotes policies to increase the penetration rate of generics to 80% by September 2020 (MHLW 2018).

Although generics are equivalent to their counterpart originators, some of them are not completely trusted by healthcare professionals and patients. That is why some generic manufacturers attempt to employ, as a business model, manufacture of "authorized generics," which are not equivalent but identical to their counterpart originators, under licensing agreements with originator manufacturers.

1.4.5   International Support and NPOs

Pharmaceutical products are also international relief supplies, which are basically essential medicines. In case natural disasters, disputes, or epidemics of infectious diseases should occur, pharmaceuticals as international relief supplies are globally delivered to affected areas, together with healthcare professionals. This delivery is undertaken by the administration of each country, international organizations, and NPOs. NPOs such as the Médicins Sans Frontiéres (MSF) and the Red Cross are concerned with the quality and enhancement of essential medicines.[8] They stand in opposition to the situation in which pharmaceutical companies have monopolizing control of medicines, and have conducted a campaign against the Agreement on Trade-Related Aspects of Intellectual Property rights (TRIPS Agreement).

The WHO has continued to run its campaign to promote vaccination in regions and states that are not self-sufficient in vaccines. The World Bank also supports countries that are not self-sufficient in essential medicines, by procuring these medicines from the market and providing them to these countries. These international support activities have created a foundation for pharmaceuticals to become international and spread across the world.

1.4.6   Technology Transfer and International Cooperation

Technology transfer is one of the factors that have contributed to spread of modern medicines across the world. It occurs when manufacturers desire to sell their products

---

[8]The Guidelines for Procurement of Medicines that are issued by the Médicins Sans Frontiéres (MSF) prescribe strict standards and procedures for procurement of medicines. The core elements of the Guidelines are: (a) to conduct on-site assessment of manufacturing plants; and (b) to assess documents related to products. The procedures for these assessments are determined. There are seven procurement routes authorized by the Guidelines. The shortest routes for procurement of medicines which have satisfied the specifications of MSF are: to procure products that have passed the prequalification of WHO; and to procure products that are officially approved by the countries participating in the ICH (the US, Japan, Australia, Belgium, Cyprus, Denmark, Finland, France, Germany, Greek, Ireland, Italy, Luxemburg, Portugal, Spain, Sweden, the Netherlands, and the UK).

outside their mother countries. Pharmaceutical products are as a rule authorized by each country. When a manufacturer explores markets outside its mother country, it establishes a local subsidiary or an affiliated company in the targeted market. The manufacturer makes an application for approval through the local subsidiary or the affiliated company and transfers its technologies on import and manufacture to these local companies. In this case, technology transfer is based on profitable activities of private companies.

Another form of technology transfer is technical guidance provided by the countries that build manufacturing plants through the utilization of the Official Development Assistance (ODA).[9] Several factors have enabled technology transfer and one of them is the technical idea of specification and standardization, which will be discussed in Chap. 4.

In addition, whether or not technology transfer takes root in the partner country constitutes an extremely important point, which determines the growth of the industry, public health, and society of the partner country.

1.5 Goods as Industries of Developed and Emerging Countries

1.5.1 Supply-Demand Relationship Linked with Global Network

Global supply-demand relationship for pharmaceutical products is multifaceted. European and North American countries have taken the lead in developing and supplying new medicines. On the other hand, for generic medicines, emerging countries have grown as important supply sources for both end products and raw materials, this occurring after the end of World War II.

India has succeeded in achieving import substitution industrialization for medicines. China has become a country supplying raw materials for medicines. The two countries have established their own positions in meeting the global supply and demand needs for both end products and raw materials for generics.

1.5.2 Pharmaceuticals as Industrial Products

At present, almost all modern medicines are industrialized products. Several decades ago, pharmacists used simple measuring devices and tools to prepare medicines, in

---

[9]The Japan International Cooperation Agency (JICA) was established in 1974 and is a Japanese ODA executing agency. The main pillars of the activities of the Agency are to provide financial support and technical cooperation, to dispatch volunteers, and to provide international emergency assistance.

the back of a pharmacy. This scene is not currently observed except for traditional medicines. As of today, pharmacists take out packaged medicines from shelves, according to prescriptions. The words "preparation and dispensing" are actually obsolete to indicate the duties of pharmacists.[10] This is because medicines have become industrialized products.

Industrialized products have great advantages in that they are adaptable to mass production, which makes it possible to meet increasing demand in a timely manner. More importantly, a possibility that novice pharmacists make errors in preparation which may jeopardize patients has been remarkably lowered.

Industrialized pharmaceutical products now accommodate the great demands of public health and in addition, their consistent efficacy and quality are secured. On the other hand, industrialization of pharmaceuticals has brought about many challenges as described below.

1.5.3 Newly Developed Medicines and Generics

Active pharmaceutical ingredients in newly developed medicines are protected by substance patents. Development of new medicines requires accumulation of data from many preclinical and clinical studies over long periods of time, which requires a large investment. In addition, the development is always associated with a risk of failure. For these reasons, the knowledge (intellectual property rights) about novel medicines is protected by patents. There is an internationally accepted cycle that during the period of protection, manufactures of originators exclusively sell the product in order to recover the investment, with which the manufacturers then invest in subsequent projects. Research-based pharmaceutical companies are always grown in this way.

Protection by patents is not unlimited. After patents for newly developed medicines expire, the knowledge about active pharmaceutical ingredients comes into the public domain as public knowledge, and third parties legitimately utilize it. Many disputes and lawsuits have occurred with regard to periods of patents and scopes of patent claims. International consensus on patents has long been discussed, but it cannot be said that the developed world completely agrees with the emerging and developing world in terms of the understanding and administration of the consensus.

Another rule to ensure protection of newly developed medicines is the right to monopolize data. Manufacturers of originator medicines submit their unique data to the regulatory authorities in the country concerned so as to obtain official approvals. The knowledge based on the data is protected separately from patents. For example,

---

[10]In Japan, the Ministry of Health, Labour and Welfare (MHLW) formulated the family pharmacists system in 2015. The MHLW expects that local pharmacies aim towards a local-oriented, new style of management, i.e., centralized management to understand what medicines individual patients take; the way in which patients take them; and responsive actions taken for 24 h a day and at the patients' home. It also expects that patients visit family pharmacies located in their immediate vicinity.

Japan has the re-examination system according to which a 10-year re-examination period is usually set for newly developed medicines.[11]

If a generic manufacturer makes an application for approval of a generic medicine before the re-examination period set for its counterpart originator terminates, the manufacturer is required to submit study results more than those which were submitted by the manufacturer of the originator. The protection under this rule is different from that by substance patents. The applicant manufacturer of the generic actually has to clear two hurdles. The period of protection for data regarding pharmaceutical products was an important agendum in the TRIPS Agreement recently adopted.

1.5.4 Confrontation Between the Developed World and the Emerging World Regarding Intellectual Property Rights

European and North American countries have taken the initiative in developing new medicines. Substance patients were first accepted in European and North American countries and because of this, development of new medicines has become a business model for research-based large-scale pharmaceutical companies. Monopolizing control of new medicines through the utilization of protection by substance patents has yielded huge profits for the manufacturers that have successfully developed the new medicines. This is epitomized by Lipitor, a lipid-lowering agent.[12]

After substance patents[13] expire, originator pharmaceuticals are incorporated as generic medicines into the industries of least developed countries. Emerging countries such as India and China have succeeded in achieving import substitution industrialization for generic medicines and on top of that, have created a structure in which these countries supply generics to other countries including European and North American ones.

In the process of building the supply-demand relationship between the developed and the emerging worlds, tension has occurred between the two worlds. One cause

---

[11]The re-examination period is one of the conditions that applicant manufacturers have to meet regarding officially approved novel medicines. In the case of a novel medicine that is a new chemical compound, the applicant manufacturer has to collect data on the novel medicine from post-marketing survey (including post-marketing clinical studies), literature investigation, and other relevant sources for a 10-year period after approval so as to verify the efficacy and safety of the medicine, and submit the data to the regulatory authorities. Until re-examination is ended, third parties are not allowed to manufacture and sell generics.

[12]Lipitor (generic name: atorvastatin), a lipid-lowering agent, was developed by Warner-Lambert's Parke-Davis. This single agent yielded so enormous sales and therefore, Liptor, together with the company, was acquired by Pfizer in 2000.

[13]Substance patents constitute a category of the intellectual properties but are different in nature from the other type of patents. Usually, one technology is protected by a combination of many peripheral patents. However, since an active pharmaceutical ingredient (API) is in many cases a single component, protection of the API by the substance patent concerned easily enables monopolizing control of the relevant medicine.

of the tension is auditing by developed countries on supply sources when they import medicines from those sources. Another, more fundamental cause of the tension is the move in which emerging countries try to take novel medicines developed by developed countries and protected by substance patents, into their own countries as generic medicines. The patent systems in emerging countries (represented by India, in particular) have long been different from those of developed countries, and as a result of this, developed countries consider that emerging countries infringe patent rights. As a matter of course, conflicts of interests have occurred between the two worlds.

The developed world understands that under the patent systems of emerging countries that are different from those of the developed world, emerging countries manufacture and export medicines developed by developed countries, without obtaining permission to do so from the developed countries concerned. The developed world thus considers that emerging countries conduct the act of counterfeiting. This consideration, coupled with the controversy about the term "counterfeiting" used in the IMPACT and its definition, has created disputes and emotional confrontation between the developed world and the emerging and developing world. These moves and events have brought about a foundation in which the developed world regards generics manufactured by emerging countries as counterfeit drugs.

1.5.5 Move of Pharmaceutical Companies Toward Globalization

In the 1990s, there was progress in mergers and restructuring of European and North American large pharmaceutical companies, to which several important factors contributed. One of them was successive development of low molecular compounds as novel medicines. Another factor was that it became evident that intensification of intellectual property rights yields enormous profits by means of monopolizing control of medicines, which was first demonstrated in the US.

Reducing the length of time necessary for development through the utilization of mergers and acquisitions was an effective strategy for pharmaceutical companies to survive international competition in development of new medicines (Fig. 1.1). Pharmaceutical giants born as a result of mergers and acquisitions had greater influential power on the WHO. This caused emerging and developing countries to have a certain sense of distrust against the WHO and developed countries in relation to the IMPACT (see Sects. 6.1 and 6.6 of Chap. 6).

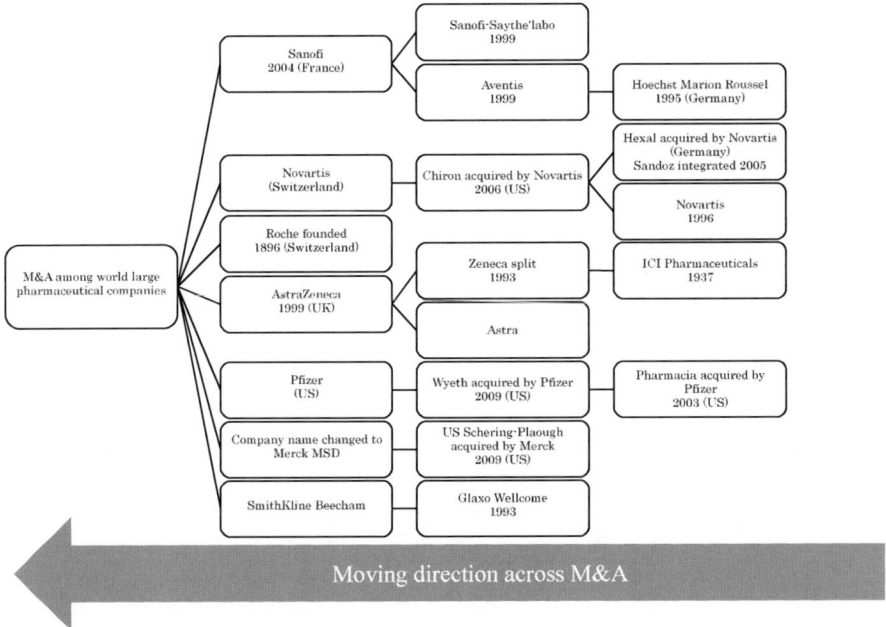

Fig. 1.1 Mergers and acquisitions among world large pharmaceutical companies starting in the 1990s. *Source* Prepared by the authors

1.6 Pharmaceutical Products as Illegally Distributed Goods

1.6.1 Concerns of the Developed World and of the Emerging and Developing World

At present, handling counterfeit goods and imitation products is a business common to the world. In this sense, distributing poor quality pharmaceuticals is not an unusual business. However, attention should be paid to the fact that the concerns of the developed world are not the same as those of the emerging and developing world.

Poor quality pharmaceuticals exploit what little money people living in poverty have and in addition, are not effective in treatment administered for the direct purpose of saving lives. For the emerging and developing world, the quality of generic medicines is a life-or-death issue. On the other hand, branded medicines are expensive and counterfeited brand drugs are expected to yield high profits. Manufacturers of originator medicines in the developed world are concerned about the smuggling of fake branded drugs and illegal distribution of them through the Internet.

1.6.2 Smuggling

Generally, expensive medicines are targeted for smuggling. Major targets are those which are not essential to health and hygiene, such as drugs to treat erectile dysfunction (ED). Several cases are described below.

In Brazil, the number of unmasked smugglings has increased year by year. For a period between January 2007 and September 2010, the vast majority of seized contraband was drugs to treat ED and anabolic steroids. None of them were indispensable to health or hygiene. Counterfeited drugs of Cialis and Viagra, both of which are medicines to treat ED, accounted for more than half of the seized contraband (Ames and Souza 2012). The fact that the drugs to treat this type of disorder are largely counterfeited and smuggled into the country may serve to indicate that there exist users and traders who do not want to use legitimate distribution routes. Ames and Souza conclude that distribution routes must be controlled and kept under close surveillance. However, as far as the demand exists and substantial profits are expected, eradication of the smuggling would be difficult.

In Canada, smuggling is a major route for the inflow of counterfeit drugs into the country. Representative ones are drugs to treat ED. In 2003, seized contraband was dealt in by not professional criminals but an airplane pilot. In 2005, detected counterfeits to treat ED were brought from China. In 2005, counterfeit drugs to treat angina pectoris and hypertension that had crept into legitimate distribution routes were first detected. These drugs did not contain active ingredients and 11 persons died. In 4 of the 11, the death might have been caused by unauthorized ingredients. Selling products through the Internet meets the demand of individuals who want to buy them anonymously (Criminal Intelligence Service Canada 2006).

Seizure of smuggled products in legitimate distribution routes is serious because it indicates the presence of blind spots in distribution management. In the US, distribution of medicines is complicated. So-called gray markets, i.e., distribution areas that are not adequately controlled by regulations, enable the inflow of counterfeit drugs into the US. One of factors contributing to the formation of gray markets is reported to be the fact that individual states set their own conditions for distributor candidates to meet so as to obtain official license.

In the US, sales through the Internet are permitted. In 2004, the FDA warned that counterfeited contraceptive patches were available on the Internet market. Some of them were significantly less expensive than the genuine patch. The survey conducted by the FDA in 2005 revealed that 85% of the medicines allegedly made in Canada were actually manufactured in other countries. Counterfeit medicines constitute a secure and highly profitable business alternative to narcotics (Stoneman et al. 2011).

Even in developed countries, loopholes exist in distribution, which allows counterfeit drugs (products) to creep in the countries. A strong independence of individual states results in these loopholes, and in this respect, the US would be similar to China and India. Free Trade Zones are considered to play a major role in provoking internationally large-scale smuggling across regions (Box 3).

Box 3: Free Trade Zone

A Free Trade Zone (FTZ) is a region subject to preferential tax treatment, e.g., no duties imposed on imported and exported goods in the region. FTZs are established to promote industries and trades in the regions concerned. More than 2,000 FTZs exist across the world.

Generally speaking, unless articles are brought into countries in which FTZs are located, or unless there is an obvious evidence indicating engagement in crimes or terrorism, no customs inspection is performed in FTZs. Consequently, repackaging or reloading makes it possible to disguise an origin of production.

1.6.3 Online Distribution

In addition to smuggling, illegal selling through the Internet functions as distribution routes provoking spread of poor quality pharmaceuticals beyond the border. Drugs to treat ED such as Viagra represent products available on the Internet market. Pfizer, a US company, purchased "Viagra" from 22 websites with the statement "You can buy Pfizer made Viagra from our website," for the purpose of finding what was actually going on (Campbell et al. 2012).

None of the websites required prescriptions. Ninety percent of the samples of the drug purchased were illegal generic Viagra. The price per tablet greatly varied from 3.28 US dollars to 33.0 US dollars. The ship from locations were Hong Kong ($n = 11$), the US ($n = 6$), the UK ($n = 2$), Canada ($n = 1$), China ($n = 1$), and India ($n = 1$). Seventeen of the 22 samples of the drug purchased were counterfeits and contained the active ingredient at 30–50% of the labeled quantity. The counterfeits delivered did not have package inserts. Only 4 samples were genuine products.

This Pfizer's report revealed that none of the websites required prescriptions. The business model on the Internet market is to protect personal confidentiality of individuals who place orders. Like the other survey results, this report has indicated that purchasing through the Internet is associated with an extremely high likelihood of unexpected delivery of counterfeit products.

Anti-obesity drugs are more frequently used for cosmetic purposes than for treatment.[14] Researchers purchased 82 anti-obesity samples of this type of drugs from 36 websites through the Internet for the purpose of finding the actual status of quality or other aspects (Khan et al. 2012). Approximately half the websites did not clearly indicate their physical addresses, and 45% of the samples did not contain package

---

[14]The drug combination fenfluramine/phentermine, usually called fen-phen, was an anti-obesity treatment that utilized two anorectics. Fenfluramine was shown to cause potentially fatal pulmonary hypertension and heart valve problems, which eventually led to its withdrawal and legal damages of over $13 billion.

inserts in the shipment. Fifty-two of the 82 samples were tested for quality in accordance with their relevant pharmacopoeias. Three of the 52 samples were counterfeits and did not contain active ingredients. Two of the 3 samples were confirmed to be counterfeit by the manufacturer of genuine products. Twenty companies were asked about genuineness of their products, and only 5 of the 20 gave their replies.

This study indicates that the Internet provides the environment optimal for dissemination of poor quality pharmaceuticals. In this study, all samples purchased were not counterfeits. However, it is true that it has been gradually noted that many of products available on the Internet market are sold illegally, which has actually formed an image that illegally sold products are all poor quality pharmaceuticals.

1.6.4 Distribution in Emerging and Developing Countries

In markets to which people in the underclass in emerging and developing countries have access, many poor quality products have been detected, although routes through which these products reach the markets are unknown.

Atemnkeng et al. analyzed the quality of antimalarial agents in Kenya and DR Congo and found that a set of medicines imported from Belgium, a developed country, contained substandard drugs (i.e., underdosed active ingredient) (Atemnkeng et al. 2007). This finding indicates that poor quality pharmaceuticals are not always manufactured in and originated from the developing and emerging world. Overdosed active ingredients are considered to have clearly resulted from human errors during manufacturing. If someone attempts to commit a perfect crime of counterfeiting so as to deceive ordinary people, then that person would not be expected to overdose with an expensive active ingredient. On the other hand, it is not possible to determine if underdosed active ingredients were caused by malice or not, because the history of process and storage control during manufacture and distribution was not available.

In this study, although active ingredients were overdosed or underdosed in some of the samples analyzed, the extent of deviation from the specifications was insufficient to induce serious health damage. A lot of precedent research reported rates of conformity to specifications. However, dividing quality into one of the two, that is, conformity or non-conformity to specifications, may misidentify the real nature and magnitude of quality-related problems. Atemnkeng et al. pointed out that "In most African nations, people have developed confidence in products developed abroad especially in Europe and the United States. Unscrupulous individuals seize this opportunity to produce illicit drugs and label them as manufactured in a European country or the United States." This agrees with the WHO's definition of counterfeit drugs; the WHO views counterfeit drugs as a problem and defines them as those which falsify legitimate and genuine pharmaceutical products.

The business model of handling counterfeit drugs does not use fictitious names or brands but utilizes the brands that are officially approved by the states and acknowledged in the markets. Nayyar et al. performed a meta-analysis on the quality of essential medicines in Southeast Asia and Sub-Saharan Africa, based on the results of 7 studies regarding quality which were conducted in Southeast Asian countries between 1999 and 2010, and on those of 21 studies regarding quality which were carried out in 21 countries in the Sub-Saharan Africa (Nayyar et al. 2012).

In this meta-analysis, the term "counterfeit" was not used because it was considered to be reminiscent of issues related to intellectual property rights, but instead the terms "falsified" (which is equivalent in meaning to "counterfeit"), "substandard" (which means out of specifications), and "degraded" (which refers to post-manufacturing or post-shipment degradation in quality) were used because these terms were considered to express quality from the neutral point of view. The proportions of poor quality drugs were high in both the regions. Measurement of the content of the active ingredient revealed that as high as 35% of the drug samples deviated from the relevant specifications in both the regions, although how much overdosing or underdosing of active ingredients deviating from the specifications was not described. The researchers commented that it was difficult to determine if the sample was falsified or substandard. Some of the samples did not contain active ingredients at all, and they may be considered to be falsified.

1.7   Discussion

This chapter functions as a warming up exercise for us to get prepared for digging down into the issue of why the theme of this book is so complicated.

Pharmaceutical products are the goods that are integrated into health care and are high in sociality and public nature and at the same time can easily be tangled in the interests of many different stakeholders. When discussing the sociality and public nature of pharmaceutical products, the qualitative and quantitative situations of patients (or individuals with illness) who are affected end users must be understood. Public health covers the greatest number. The reasons why pharmaceutical products are controlled, supervised, and regulated by the state are because they are the essential goods for public health and in addition, the prevalence of illegal and or the inappropriate use of pharmaceuticals can damage society. Therefore, the state possesses the right to grant approval and license to pharmaceuticals and the law enforcement power on them.

When acts that are considered to be linked with counterfeiting actually involve the goods that are under the control of the state, such acts are no more merely counterfeiting but regarded as defiance against the authority and power of the state. Furthermore, when the quality of a pharmaceutical product fails to achieve expected outcomes that should have been attained, such failure is regarded as a double-meaning crime against the state and the public interest whatever the reason may be. In addition, the inflow of poor quality pharmaceuticals into a country from other countries may easily create hostile feelings against them.

Japan's first circulated coinage was minted in 708 and only one year later, the order to prohibit counterfeiting, that is, to prohibit the act of minting the coinage without obtaining the approval from the state, was issued. A famous physicist Sir

Isaac Newton persistently hunted down criminals who counterfeited money, when he was the director of the UK Mint Bureau, and sent them to an execution platform for hanging (Levenson 2009). This clearly illustrates how serious the act of counterfeiting is and how robustly the state saves its face against criminals.

We need to discuss whether or not we can place complete confidence in the practical effectiveness of the state's regulations. The presence of regulations in the form of provisions or orders cannot ensure that these regulations are actually effective. If things are left as they are, they will not be in the desirable form. That is why we have to formulate and intensify regulations. The private sector is responsible for the vast majority of supply of pharmaceutical products. Even in the private sector, pharmaceutical companies which concentrate their resources on development of new medicines have a different business model from that of those which supply generics and or raw materials for medicines. Different business models lead to different product portfolios and incentives to quality. We should discuss what gives suppliers incentives to improve quality.

The global pharmaceutical industry has so massively grown to be able to stand face to face with the state[15] and it strongly attempts to eliminate the risk of private companies losing their profits due to third parties' acts. They try to combat all acts that obstruct lawful sales by officially authorized companies and these acts include, among others, selling unregistered drugs, conducting unlicensed manufacture and/or distribution, not complying with laws and regulations, and overlooking and/or hiding deviations. They fight against not only obvious crimes but also act in legally gray areas. Both officially registered pharmaceutical products and poor quality medicines have spread and disseminated across the world. We have to discuss whether these phenomena on the two types of medicines are attributable to different causes or the same cause. Pharmaceuticals are industrial products having specifications, and therefore, there is the premise that the same level of quality will be achieved anywhere in the world. In reality, however, the technical levels of manufacturing and the systems to ensure the practical effectiveness of regulations on distribution vary depending on individual countries. We also have to discuss what is brought about by the gap between the premise and the reality from the global viewpoint.

The WHO's policies for medicines involved stakeholders in various fields, under the situations in which Member States individually addressed their own challenges and global-scale conflicts of interests occurred. The IMPACT was the product born under these circumstances. Discussing why and how the IMPACT reached the deadlock may provide us many insights and lessons (see Chap. 6).

Fake brand drugs, which are not used for lifesaving, distributed through the Internet or smuggling need to be considered as different in nature from the problem of poor quality generic medicines distributed in rural areas in developing countries. The former group of drugs is expensive and highly profitable, whereas the latter group of medicines is affordable and of low profitability. It would be straightforward to argue

---

[15]The Mainichi Newspapers Co., Ltd., one of the major Japanese newspaper publishing companies, reported that a US company Pfizer abandoned a merger with an intention to avoid taxes (2016).

that both groups are lumped into one category of acts done by criminals, provided that the rationale for such lumping is clarified.

Poor quality pharmaceuticals are always associated with overdosing or underdosing of active ingredients and contamination. If the content of an active ingredient is lower than the specification, then therapeutic efficacy cannot be expected. On the contrary, overdosing of active ingredients may cause adverse drug reactions.[16] Contamination also jeopardizes patients. The extent to which overdosing, underdosing or contamination is problematic varies depending on individual cases. Accordingly, handling quality in a generalized manner needs to rely on conformity to specifications. However, a lot of precedent research reports utilized data on rates of conformity to specifications. This would be inadequate to indicate the magnitude of the problem of poor quality pharmaceuticals and to make matters worse, would be likely to cause great misunderstanding.

References

Ames, Joseane, and D.Z. Souza. 2012. Counterfeiting of drugs in Brazil. Revista de Saúde Pública. http://dx.doi.org/10.1590/S0034-89102012005000005. Accessed 1 Sept 2018.

Atemnkeng M.A., K. De Cock, and J. Plaizier-Vercammen. 2007. Quality control of active ingredient in artemisinin-derivative antimalarials within Kenya and DR Congo. *Tropical Medicine & International Health* 12 (1): 68–74. https://doi.org/10.1111/j.1365-3156.2006.01769.x. https://www.ncbi.nlm.nih.gov/pubmed/17207150. Accessed 1 Sept 2018.

Campbell, N., J.P. Clark, V.J. Stecher, et al. 2012. Internet-ordered Viagra (sildenafil citrate) is rarely genuine. *The Journal of Sexual Medicine* 9 (11): 2943–2951. https://doi.org/10.1111/j.1743-6109.2012.02877.x. https://www.ncbi.nlm.nih.gov/pubmed/22925379. Accessed 1 Sept 2018.

Criminal Intelligence Service Canada, Counterfeit pharmaceuticals in Canada. http://publications.gc.ca/collections/collection_2013/sp-ps/PS64-108-2006-eng.pdf. Accessed 6 March 2016.

Doi, Osamu, Satoru Kimura, et al. 2013. *Drug-Induced Suffering in Japan*. Tokyo: Yakuji Nippo. (Parallel in Japanese and English).

Illich, Ivan. 1976. *LIMITS to medicine medical nemesis: the expropriation of health*. London: Calder & Boyars Ltd.

Kawakita, Airo. 1977. *Kindai Igaku no Shiteki Kiban (Jo)* [Historical Groundwork of Modern Medicine, vol. 1]. Tokyo: Iwanami Shoten. (In Japanese).

Khan, Mohiuddin Hussain, Tsuyoshi Tanimoto, Yoko Nakanishi, et al. 2012. Public health concerns for anti-obesity medicines imported for personal use through the internet: a cross sectional study. BMJ Open. 2, e000854. https://doi.org/10.1136/bmjopen-2012-00854. https://bmjopen.bmj.com/content/2/3/e000854. Accessed 1 Sept 2018.

Levenson, T. 2009. *Newton and the counterfeiter*. New York through: Thomas c/o The Park Literacy Groug, LLC.

---

[16]The therapeutic index is the ratio of the lethal dose of a drug to the dose at which the drug exhibits its therapeutic effectiveness, and usually expressed as LD_{50}/ED_{50} (LD_{50}: Median lethal dose refers to the dosage of a given drug required to kill 50% of a test population; ED_{50}: Median effective dose refers to the dosage of a given drug at which the minimum effectiveness is observed in half of a test population). The larger the index, the safer the drug is. For example, the therapeutic index is approximately 100 for diazepam (anti-anxiety agent) and 2–3 for digoxin. The margin of safety is narrow for digoxin, indicating that an overdose of digoxin may be associated with high risks of toxicity.

MHLW. 2018. Jenerikku Iyakuhin no Shiyo Sokushin ni tsuite [Promotion in Use of Generic Medicines]. https://www.mhlw.go.jp/stf/seisakunitsuite/bunya/kenkou_iryou/iryou/kouhatu-iyaku/index.html. Accessed 12 Aug 2018. (In Japanese).

Nayyar, G.M., J.G. Breman, P.N Newton, et al. MRCP. 2012, Poor-quality antimalarial drugs in Southeast Asia and sub-Saharan Africa. *The Lancet Infectious Diseases* 12 (6): 488–496. https://doi.org/10.1016/S1473-3099(12)70064-6. Accessed 1 Sept 2018.

Nihon Yakkyokuho Kofu Hyakunen Kinen Jigyo Jikko Iinkai. 1987. *Nihon Yakkyokuho Hyakunenshi* [The Hundred Years History of Japanese Pharmacopeia]. Tokyo: Nihon Kohteisho Kyokai. (In Japanese).

Stephens, Trent and Rock Brynner. 2001. *Dark remedy the impact of thalidomide and its revival as a vital medicine*: Trans. New York: Perseus Publishing.

Stoneman, A., S. Simon, and J. Trahan. 2011. Counterfeit medicines: impurities in the American drug supply. *Journal of Midwifery & Women's Health* 56 (6): 636–638. https://doi.org/10.1111/j.1542-2011.2011.00108.x. Accessed 1 Sept 2018.

Umetani, Noboru. 2007. *Oyatoi Gaikokujin –Meiji Nihon no Wakiyakutachi* [The Foreigners Hired by The Japanese Government -Supporting Players in Meiji Era -]: Tokyo: Kodansya Gakujutsu Bunko. (In Japanese).

Uzawa, Hirofumi. 2000. *Shakaiteki Kyotsu Shihon* [Social Common Capital]. Tokyo: Iwanami Shinsyo. (In Japanese).

WHO. 1975. WHA28.66. Handbook of resolutions and decisions of the World Health Assembly and the Executive Board Volume II 1973–1984. http://apps.who.int/iris/bitstream/10665/79012/12/9241652063_Vol2.pdf. Accessed 3 July 2018.

WHO. 1988. WHA41.18. Handbook of resolutions and decisions of the World Health Assembly and the Executive Board Volume III 1985–1992. http://apps.who.int/iris/bitstream/10665/79012/12/9241652063_Vol2.pdf. Accessed 3 July 2018.

WHO. 1992. WHA45.29. Handbook of resolutions and decisions of the World Health Assembly and the Executive Board Volume III 1985–1992. http://apps.who.int/iris/bitstream/10665/79012/12/9241652063_Vol2.pdf. Accessed 3 July 2018.

Part I
Pharmaceuticals in Globalization

Firstly, it is clearly understandable that international organizations and developed countries maintain that poor quality pharmaceuticals must be combated and eradicated. Secondly, the WHO's policies on pharmaceutical products have brought about tension between the developed and the emerging and developing worlds. Thirdly, the distribution of modern medicine across the world may be strongly associated with dissemination of the problems noted with poor quality pharmaceuticals. The authors discuss the association from the viewpoints of the roles of specification and standardization, which specify quality. Fourthly, the problem of poor quality pharmaceuticals is linked with events that occurred during the era of so-called globalization.

The final topic of Part I is the deadlock of IMPACT.

Chapter 2
Global Circulation of Imitated Products, Poor Quality Pharmaceuticals, Fake Products, and Health Problems

2.1 Business Handling Imitations in the World

2.1.1 Definition of Imitation

Counterfeit drugs unlawfully take advantage of the existing branded medicines. In other words, they imitate or duplicate officially authorized products or genuine products.

The report issued by the Japan External Trade Organization (JETRO) (JETRO Singapore Center 2009) states that the acts of imitating and manufacturing/distributing imitations refer to a series of illegitimate activities which infringe intellectual property rights. These acts are in most cases deliberate, although some of them are not intentional. The typical examples of infringement are described below.[1]

(a) A precisely duplicated article with a high degree of perfection that can be sold at prices close to those of the authentic ones, and misleads consumers into believing that the duplicate was a genuine article.
(b) An article that is similar to the authentic one in terms of appearance and functions but is considerably less expensive. Consumers purchase in many cases the article knowing that it is an imitation.
(c) An article with an existing brand or trademark, although the article is not actually marketed by the brand/trademark holder.
(d) Articles which are similar to but actually different from products of brand holders, or articles which are sold under similar names to the authentic brand names.
(e) Products manufactured utilizing patented technologies, manufacturing methods or processes, without obtaining permission to do so from the patent holders.

---

[1] This report covers the infringement of intellectual property rights, trademark rights, copyrights, patent rights, and design rights in the TRIPS Agreement of the World Trade Organization (WTO), and focuses on infringement cases in the automotive and electrical appliances industries.

© Springer Nature Singapore Pte Ltd. 2020
S. Kimura and Y. Nakamura, *Poor Quality Pharmaceuticals in Global Public Health*, Trust 5, https://doi.org/10.1007/978-981-15-2089-1_2

(f) So-called "no-brand" and "generic" products that are "lawfully" duplicated under national laws.

Which case (s), among (a) through (f) above, is (are) applicable to what are called counterfeit medicines, among poor quality pharmaceuticals actually available in markets?

Case (a) is in fact not applicable to pharmaceutical products. If counterfeit medicines were to have the same level of efficacy and safety as that of officially authorized medicines, such counterfeits could be problematic because they may infringe private rights or are not officially licensed or approved and they are therefore illegal, although they would not be actually problematic from the viewpoint of public health. The WHO describes that typical counterfeit medicines do not contain active ingredients at all or contain toxic substances, leading to serious health damage including deaths.

Case (b) is sometimes applicable to pharmaceutical products. Functions of medicines may decline even though they are manufactured and marketed by legitimate companies. These deteriorated products are not imitations, however both legitimacy and meeting specifications are essential for patients to accept them as authentic ones. Otherwise such products are not different from imitations. Some medicines are supplied at lower prices because their quality is below the specifications for some relevant reasons, e.g., their expiration dates have passed or the quality has been deteriorated during transportation. They have lower quality and are supplied at lower prices. There are a great number of consumers who can only afford less expensive medicines as substitute option. As discussed in Chap. 8, there are many temptations for legitimate manufacturers to sacrifice the quality to ensure their profit.
When lawful companies manufacture and distribute medicines to which Case (b) applies, such an act can be regarded as illegal but not criminal. Furthermore, it is impossible in many cases that third parties could retrospectively determine whether such acts were deliberate or not. To the knowledge of the authors, no empirical data are available regarding how much health damage or therapeutic problems occurred in this case.

Case (c) is sometimes applicable to pharmaceutical products. In Japan, there was an incident in which fake drugs were seized because labeling with Kanji (Chinese) characters mislead consumers into believing that they were authentic herbal medicines. The Japanese people usually have a good image that "China equals the tradition of herbal medicines," and this image was utilized in this incident.

Case (d) is applicable to pharmaceutical products. For example, the name "Ponstan" was intentionally changed to "Postan," which takes advantage of visual misidentification of ordinary people.

Case (e) is obviously illegal from intellectual property rights. The manufacturers may not be official license holder or habitual offenders. If so, we have no grounds to trust that their products are well quality-controlled.

Case (f) is controversial. Lawfully manufactured generic products are widely available, however, generic products, in particular, distributed in emerging and developing countries are often discussed in the context of conflict in the patent system between developed countries and emerging countries.

The above-described case was regarded as infringement in developed countries but was lawful in emerging and developing countries. The problem of poor quality pharmaceuticals has been deeply associated with international conflicts of interests because of inconsistencies in international systems regarding intellectual property rights. This is the most important background that caused the International Medical Products Anti-Counterfeiting Taskforce (IMPACT) to reach a dead end, as discussed in Chap. 6: A Dead End of IMPACT.

2.1.2 Size of Counterfeit/Piracy Business

Counterfeits are produced and consumed in all countries across the world. The size of business of handling pirated and counterfeit goods has grown year by year (Table 2.1). The total value of counterfeit and pirated goods as a result of this illegal business was estimated to be 923 billion to 1.13 trillion US dollars in 2013 and is forecasted to expand to 1.9–2.8 trillion US dollars in 2022, 10 years later (Frontier economics). This counterfeiting business not only displaces the legitimate business but also removes employment opportunities.

In the survey report issued by the Organization for Economic Cooperation and Development (OECD) in 2007, OECD concluded that up to 200 billion US dollars of worldwide trade could be in counterfeit or pirated products (OECD 2007). The report described that "the figure does not include counterfeit and pirated products that are produced and consumed domestically, nor does it include the significant volume of pirated digital products that are being distributed via the Internet."

This illegal business is expanding worldwide. In particular, Asia is the largest source of counterfeit and pirated products. It is reported that the amount of these products supplied by 12 Asian countries accounts for 70% (volume-based) of the world total (Table 2.2).

Especially, made in China counterfeit and pirated products are disseminating throughout the world. In many countries, China ranks first (volume-based) as the supply source of these products (Table 2.3) (OECD 2008).

2.2 Databases for Poor Quality Pharmaceuticals

Regarding the status of occurrence of poor quality pharmaceuticals across the world or the size of business involving these medicines, there is no database that is reliable, comprehensive, and commonly available. Even in countries with well-established statistics, it is not easy to collect all the problematic cases that occur in the market of healthcare services.

Table 2.1 Summary of estimates of counterfeiting and piracy

Quadrant	Estimate	2013	2022 (forecast)
1	Total international trade in counterfeit and pirated goods	$461 Billion	$991 Billion
2	Total domestic production and consumption of counterfeit pirated goods	$249–$456 Billion	$524–$959 Billion
3	Digital piracy in movies, music, and software	$213 Billion	S384–$856 Billion
	– Digital piracy in film	$160 Billion	$289–644 Billion
	– Digital piracy in music	$29 Billion	$53–117 Billion
	– Digital piracy in software	$24 Billion	$42–95 Billion
	Total value of counterfeit and pirated goods	**$923 Billion–1.13 trillion**	**$1.90–$2.81 Trillion**
4	Wider economic and social costs		
	– Displacement of legitimate economic activity	$470–$597 Billion	$980–$1244 Billion
	– Estimated reduction in FDI	$111 Billion	$231 Billion
	– Estimated fiscal losses	$96–130 Billion	$199–$270 Billion
	– Estimated reduction in FDI	$60 Billion	$125 Billion
	Total Wider economic and social costs	**$737–$898 Billion**	**$1.54–$1.87 Trillion**
	Estimated employment losses	**2–2.6 Billion**	**4.2–5.4 million**
	Foregone economic growth in OECD 2017	**$30 Billion–$54 Billion**	

Source Frontier estimates based on OECD 2013 data on counterfeiting in international trade, and UN trade and GDP data to derive estimates for domestic production and consumption. Data for Piracy based on latest industry sources (2015)

Monitoring the status of the market of healthcare services is a basic element for pharmaceutical regulatory administration. In reality, however, underreporting and oversights always occur. In particular, data for countries with inadequate capacities to establish statistics are inevitably sporadic. In this section, five databases are introduced below.

Table 2.2 Seizure of imported products which infringe copyrights or counterfeit and pirated products: seizure percentage by source economies

Region of top 20 source economies	Number of source economies in region	Seizures (% of total)
Asia (excl. Middle East)	12	69.7
Middle East	2	4.1
Africa	2	1.8
Europe	2	1.7
North America	1	1.1
South America	1	0.8
Top sources	**20**	**79.2**

Note The seizure percentages are based on trade-weighted data from 19 reporting economies
Source The Economic Impact of Counterfeiting and Piracy Executive Summary 2007

Table 2.3 Source of seizures of counterfeit and pirated products in recent years, by economy

Economy reporting seizures	Origin of seized items and share of total seizures (of known sources)
Andorra	Malaysia(57%), Korea(25)%, Mauritius(11)%, Morocco(4)%, China(2)%
Angola (a)	Morocco(43)%, UAE[*](14)%, Thailand(14)%, China(14)%, South Africa(7)%, Congo(7)%
Australia (a)	China(26)%, Malaysia(20)%, Thailand(15)%, Indonesia(14)%, Hong Kong, China(8)%
Cyprus	China(49)%, Philippines(13)%, Hong Kong, China(11)%, UAE[1](6)%, Korea(5)%
Estonia (a)	China(41)%, Russian Federation(29)%, Bulgaria(8)%, UAE[1](6)%, Turkey(6)%
Fiji (a)	India(96)%, China(4)%
Gabon (a)	China(100)%
Germany	China(46)%, Hong Kong, China(5)%, Vietnam(4)%, Chinese Taipei(13)%, Thailand(4)%
Ghana	Nigeria(100)%
Korea	China(94)%, Hong Kong, China(2)%, Belgium(1)%, Chinese Taipei(1)%, Vietnam(1)%
Latvia	China(56)%, Korea(26)%, Chinese Taipei(10)%, Thailand(7)%, Latvia(<1)%
Mauritius	China(92)%, Thailand(4)%, Indonesia(2)%, India(2)%

(continued)

Table 2.3 (continued)

Economy reporting seizures	Origin of seized items and share of total seizures (of known sources)
Netherlands (b)	China(48)%, Hong Kong, China(10)%, Turkey(3)%, Nigeria(3)%, Chinese Taipei(28)%
New Zealand (a)	China(52)%, Thailand(19)%, Korea(5)%, Hong Kong, China(4)%, Indonesia(3)%
Portugal	China(68)%, Korea(11)%, Malaysia(7)%, Portugal(4)%, Brazil(3)%
Romania	China(38)%, Iran(24)%, Moldova(16)%, Turkey(12)%, UAE[1](7)%
Spain	China(58)%, Thailand(9)%, United States(8)%, UAE[1](5)%, Hong Kong, China(4)%
Thailand	China(100)%
United States	China(69)%, Hong Kong, China(6)%, UAE[1](2)%, India(2)%, Pakistan(2)%
European Union (c, d)	China(38)%, Thailand(10)%, Hong Kong, China(8)%, Turkey(7)%, Malaysia(4)%, United States(4)%

(a) Based on number of seizures
(b) Based on top 100 sources
(c) A number of EU member states provided data; this is reported separately, above
(d) Calculations based on total seizures, including those from unknown sources
* United Arab Emirates
Note Except as noted, percentages represent the share of total seizures where sources are known; some respondents reported a significant level of seizures where the source was unknown. The data are based on reported values, except as noted
Source European Commission, 2006*b*; OECD, 2005*b*; OECD 2006; and United States Department of Homeland Security, 2006
Source OECD The Economic Impact of Counterfeiting and Piracy 2008

2.2.1 WHO Database

2.2.1.1 Rapid Alert System

The WHO has established the Rapid Alert System for counterfeit medicines. The System compiles reports on counterfeit/substandard drugs detected in individual regions across the world. Two pie charts introduced below (Figs. 2.1 and 2.2) break down 771 cases reported to the WHO for a period between 1982 and 1999 (WHO 1999).

Although the reports were collected from across the world, the Western Pacific Region (Asian countries) accounted for approximately half, followed by the Region of Africa and the Region of Europe (Fig. 2.1). Of the nine regions, the total of industrialized countries accounted for 21.1% and the balance of 78.9% was taken by the developing countries. As is shown, the number of reports was smaller in developed countries and was greater in emerging and developing countries. However,

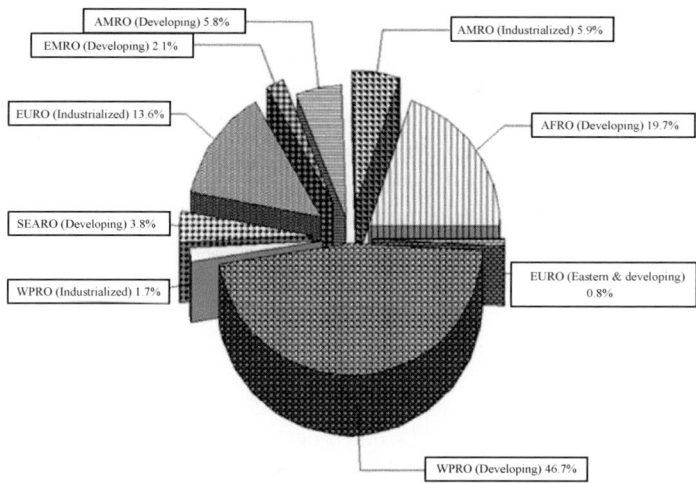

*Countries classified according to WHO Regional Offices:

AFRO - Regional office for Africa
AMRO - Regional office for the Americas
EMRO - Regional office for the Eastern Mediterranean
EURO - Regional office for Europe
SEARO- Regional office for South-East Asia
WPRO - Regional office for the Western Pacific

Fig. 2.1 The number of region-specific reports on counterfeit/substandard drugs. Geographical origin of cases (1982-April 1999; total: 771). *Source* WHO (1999). Counterfeit and Substandard Drugs in Myanmar and Viet Nam

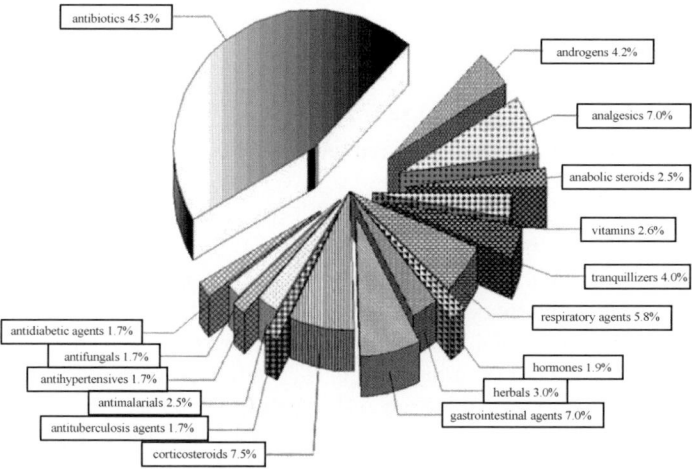

Fig. 2.2 Pharmaco-therapeutic classes of cases reported (1982-April 1999; total 771). *Source* WHO (1999). Counterfeit and Substandard Drugs in Myanmar and Viet Nam

since medicinal products cross the border by means of export and smuggling, it is not always true that manufacturers (criminals) of counterfeit drugs are based on the region where the counterfeits were detected or reported on. There is no information about how the reported articles were determined to be counterfeit or substandard.

Antibiotics accounted for almost half the counterfeit/substandard drugs, followed by steroids, drugs to treat gastrointestinal disorders, and analgesics. Thus, counterfeit/substandard drugs cover a wide range of therapies (Fig. 2.2). The fact that almost half the counterfeit/substandard drugs are antibiotics may be closely related to the demand based on the disease structure in emerging and developing countries, that is, the demand for drugs to treat infectious diseases.

The United Nations Interregional Crime and Justice Research Institute (UNICRI) regards handling counterfeit medicines as a highly profitable business. However, unlike drug-related crimes such as handing narcotics, counterfeit medicines do not always constitute a highly profitable business because medicines are goods used only when they are necessary and counterfeits are competitive pricewise with officially authorized medicines in the market.

Of the 771 reported cases, 325 (42%) had labeling for the quality of active ingredients. Among those, 59% did not contain active ingredients, and 7% contained the active ingredients as specified. The amount of active ingredients contained was wrong in 17%, and different active ingredients were contained in 16%.

These two pie charts provide the number of reported cases and the therapeutic categories of reported counterfeit and substandard drugs but do not provide the total volume. The size of business handling counterfeit medicines was estimated to correspond to 7 trillion and 500 billion Japanese Yen over the world in 2010 (Kimura 2009), which makes us consider that the total of 771 reported cases for a 17-year period is too small. However, since the total volume for the reported cases is unknown, we cannot make a judgment.

2.2.1.2   Global Surveillance and Monitoring System (GSMS) for Substandard and Falsified Medical Products

This database was established after the IMPACT had reached a dead end, and contains data for a period between 2013 and 2017 (WHO 2017a). In 2017, the WHO revised its definition of poor quality pharmaceuticals from "counterfeit medical product" to "substandard and falsified medical products" (WHO 2017b).

Interestingly, we can infer the disease structure across the world and how it changes from the reported status of poor quality pharmaceuticals. When compared with the results of Rapid Alert System introduced above, this database shows a peak for both antibiotics and antimalarial drugs, although the two together totaled, 36.5% and their relative importance reduced (Table 2.4).

Alternatively, lifestyle products accounted for 8.5% and cancer medicines, 6.8%. The higher ranking of these drugs may serve to indicate that lifestyle-related diseases and cancer have spread also in low- and middle-income countries.

Table 2.4 Examples of substandard and falsified products reported to the GSMS (2013–2017)

Type of product	Number of Member States reporting	Total no. of product reports	Percentage of all products reported to database[a]
Anesthetic and painkiller	29	126	8.5
Antibiotics	46	244	16.9
Cancer medicines	19	100	6.8
Contraception and fertility treatments	19	29	2.0
Diabetes medicines	7	11	0.8
Heart medicines	22	75	5.1
HIV/hepatitis medicines	9	43	2.9
Lifestyle products[b]	37	124	8.5
Malaria medicines	26	286	19.6
Mental health medicines	19	45	3.1
Vaccines	11	29	2.0

[a]Since only selected products are reported in this table, the percentages in this column do not add up to 100%. A table showing the breakdown of all reports using the anatomical therapeutic chemical classification is provided in the Annex to the main report
[b]So-called lifestyle products include products for cosmetic use, erectile dysfunction, bodybuilding, and dieting
Source WHO Global Surveillance and Monitoring System

If the trend in poor quality pharmaceuticals moves in conjunction with changes observed in the disease structure of a certain region, two possibilities could be considered; one is that traders handling poor quality pharmaceuticals as a business might carry out marketing activities; and the other is that characteristics of the market in that region might allow poor quality pharmaceuticals to be manufactured and distributed.

Poor quality pharmaceuticals are detected in countries with high- through to middle- and low-income countries (Fig. 2.3). Some countries are not reported to the WHO GSMS since they are not applicable, but some of them are reported in other databases or literature. It should be assumed that poor quality medicines are disseminated across the globe.

In Japan also, detection of poor quality pharmaceuticals was reported, which will be discussed in more detail in Chap. 9.

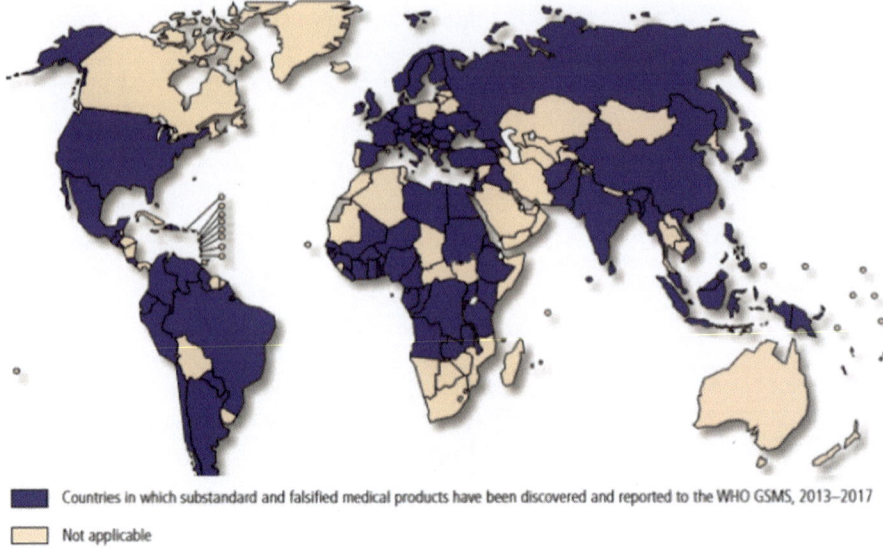

Countries in which substandard and falsified medical products have been discovered and reported to the WHO GSMS, 2013–2017

Not applicable

Fig. 2.3 Countries in which substandard and falsified medical products have been discovered and reported to the WHO GSMS, 2013–2017. *Source* WHO Global Surveillance and Monitoring System

2.2.2 Database of the Pharmaceutical Security Institute (PSI)

The Pharmaceutical Security Institute (PSI) is one of the non-government organizations (NGOs) established by security directors of research-based global pharmaceutical companies in developed countries. At present, 28 companies, government agencies, and international organizations participate in the PSI.[2]

Figure 2.4 shows the reported incidents involving counterfeit medicines that are published on the website of PSI. The number of product items per incident or the types of products engaged in each incident is not disclosed (Pharmaceutical Security Institute 2016).

The number of incidents had been steady at around 2000 since 2011, and then substantially increased in 2015. The number of counterfeit medicines per incident is not published and the total volume of counterfeits involved in these incidents is unknown.

---

[2]Twenty-eight companies, government agencies, and international organization participate in the PSI.

Government: European Commission, INTERPOL, Medicines and Healthcare Products Regulatory Agency (MHRA), U.S. Dept of Justice—CCIPS, U.S. Food and Drug Administration (FDA), U.S. Immigration & Customs Enforcement, WHO-IMPACT.

Non-Government: Abbott Laboratories, AstraZeneca, Bristol-Myers Squibb, GlaxoSmith Kline, Eli Lilly and Company, International Federation of Pharmaceutical Manufacturers Associations (IFPMA), Novartis, Partnership for Safe Medicines, Partnership for Safe Medicines India, Pfizer, Roche, RxPatrol, Sanofi.

Fig. 2.4 The number of reported incidents involving counterfeit medicines (2011–2015). *Source* PSI[a]

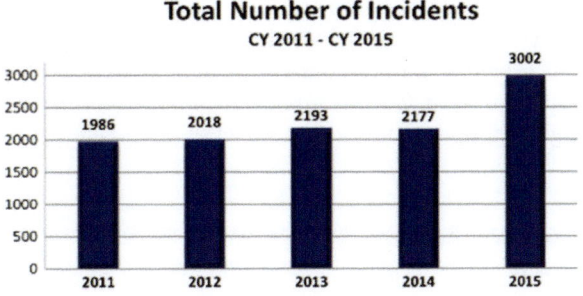

Fig. 2.5 The number of reported incidents involving counterfeit medicines, by region. *Source* PSI[b]

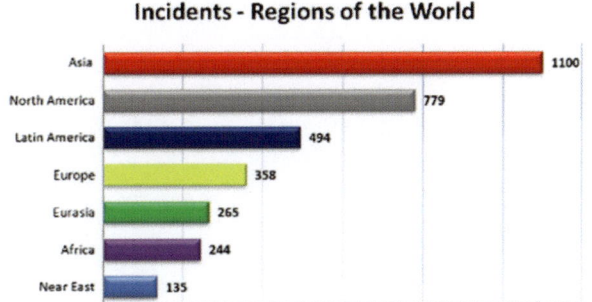

Another report issued by the PSI demonstrates that reported incidents involving counterfeit medicines have spread across the world (Pharmaceutical Security Institute 2014). As the JETRO's report demonstrated, the largest number of incidents was reported from Asia. The regions of Europe and North America, in which pharmaceutical regulations have been advanced, showed a larger number of incidents than in Africa (Fig. 2.5).

It should be noted, however, that this type of incident reporting is greatly affected by differences in capacities which regulate pharmaceutical affairs. As it is always true for counterfeit products, regions in which counterfeits are detected and reported on are different from regions in which they are manufactured, which implies that there may be a huge gap between the compiled data and the actual status in individual countries.

2.2.3 Media Reports on Medicine Quality: Database of the US Pharmacopeia

This database shows what is summarized by the US Pharmacopeia (2008–2012) (McGinnis 2013). This list compiles a series of incidents specified by region, name of medicine, brief summary, and reference (URL on websites are indicated for all incidents).

This database covers incidents of counterfeit and substandard medicines reported in the media across the world. References adopted are media including newspapers and scientific journals such as magazines. Credibility of incidents is not verified. Analyses by editors are not published, either. Despite these limits, this database regularly updates the status of individual countries across the world and is useful when trying to understand the global situation from a bird's-eye view.

The Media Reports on Medicine Quality are outlined as described below.

For a period between 2008 and 2014, problematic incidents were reported worldwide from developing to developed countries. Region-specific analysis revealed the greatest number of reports in Asia, in particular, the prominence of China.

The reported medicines widely ranged from affordable essential medicines to expensive medicines such as anticancer agents. Medicines not used for lifesaving, such as drugs to treat Erectile Dysfunction (ED) and slimming drugs, were not infrequently reported. Although chemical analysis results were not stated for all incidents, some reports indicated that no active ingredients were contained at all.

Smuggling is one of the channels used to invade other countries. Incidents in Japan were also reported, and it would be assumed that these Japanese incidents were not related to legitimate distribution channels but to illegal private importation or online distribution channels.

Box 4: YouTube

YouTube is one of the influential media platforms. On YouTube, political parties upload what they want to appeal to the people or someone uploads content to accuse those in power. In addition, content of hate speeches, violations of human rights, or racial discrimination is uploaded. For some themes uploaded, some would criticize that they mainly aim at creating sensations and are never worthy of scientific discussion. However, aside from whether content conveys exactly fact or not, we need to recognize that YouTube is one of the media having an impact on the awareness and knowledge of people.

When YouTube was searched using "counterfeit drug" as a key word, 26,500 movies were retrieved (on February 11, 2018). Each movie got several thousands of clicks to hundreds of thousands of clicks, although the number of views varied depending on when the movies were uploaded. Those who upload movies on YouTube include media, pharmaceutical companies, and NGOs. Some examples are introduced below. What is stressed is the viewpoint of cracking down because "counterfeit drugs" are crimes causing many deaths. Although a sensational incident could easily incite only one viewpoint, YouTube can further accelerate the incitation by the power of movies.

- Undercover Agents Go on the Hunt for Counterfeit Drugs
  ABC News: 273,000 views, uploaded in 2016
  Part 1: As part of a nearly year-long investigation, ABC News' "20/20" joined police on a **counterfeit medicine** raid.
- Combating the Counterfeit Drug Trade: Ashifi Gogo at TEDxBoston
  TEDx Talks: 9,500 views, uploaded in 2013

> "Over 700,000 people die every year. That's equivalent to four fully packed jumbo jets crashing every day.
> - Detecting Fake Drugs With A Piece Of Paper—Headline Science
>   American Chemical Society: 21,000 views, uploaded in 2017
>   Each year, **fake** or substandard **medications** kill more than 300,000 people worldwide.

2.2.4 Medicine Quality Database & Poor Quality Medicines Alert

This database was established in support of the United States Agency for International Development (USAID) and the US Pharmacopeia (USP). This database compiles data on quality of essential medicines in a total of 12 countries[3] in Africa, Asia, East Europe, Latin America, and the Caribbean, in which the distribution of poor quality medicines is regarded as a problem.

Quality tests are conducted and assessed in accordance with the standards of the participating states. Some states set the permissible width of specification for an active ingredient at 80–120% but others, at narrower ranges. It is also pointed out that the method of determining whether a drug is substandard or counterfeit varies depending on the participating states. Samples submitted for the tests are collected from the public, private, and informal sectors, although whether or not the indicated product information (such as country of manufacture, name of manufacturer, etc.) is true or not, is not verified. Test results indicate the following items: Region, Country, Province, Medicine/Brand name, Final test results (accepted or rejected), Type of test, Reason for failure, and Judgment result on whether the drug sample tested results from counterfeiting or not.

This database contains test results for only 13,000 samples as of 2013. This number of 13,000 is that of samples tested after they were obtained by sampling from the markets. Not all of these sampled drugs conformed to the relevant specifications or were counterfeited. The testing methods and acceptance criteria of this database are not common to those of the other databases. This database has a limited capacity to provide information leading to an exact understanding of the world situation. However, this database has encouraged the participating states to start a fixed-point observation regarding the quality of essential medicines and in this respect, it is significant for the health administration of these countries.

---

[3]The 12 countries are Cambodia, Colombia, Ecuador, Ghana, Guyana, Kenya, Laos, Mozambique, Peru, the Philippines, Thailand, and Vietnam.

2.3 Definition and Actual Status of Poor Quality Pharmaceuticals

2.3.1 Definition by the IMPACT and the Actual Status of Poor Quality Pharmaceuticals

How the IMPACT recognized counterfeit medicines came down to its definition, which is introduced below (IMPACT Secretariat 2011).

> Counterfeit medical product: a medical product is counterfeit when there is a false representation (NOTE 1) in relation to its identity (NOTE 2) and/or source (NOTE 3). This applies to the product, its container or other packaging or labeling information.
>
> Counterfeiting can apply to both branded and generic products and counterfeit products may include products with the correct components (NOTE 4) or with the wrong components, without active ingredients, with incorrect amounts of active ingredients or with fake packaging.
>
> Violations or disputes concerning patents must not be confused with counterfeiting of medical products.
>
> Medical products (whether generic or branded) that are not authorized for marketing in a given country but authorized elsewhere are not considered counterfeit.
>
> Substandard batches of or quality defects or noncompliance with good manufacturing practices/good distribution practices (GMP/GDP) in legitimate medical products must not be confused with counterfeiting.
>
> NOTE 1: Counterfeiting is done fraudulently and deliberately. The criminal intent and/or careless behavior shall be considered during the legal procedures for the purpose of sanctions imposed.
>
> NOTE 2: This includes any misleading statement with respect to name, composition, strength, or other elements.
>
> NOTE 3: This includes any misleading statement with respect to manufacturer, country of manufacturing, country of origin, marketing authorization holder or steps of distribution.
>
> NOTE 4: This refers to all components of a medical product.

The core of the definition is described in only the first three lines and the remaining merely lists the cases. Although this is called the definition, it would be assumed the IMPACT might attempt to encourage people to understand the issue by means of non-specific words but by the image created by the cases listed. The reminder that "violations or disputes concerning patents must not be confused with counterfeiting of medical products" strongly suggests that some factors within the problem of poor quality pharmaceuticals are easily linked to the area of patents.

This definition states that substandard batches must not be confused with counterfeiting, which means that it is understood that the act of counterfeiting is different from the acts of manufacturing and distributing that brought about substandard medicines. In this respect, a specialist who was sent from his Japanese pharmaceutical company to the WHO to be engaged in the counterfeiting-related problems (as of 2011) commented as described below.[4]

---

[4]Interview conducted by the author 19 November 2014 in Tokyo.

The WHO made its position clear, that is, the Organization addressed the health-related problems alone and did not get involved in criminal acts or patent-related problems. Therefore, the Organization drew a line in the discussion at which health damage occurs or not.

Drug regulatory authorities understood as follows: counterfeit drugs were made by criminals so that they looked exactly the same in appearance as authentic ones, although they contained fake substances, and were intentionally distributed into the lawful distribution channels; and substandard medicines constituted a problem of deviations from the GMP and were not related to malicious intent.

Subsequently, it became considered that what is ideal is to secure distribution of genuine products and something should be done to eliminate the other distribution mechanisms.

The WHO stated that regarding counterfeit drugs, it was necessary to exchange information among countries and to establish a universal definition for the purpose of identifying the magnitude of the problem on a global scale. The first definition was developed by the WHO in 1992 and discussion to revise the definition continued.

The IMPACT definition alone is not sufficient enough to understand what types of quality-related problems exist in poor quality pharmaceuticals. Quality-related problems consist of overdosing and underdosing of active ingredients and in addition, other items related to efficacy and safety (e.g., solubility, equivalency, contamination, and inadequate sanitation). Items determining poor quality are wide-ranging.

For example, the following incidents were reported (Caudron et al. 2008): overdosing and underdosing of active ingredients (for antituberculosis drugs and antimalarial drugs); inadequate vial filling (for paracetamol, etc.); contamination (for purified water, solution for injection, etc.); misleading labeling; inadequate dissolution and biological equivalence (rifampicin); contamination with diethylene glycol (for cold remedies); poor stability (for antibiotics, vaccines, etc.); excessive or insufficient dissolution rates (for antidiabetic drugs). Many of these incidents were discovered in low- and middle-income countries but were also found in the United Kingdom and France. This indicates the spread of poor quality pharmaceuticals across the world.

These cases are not merely deviations from specifications but even worse, adversely affect patients' recovery from diseases and jeopardize patients.

If quality-related problems are not so major to lead to health damage, then the medicines concerned are highly likely to be substandard rather than counterfeit. The extent of health damage varies. Among the fatal incidents, those attributable to additives such as diethylene glycol attract attention. For these incidents, what exactly happened is unknown, which causes ordinary people to fear that they may be malicious acts of terrorism or be committed by criminals for fun.

When drugs contain no active ingredients at all, it might be acceptable that such drugs are regarded as counterfeits because a clear intent "to commit a fraud" is assumed. However, if overdosing or underdosing of active ingredients is used as a criterion to determine the presence or absence of counterfeiting, such criterion may be unavoidably arbitrary about a line drawn to determine if drugs are counterfeits or not.

In 2006, the abbreviation used by the WHO to express counterfeit drugs was SSFFC (Substandard/Spurious/Falsely-labelled/Falsified Counterfeit medicine) and included substandard medicines. At that time, Brazil and India expressed their concern about the definition of counterfeit medicines, whereas African countries suffered from health damage caused by poor quality drugs. Under these circumstances, both substandard and falsified medicines were included in the abbreviation, for the purpose of discontinuing the wandering discussion that was too obsessed with the definition.[5]

The WHO describes that if legitimate manufacturers get involved in crime and deliberately manufacture substandard medicines, such substandard medicines might be considered as counterfeits. The WHO regards counterfeiting products as criminal. However, even under this definition, it is quite difficult to retrospectively determine whether suspected products were lawful or criminal. The dissatisfaction of emerging and developing countries with the definition was one of the causes for IMPACT to reach a deadlock within a short period of time.

Box 5: The Core Part of the Problem with the Definition of Counterfeit Medicines

The reason why the definition of counterfeit medicines caused confusion was because the definition was based on type classification. The methods for classification include among others, classification by type, specification, genealogy, and dynamic. The classification by type starts at images, and is commonly used in every aspect; it is regarded as the king of the classification. This method is applicable to any type of event in which standards for the classification can be freely chosen. Its disadvantage is that the boundary between one taxon (which is a taxonomic unit set in accordance with a given system) and its adjacent taxon remains intrinsically unclear.

The definition of counterfeit medicines issued by the IMPACT creates the image by means of the cases listed. The classification by specification clarifies boundaries between taxons, but the taxon established there has a problematic relationship with the image (Nakao 1992). When even a small extent of deviation is noted from the permissible range of specification between 90% and 110%, whether such minor deviation is judged to be a dangerous counterfeit or be of no clinical significance varies depending on individuals and cases. In other words, the relationship with the image becomes a problem.

Almuzaini et al. conducted a systematic literature review and reported "the lack of evidence available that specifically differentiates between substandard and counterfeit medicines" (Almuzaini 2013). In a study conducted with the support from research-based global pharmaceutical companies, Johnston et al. reported that it is difficult to differentiate substandard from counterfeit medicines and that the problem of substandard drugs is greater than that of counterfeits (Johnston and Holt 2014). These reports are valuable because

---

[5]Interview conducted by the author with a person working for the Japanese Ministry of Health, Labour and Welfare (MHLW) who was sent to the WHO, 18 November 2014 in Tokyo.

they empirically verified the problem of the recognition created by the image based on type classification.

2.3.2 New Definition for Poor Quality Pharmaceuticals

In 2017, the WHO renewed the definition of poor quality pharmaceuticals (WHO 2017b). The background behind this renewal was that the previous definition of counterfeit medicines was criticized in particular by emerging and developing countries, which was one of the causes for the deadlock of IMPACT.

The new definition is introduced below. When compared with the definition of IMPACT, the new definition first describes "substandard" and gives a simple description about "fake drugs." This indicates that the WHO has shifted the center of its concern from counterfeiting to substandard medicines.

WHO definitions of substandard, unregistered/unlicensed and falsified medical products

For many years, the response to this important threat to public health was embroiled in a discussion of complex definitions that meant different things to different people. Reflecting this complexity, until May 2017, WHO used the term "substandard/spurious/falsely-labelled/falsified/counterfeit medical products". The WHO Member State mechanism on substandard and falsified medical products was tasked with revising these definitions to ensure that they were based on a public health perspective, with no account taken of intellectual property concerns. Based on these deliberations, the World Health Assembly, which governs WHO, adopted the following definitions.

Substandard medical products

Also called "out of specification", these are authorized medical products that fail to meet either their quality standards or their specifications, or both. Unregistered/unlicensed medical products: Medical products that have not undergone evaluation and/or approval by the national or regional regulatory authority for the market in which they are marketed/distributed or used, subject to permitted conditions under national or regional regulation and legislation. Falsified medical products are medical products that deliberately/fraudulently misrepresent their identity, composition, or source.

2.3.3 Discussion About Reasons for Production of Poor Quality Pharmaceuticals

There has so far been a lot of discussion about the reasons why poor quality medicines are produced. The arguments can be divided into several patterns.

Firstly, there is an argument that poor quality medicines are produced by criminals. In the case of fatal incidents, in particular, where toxic substances are detected, this argument may easily be accepted. If toxic substances are deliberately combined, then such combination is an extremely vicious crime. If they are mixed unintentionally, i.e., inadvertently or by ignorance, then such mixture can be an accident. However, since it is difficult to retrospectively determine whether this is deliberate or not, it is likely to be concluded that this is attributable to criminal activity.

Secondly, there is an argument that legitimate manufactures fail to comply with GMP, resulting in the production of substandard medicines. It is difficult to retrospectively determine whether such failure is deliberate or due to immature skills.

Thirdly, one of the arguments is that medicines which are produced up to standard may deteriorate in quality due to the impact of bad transportation or storage.

Fourthly, there exists a combination of the second and third cases.

Whether poor quality medicines result from counterfeiting or out-of-specification has been long controversial, and even as of today, it would be assumed that the controversy has not been completely settled. Regarding this controversial issue, Caudron et al. performed a literature review and organized the relevant prior research studies as described below (Caudron et al. 2008).

> Omer (1990) and Arya (1995) discussed the necessity of performing stability tests for medicines in the tropics. O'brien (1997) reported that contaminated active ingredients may cause fatal toxicity.
>
> In 1997, Andriollo reported the problems in the manufacture of medicines to be exported from European countries to developing countries, and in addition, only occasional quality control and lack of regulatory control performed on medicines destined for international aid and for programs targeted to developing countries. Moride (1997) reported that there is a problem in the awareness of healthcare professionals about the dangers posed by substandard drugs.
>
> Not a few investigators reported that substandard and counterfeit drugs are confused, and they are Verduin (1998), Laserson (2001), Po (2001), Figueras (2002), Wertheimer (2003), Rassool (2004), Videau (2006), and Atemnkeng (2007).
>
> Wondemagegnehu (1999) went as far as to tackle this issue and reported that "the majority of poor quality drugs were genuine and not the result of counterfeiting." According to Maponga (2003), one WHO study found that 18 out of 19 poor quality medicines were genuine products, yet the WHO cited this study as evidence of counterfeiting. Syhakhang (2004) and Atemnkeng (2007) reported that the majority of poor quality drugs were not the result of counterfeiting but were genuine.

As described above, it is difficult to determine whether poor quality drugs are the result of criminal counterfeiting or are substandard but genuine, and this difficulty is another cause to make it even harder for us to understand the magnitude and seriousness of the problem of poor quality pharmaceuticals. What we need to pay our attention to is that there is a risk of falling into thinking that we have to choose one of the two, counterfeiting or substandard.

2.3.4 To Whom Are Poor Quality Pharmaceuticals the Problem?

The WHO expressed its understanding that counterfeit drugs are copies of genuine medicines and are inferior in quality than that of the genuine, and in addition, are problematic in terms of legitimacy. This may have serious impacts on many stakeholders as described below.

However, there are different estimates by experts or organizations on the impact of poor quality products, counterfeiting in particular. That is because no reliable database is available. Developed countries may tend to overestimate to appeal the problem and conversely developing/emerging countries may tend to underestimate not to lose their face. This is one of the reasons why the quality issue has become complicated and emotionally concerned.

For pharmaceutical companies, counterfeit medicines cause several serious problems related to their management. Firstly, infringement of intellectual property rights including patent rights by third parties adversely affects their management. Secondly, opportunities to sell genuine products are reduced. Thirdly, the products of the company that are attacked by counterfeit drugs lose the trust of consumers and healthcare professionals.[6]

For patients, counterfeit medicines are not effective and deprive them of the chance to receive adequate therapy, or even worse, put them at risk of serious health damage, including death. In addition, patients suffer economic losses. In many countries of the world, greater proportions of citizens have to pay medical expenses out of their own pockets.

Risks posed to patients' impact on healthcare professionals, who cannot ensure the efficacy and safety of treatment administered to patients, which threatens the foundation of treatment plan.

For the pharmaceutical regulatory agencies of each country which approve pharmaceutical products, counterfeiting is an illegal act, which diminishes public confidence in the administrative agencies engaged in crackdown of crimes.

For the WHO and the health administrative agencies of each country, poor quality of the pharmaceuticals essential to public health, including but not limited to antibiotics, anti-HIV/AIDS drugs, and vaccines, lowers the social function to defend against infectious diseases on a global scale, due to development of drug resistance.

Namely, the quality-related problems do not merely cause all stakeholders to suffer from losses. The WHO has a sense of danger against the possibility that deterioration

---

[6]As far as the authors know, no empirical research has demonstrated the amount of loss pharmaceutical companies suffer because of counterfeit medicines.

in the quality of healthcare may increase the burden of disease and health cost (WHO 2018). Poor quality pharmaceuticals surely lower the quality of healthcare.

2.4   Health Damage Caused by Poor Quality Pharmaceuticals

2.4.1   Serious Incidents of High Criminality

2.4.1.1   Counterfeit Heparin Incident in Europe and North America

The counterfeit heparin incident was triggered by the occurrence of serious allergic reactions caused by heparin preparation at US dialysis centers in December 2007. The damage expanded and in the end, at least 80 persons died and more than 800 non-fatal adverse drug reactions occurred. In Germany also, dozens of victims were reported (Bogdanich 2008).

This heparin preparation was manufactured by Baxter in the US, and the active ingredient in heparin was imported from Scientific Protein Laboratories (SPL) and its Changzhou SPL plant in Changzhou City, China. The substance that caused the health damage was initially unknown. The US FDA discovered the presence of oversulfated chondroitin, a compound that mimics heparin that should not have been contained in the preparation. At that time, this substance was recognized as an authentic ingredient of heparin when tested in accordance with any pharmacopoeia of the world. Namely, it passed the specification test. It became evident that even if a specification was set, such setting could not perfectly guarantee quality, and the detection method for oversulfated chondroitin was additionally included in the pharmacopoeia. This incident might have been committed by a person having a good knowledge of pharmacology.

In this incident, the manufacturer of the final product was the legitimately approved marketing authorization holder in the United States and manufactured the product in accordance with GMP. SPL was also a legitimate company. Nevertheless, the counterfeit heparin was produced and distributed. As the result of this incident, pharmacopoeias of major countries, including Japan, were revised.

This incident reveals pitfalls of globalization. In the field of generic medicines, outsourcing of operations as well as complication and elongation of the supply chain have been enhanced for the purpose of looking for inexpensive chemical compounds. It has, therefore, become difficult to verify manufacturing, quality control, and quality assurance system of companies from which those chemical compounds are procured. Consequently, there are intrinsic dangers making quality assurance systems vulnerable and it is not simple anymore to draw a line at which drugs are judged to be counterfeit or substandard. Lessons from this incident are that at some points in the life cycle of medicines, there are opportunities for not only legitimate companies alone but also illegal companies to be get involved in critical aspects.

2.4.1.2 Counterfeit Cold Remedy Incident

As procurement of raw materials for generic medicines has spread across the world, incidents caused by money laundering-like activities were reported (Franco 2007).

In Panama, at least 100 deaths were caused by diethylene glycol contained in cold remedies. The glycerin contaminated with diethylene glycol that was imported into Panama was manufactured in China and was labeled as 99.5% pure glycerin. The counterfeit glycerin passed through three trading companies from its beginning trade located near the Yangtze Delta in a place local Chinese people call "chemical country," to the second one in Beijing, and the third one in Barcelona. Purity test results were repeatedly falsified and no one knew who made it and where it came from.

This incident indicates that active ingredients of pharmaceutical products are regulated for medicines, whereas additives such as excipients are not under regulation as medicines; inexpensive additives or excipients, even if they are of unknown origin, can be used for manufacture of pharmaceutical products. Manufacturers must conduct incoming inspection of the ingredients. In this incident, however, whether or not the manufacturer was able to conduct an incoming inspection adequately and actually did it is unknown. China is a great supply source for raw materials, although it might be assumed that not a few companies would have inadequate awareness about business ethics.

2.4.1.3 Overview of Health Damage

It is impractical to conduct clinical studies using poor quality medicines such as counterfeits, and a survey based on literature search was performed with an attempt at identifying the actual status of health damage.

This survey (Kimura 2013) used PubMed and retrieved papers with English written abstracts using the following retrieval formula: (counterfeit OR fake OR falsified OR spurious OR bogus) AND (medicine OR drug). A total of 1,608 articles were hit and among them, 136 reports involving health damage were identified (fake drugs were clearly stated in 71 reports and not, in 66 reports). In 24 out of the reported incidents, the year and country of occurrence as well as the details and cause of damage were described. The 24 incidents are summarized below.

- 15 incidents occurred in developing countries and 9 in developed countries.
- The causative fake drugs (counterfeit drugs) were antipyretic analgesics and antitussive drugs in a total of 8 incidents, and antidiabetic drugs in 3.
- In 10 incidents, unlabeled ingredients were contained. In 7 incidents, active ingredients were not contained or underdosed.
- The number of victims suffering from health damage was 5,642 and among them, there were 3,534 deaths (62.4%).

In this survey, comprehensive screening and meta-analysis were conducted for published papers regarding health damage caused by counterfeit medicines. The survey outcome is characterized by the finding that the combined trends fall into the definition proposed by the WHO, but whether medicines were counterfeit or not was based on the subjective judgment by authors of the papers. This bias, coupled with the reporting bias in those reports on health damage extracted might have resulted in high mortality rates.

Interestingly, the number of health damage cases caused by diethylene glycol, ethylene glycol, and glycerin was large whether health damage was reported to be caused by imitated drugs (=counterfeit drugs) or non-imitated drugs in the papers under survey. Many of these cases were related to syrups, which are for pediatric use and are frequently given a sweet taste. These excipients might have been used to give the taste.

It was not determined if contamination with these excipients in the reported cases was intentional, accidental, or ignorant. However, the large number of incidents due to syrups contaminated with diethylene glycol may indicate a possibility that the contamination might have been related to ignorance or human error. The absence of incoming inspection for raw materials received or the presence of counterfeited certificates of analysis results in contamination with toxic substances or impurities, which is included in the category of human errors.

Diethylene glycol, ethylene glycol, and glycerin frequently caused major problems in the food industry, in addition to the field of pharmaceutical products. Diethylene glycol is not percutaneously absorbed and an excellent solvent is used in cosmetics and other such substances. The compound is dangerous because when orally taken, it exerts toxic effects on the liver, kidneys, and central nervous system.

A poisoning incident using diethylene glycol occurred, in which wine and other drinks were intentionally contaminated with the compound as an additive to give a sweet taste and increase mellowness (Suzuki 2011). This incident is known in Japan as the incident of poisoned wine produced in Australia in 1985. The compound was used in juice, champagne, and fruit liqueur.

2.4.2   Estimation of Invisible Health Damage and Its Limitation

It is almost impossible to compile data on the actual status of health damage caused by poor quality pharmaceuticals on a global basis. What we can do is to estimate what is going on, on the basis of several hypotheses formulated. At a meeting of the Executive Board of WHO held in 2009, emerging and developing countries criticized the WHO/IMPACT, claiming that "data on the problems associated with counterfeit medicines are insufficient".

In 2017, the WHO published its report on the impact of poor quality pharmaceuticals on public health and socioeconomic factors (the report entitled "A study on the public health and socioeconomic impact of substandard and falsified medical products") (WHO 2017b). This report is concerned with meta-analysis on the prevalence

Table 2.5 Findings on excess deaths due to substandard and falsified antibiotics in hospitals and community settings

Prevalence of substandard and falsified products (%)	Number of excessive death in most likely case scenario (twofold increase in CFR)	Number of excessive death in alternative scenario (fourfold increase in CFR)
1	8,688	18,372
5	37,018	85,438
10	72,430	169,271

Source WHO. A Study on the Public Health and Socioeconomic Impact

of poor quality pharmaceuticals, and presents two models regarding their socioeconomic impact on the basis of meta-analysis results (the extraction from "Executive Summary" of this report is introduced below).

The first model: Childhood pneumonia.[7]

This model provides a first estimation of the potential impact of substandard and falsified antibiotics on mortality from pneumonia among children aged 0 to 5 years.

The estimation of the impact of substandard and falsified antibiotics on childhood pneumonia mortality considered different levels of global prevalence of substandard and falsified antibiotics used for the treatment of this illness. Table 2.5 summarizes the estimates for excess deaths from severe pneumonia due to substandard and falsified antibiotics at prevalence levels of 1%, 5% and 10% (assuming that use of substandard and falsified medicines results in a two-fold or a four-fold increase in case fatality rate (CFR)).

Based on a 10% prevalence of substandard and falsified antibiotics, this model estimates that

- Up to 72,430 deaths from childhood pneumonia can be attributed to the use of substandard and falsified antibiotics that have reduced antibiotic activity.
- This increases up to 169,271 deaths if substandard and falsified antibiotics have no activity.

The second model: Malaria in sub-Saharan Africa

The prevalence of substandard and falsified antimalarials was based on a literature review of studies of antimalarial quality in sub-Saharan Africa. The analysis modeled the incremental impact of their prevalence on treatment effectiveness. Health impact was measured in terms of deaths and disability-adjusted life years, and economic impact in terms of patient and provider costs related to additional treatment and further care needed due to failure of initial treatment. Table 2.6 summarizes these estimates.

For both the base case and CFR-adjusted case, it is estimated that incremental deaths in sub-Saharan Africa due to substandard and falsified antimalarials comprise

- Approximately 2.1–4.9% of total malaria deaths, or
- Approximately 3.8–8.9% of malaria deaths relating to patients seeking treatment.

---

[7]Pneumonia in this model refers to acute lower respiratory infection in children aged 0–5 years.

Table 2.6 Health and economic impact due to reduced effectiveness of substandard and falsified antimalarial products

	Incremental health impact (deaths)		Incremental economic impact (million USD 2017)	
	WMR cases	CHAI cases	WMR cases	CHAI cases
Base case	72,000 (40,000–98,000)	266,906 (147,000–364,000)	12.1 (6.7)	44.7 (24.8–60.8)
CRF adjusted case	31,000 (17,000–43,000)	116,000 (64,000–158,000)	10.4 (5.8–14.2)	38.5 (21.4–52.4)

Source WHO. A Study on the Public Health and Socioeconomic Impact

2.5 International Awareness of Poor Quality Pharmaceuticals

2.5.1 Acknowledgement by the WHO

Dr. Margaret Chan, the 7th Director-General of WHO, expressed her opinions on the problems related to counterfeit medicines in her opening remarks at the first meeting on Member State Mechanism[8] on substandard/spurious/falsely-labelled/falsified/counterfeit (SSFFC) medical products that were held in November 2012, as introduced below (WHO 2011).

> The goal, objectives, and terms of reference for this meeting were established in an annex to resolution WHA65.19, approved by the World Health Assembly in May. The objectives recognize the need to strengthen regulatory capacity and quality control laboratories at national and regional levels. The need to ensure the integrity of the supply chain is clearly stated. The Member State mechanism may also further develop definitions of substandard/spurious/falsely-labelled/falsified/counterfeit medical products.
>
> Ways must be sought to ensure that combatting these products does not result in hindering the availability of legitimate generic medicines. The emphasis is firmly placed on looking at problems from a public health perspective.
>
> WHO and its Member States must be concerned whenever harmful products enter the supply chain, regardless of the motive or cause, and regardless of whether the cause reflects deliberate deception, negligence, or weak capacity for quality assurance and regulatory control.
>
> A study published in June of this year examined samples of malaria medicines from several countries in South-East Asia and sub-Saharan Africa. In both regions, 35% of the samples failed chemical analysis. In South-East Asia, 46% failed packaging analysis and 36% were classified as falsified. In sub-Saharan Africa, 35% failed packaging analysis and 20% were classified as falsified. We cannot let poor quality medicines undermine the huge progress being made against malaria and so many other diseases. Patients in the developing world are at greatest risk from the proliferation of harmful medical products, but patients everywhere are vulnerable.

---

[8]The Member State Mechanism was established within the WHO after the IMPACT reached the deadlock, with the aim of encouraging all Member States to address the problem of poor quality pharmaceuticals.

What the above-introduced four points appealed by Dr. Margaret Chan would mean might be understood as described below.

Firstly, she emphasizes that the Member State mechanism is legitimate, although the IMPACT was not. Clearly, this emphasis was made in response to the criticism from emerging and developing countries that the precedent IMPACT had not been legitimately entrusted by the Health Assembly of WHO (see Chap. 6).

Secondly, the IMPACT's definition of 2006 clearly indicated that legitimate generic medicines are not included in the problem of counterfeit medicines. Nevertheless, she mentioned this issue in the above-introduced opening remarks, which might serve to demonstrate that as a background situation, confrontations, and distrustfulness between the developed and the emerging/developing worlds had existed with regard to intellectual property rights.

Thirdly, by saying "regardless of whether the cause of manufacturing and distributing poor quality pharmaceuticals reflects deliberate deception or negligence," she clarified her position that risks posed by counterfeit medicines are not distinguishable from those due to substandard medicines. However, it should be distinguished which is the major cause bringing about poor quality pharmaceuticals, a criminal or a legitimate trader. Pharmaceutical products are supplied by lawful business organizations. Why do lawful business organizations manufacture and distribute poor quality pharmaceuticals? This question is more important in essence than the definition of poor quality pharmaceuticals.

Fourthly, she emphasizes that people living in poverty who are vulnerable are victims, clarifying the WHO's position that this problem is inseparable from the challenge regarding access by the poor and needy to medicines.

2.5.2 Acknowledgement by the Other International Organizations

2.5.2.1 United Nations

The United Nations Office on Drugs and Crime (UNODC) is responsible for conducting survey and analysis on illicit drugs and crime, and assisting Member States of the United Nations in concluding and implementing treaties concerning illicit drugs, crime, and terrorism as well as in facilitating establishment of national laws concerning these issues. The UNODC regards counterfeit medicines as crime. In the "Fact sheet: Transnational Organized Crime-The Globalized Illegal Economy," counterfeit medicines are described as one of the items, as introduced below (UNODC).

> The sale of fraudulent medicines is a worrying business, as it represents a potentially deadly trade for consumers. Piggybacking on the rising legitimate trade in pharmaceuticals from Asia to other developing regions, criminals traffic fraudulent medicines from Asia, in particular to south-East Asia and Africa to the value of $1.6 billion. Instead of curing people, however, they can result in death or cause resistance to drugs used to treat deadly infectious diseases like malaria and tuberculosis.

In addition to build a lucrative online trade in fraudulent medicines targeting developed and developing countries alike, which can also lead to health implications for consumers.

The UNODC has a concern about the increase in counterfeit medicines in proportion to the rising legitimate trade in pharmaceuticals from Asia to other developing countries (which may refer, in particular, to African countries) and about an online trade targeting even developed countries. What is specifically meant by the increase in counterfeit medicines in proportion to the rising legitimate trade is unknown. However, it might be considered that this would indicate the presence of counterfeit medicines which pretend to be authentic and are slipped into the trade.

The United Nations Interregional Crime and Justice Research Institute (UNI-CRI) prepared its report entitled "Counterfeit Medicines and Organized Crime" in 2012. The reasons why this report was prepared is as described below (UNICRI 2012).

The definition of counterfeit medicines is based on that proposed by the WHO in 1992. Counterfeit medicines are fake products with the greatest potential for harming the health of consumers. Nevertheless, the threats posed by counterfeit medicines and even counterfeits by themselves have not attracted attention of media and those engaged in public health.

Counterfeiting of medicines has become a profitable crime industry run by transnational criminal organizations, and has affected the international society in a wide range of aspects, including but not limited to people's safety, people's living conditions, social development, commercial activities, and economic growth. For the purpose of warning the public about the existence of this situation and spreading information about this issue, the UNICRI prepared a report entitled "Counterfeit Medicines and Organized Crime." This report made special mention of the Internet's role as an unregulated medicine market.

The UNICRI adopts the WHO's definition of counterfeit medicines. Like the above-described UNODC, the UNICRI has a concern about an unregulated online trade run by criminals. It understands that counterfeiting of medicines is a profitable crime industry run by transnational criminal organizations, as in drug trafficking. It is also emphasized in this report that the problem of counterfeit medicines has rarely been recognized among ordinary people and the media.

2.5.2.2 World Bank

The extraction from the document entitled "Assuring the Quality of Essential Medicines Procured with Donor Funds" (2012) is introduced below (Moore et al. 2012). This paper summarizes the ongoing discussion on the basis of understanding about how the Global Fund, UNICEF, the World Bank, NPOs, and NGOs currently procure medicines for the sake of developing countries through the use of various policies and strategies.

The donor community spends millions of dollars annually on procuring essential medicines as part of development assistance for health. Defining and enforcing quality standards for these medicines continues to prove challenging as this involves complex regulatory processes.

While developed countries with stringent regulatory authorities in place have the capacity to comply with strict regulatory requirements, the essential medicines procured for developing countries are either not available in developed country markets, or are not the most competitively priced medicines internationally. Donors have therefore been forced to independently develop systems to purchase at lowest feasible cost, essential medicines for the developing world without compromising quality.

The World Bank has a concern about the essential medicines from the viewpoint of donors which provide aids to the developing world, and this perspective is different from those of the other organizations. The World Bank focuses on the balance between the quality of essential medicines and the pricing that enables those living in poverty to access them.

2.5.2.3 International Criminal Police Organization Referred to as INTERPOL

Every year, INTERPOL carries out, in collaboration with the WHO and police forces of national governments, international crackdowns on the online market. INTERPOL understands that illicit online pharmacy networks create hotbeds of distribution of counterfeit medicines. Its understanding is as described below (Interpol).

Pharmaceutical Crime: Criminals involved in pharmaceutical crime are operating through traditional organized crime groups or creating informal networks across the globe. These criminal networks are engaged in all types of pharmaceutical crime.

The examples include counterfeiting, diversion, theft, and illegitimate selling through the Internet. Transactions among transnational criminal enterprises yield huge profits. One illicit online pharmacy network earned 55 million US dollars during 2 years of operation.

INTERPOL fights against these criminal networks, intensifies collaborations among the key organizations such as police, customs, and health authorities, and thus, confronts the threats to public health and safety. In several regions in Asia as well as in Africa and Latin America, counterfeit medicines account for as large as one-third of the national or local markets.

Many of these counterfeit medicines contain incorrect ingredients, overdose or underdose active pharmaceutical ingredients (APIs), or do not contain APIs at all, and consequently, pose a grave danger to health. Counterfeit medicines sometimes are fatal. It is, therefore, extremely critical to combat counterfeit medicines, for the purpose of protecting global public health and safety.

INTERPOL is a partner of the IMPACT and understands that counterfeit medicines constitute part of pharmaceutical crime and must be combated. This understanding is consistent with the definition and policy of IMPACT. INTERPOL agrees with the IMPACT on the understanding that counterfeit medicines should be regarded as a public health issue on a global scale.

2.5.2.4 World Intellectual Property Organization (WIPO)

The World Intellectual Property Organization (WIPO) posts the "Fact sheet on Counterfeit medicines" prepared by the WHO in 2006, as it is on its website to explain counterfeit medicines (WIPO 2006). It might be assumed that it would be difficult for emerging countries to understand why the WIPO is engaged in tackling the problems associated with counterfeit medicines. The WHO's definition of counterfeit medicines does not contain words directly referring to intellectual property rights. We need to understand complex background behind this reality.

2.5.3   Acknowledgement by Individual National Governments

2.5.3.1   United States Food and Drug Administration (US FDA)

The Food and Drug Administration (FDA) is an administrative agency of a country, i.e., the United States of America, but has an extremely great impact on the globe. The statements posted on the website of US FDA are introduced below (FDA).

> Counterfeit medicine is fake medicine. It may be contaminated or contain the wrong or no active ingredient. They could have the right active ingredient but at the wrong dose. Counterfeit drugs are illegal and may be harmful to your health.

> FDA takes all reports of suspect counterfeits seriously and, in order to combat counterfeit medicines, is working with other agencies and the private sector to help protect the nation's drug supply from the threat of counterfeits.

The idea of the US FDA to fulfill its responsibilities is in accordance with the IMPACT's definition of counterfeit drugs. The FDA audits companies which export pharmaceutical products to the US and whenever necessary, issues warnings to audited exporters and bans on the import of their products. Its international capacity to implement pharmaceutical regulatory surveillance serves as a model which other countries follow.

2.5.3.2   European Medicines Agency

The commentary posted on the website of European Medicines Agency (EMA) is introduced below (European Medicines Agency). The EMA distinguishes "counterfeit" from "falsified" and expresses its opinion that what the IMPACT regards as "counterfeit" is "falsified." This may reflect the argument of emerging and developing countries that the term "counterfeit" is used in the context involving infringement of trademark rights.

Falsified medicines are fake medicines that are designed to mimic real medicines, and may

- contain ingredients of low quality or in the wrong doses;
- be deliberately and fraudulently mislabeled with respect to the identity or source;
- have fake packaging, the wrong ingredients, or low levels of the active ingredients.

Until, recently, the most frequently falsified medicines in wealthy countries were expensive "lifestyle" medicines, such as hormones, steroids, and antihistamines. In developing countries, they have included medicines used to treat life-threatening conditions such as malaria, tuberculosis, and HIV/AIDS. The phenomenon of falsified medicines is on the increase, with more and more medicines now being falsified. These include expensive medicines, such as anticancer medicines, and medicines in high demand, such as antivirals. Counterfeit medicines are medicines that do not comply with intellectual property rights or that infringe trademark law.

The EMA essentially follows the same profile of awareness with the WHO/IMPACT on the issue of poor quality medicines. Its concern is targeted at not only medicines important for public health in developing countries but also expensive fake drugs detected in developed countries. It might be assumed that the EMA carefully distinguishes between "counterfeit" drugs and the problem involving public health, by highlighting the implication that the term "counterfeit" is suggestive of infringement of intellectual property rights.

2.5.3.3   Japanese Ministry of Health, Labor and Welfare

"Approach to Counterfeit Medicines and Designated Substances by the Ministry of Health, Labor and Welfare (MHLW)"

In Japan, it can be said that counterfeit medicines-related problems extremely rarely occur in legitimate distribution channels and are not an urgent issue. Counterfeit medicines are discussed in linkage with the social problem of dangerous drugs (which were initially called quasi-legal drugs).

The Compliance and Narcotics Division, Pharmaceutical and Food Safety Bureau, MHLW adopts the WHO's definition of SSFFC to express counterfeit medicines. This means that the Division has the following common understanding: "Distribution of counterfeit medicines causes problems including the occurrence of health damage among the people and worsening of disease condition due to loss of the opportunity to receive treatment and in addition, forces companies to fail to receive legitimate profits for their development of pharmaceutical products (or to suffer from disadvantages due to damaged images of products)" (MHLW Japan 2014).

The MHLW expresses concern about the possibility that counterfeit medicines may make companies lose legitimate profits they should have received for their development. However, as far as the authors know, there is no empirical research regarding these lost profits.

2.5.4 Acknowledgement by Associations Representing Research-Based Pharmaceutical Companies

2.5.4.1 International Federation of Pharmaceutical Manufacturers & Association

The four associations, that is, the International Federation of Pharmaceutical Manufacturers & Association (IFPMA), the Pharmaceutical Research and Manufacturers of America (PhRMA), the European Federation of Pharmaceutical Industries and Associations (EFPIA), and the Japanese Pharmaceutical Manufacturers Association (JPMA) announced the joint statement on July 23, 2012, as outlined below (IFPMA et al. 2012).

> This joint statement to crack down on counterfeits from illicit Internet pharmacies and other sources was issued as a group of private US companies (including Google, Go Daddy, and several others) launched the Center for Safe Internet Pharmacies (CSIP) initiative to target illegal Internet pharmacies.

> The four associations support and encourage the individual and cooperative work for the United States Government, the European Union (EU), individual EU member states, the Japanese Government, and international organizations to reduce illegal sale of medicines by illegitimate online drug sellers that endanger public health.

The IFPMA is the global non-profit organization representing the research-based pharmaceutical companies in Japan, the United States, and the EU and has an influential power. The IFPMA has concern about illegal sale of medicines by unlawful online drug sellers because expensive pharmaceuticals contributing to profits are targeted by this illegal sale and intellectual property rights are threatened.

2.5.4.2 Japanese Pharmaceutical Manufacturers Association

On its website, the Japanese Pharmaceutical Manufacturers Association (JPMA) posts the commentary as described below (JPMA 2012).

> Action policy for countermeasures against counterfeit medicines: The threat of counterfeit medicines is increasing worldwide, and it is reported that between 10% and 30% of distributed medicines in developing countries are counterfeit, which poses a serious threat to patient safety.

> Manufacturing and distributing counterfeit medicines while deliberately disguising them as genuine authorized medicines not only fails to provide patients with the desired treatment effect but also brings about risks of physical disability or death due to unexpected adverse reactions. Health damage caused by counterfeit medicines has increased year by year across the world, and the member companies running their businesses abroad are exposed to consequent risks of damage.

> At present, counterfeit medicines have not yet been detected in distribution channels within Japan. However, counterfeits inflowing into Japan through private importation via the Internet from abroad and associated health damage have been confirmed. The volume of transactions for counterfeit medicines is growing (the Japan Customs reported that the number of seizures was about 390,000 articles in 2012, which was as high as 7.3 times greater than that in 2011).

The Japanese Ministry of Health, Labour and Welfare (MHLW) has established the "Suspicious Drugs Reporting Network," a website for educating the general public on counterfeit medicines. The MHLW announced that they will promote countermeasures against counterfeit medicines, in collaboration with the private sector, consumers, and other relevant associations.

The above-stated facts indicate that across the world including Japan, the awareness of the need to intensify actions to combat counterfeit medicines has been enhanced. The JPMA and its member companies will address the challenge of eradicating counterfeit medicines, in collaboration with the government, customs, and law enforcement agencies.

The JPMA is a member of the IFPMA, and basically has the same stance as that of IFPMA regarding illegal sale through the Internet. The JPMA considers that "eradication" is a solution.

The document used at a meeting of the Quality Committee of JPMA (date unknown) entitled "Combating Counterfeit Medicines: What Pharmaceutical Companies Can Do" lists Viagra, Levitra, and Cialis (all of which are drugs to treat ED) as examples of counterfeit medicines which are within the immediate grasp of ordinary people. In an incident of illegal sale of medicines through the Internet, an unlicensed import agent for medicines illegally imported drugs containing the active ingredient of Viagra, sold them to 8,000 persons for two and a half years, and attained the sales of about 200 million Japanese Yen.

It is described in the website of JPMA that distribution of counterfeit medicines leads to the following: patients lose opportunities to receive treatment; patients may suffer from health damage; adverse effect on the financial situations of pharmaceutical companies, which may delay development of new medicines; and if a recall from the market is unavoidable, then such recall may cause social turmoil. However, such cases were not reported by the JPMA. It is also stated in the JPMA's website that countermeasures of pharmaceutical companies include securing technologies to avoid counterfeiting and make an easy judgment on authenticity possible, ensuring security of distribution channels outside Japan, cooperating for crackdown, and conducting activities to raise the awareness of patients and healthcare professionals.

2.5.4.3   Pharmaceutical Security Institute

According to the statement in its website, the purposes of the Pharmaceutical Security Institute (PSI) is to achieve the following goals, by exchanging information about counterfeit medicines, illegally produced drugs, and pharmaceutical thefts: (a) to help member pharmaceutical companies, law enforcement agencies, and authorities responsible for implementing pharmaceutical administration and regulations to combat counterfeit medicines; (b) to arrange liaison and coordination among international and national organizations engaged in the areas of counterfeit and illegitimate medicines; (c) to collect information about all aspects of illegal medicines; and (d) to call attention to enforcement of laws regarding pharmaceutical crime and assist those concerned in providing training about the law enforcement.

The PSI collaborates with INTERPOL, World Trade Organization, European Commission, regional and national police, customs, authorities responsible for pharmaceutical administration and regulations, and industries. The PSI acts on a global scale and places importance on sharing information with the private sector (large-scale global pharmaceutical companies). However, the details of collected information do not appear to be made publicly available.

The international organizations including WHO and the administrative authorities as well as research-based pharmaceutical companies in developed countries (in particular, Japan-United States-EU trilateral world) have the common understanding that counterfeit medicines constitute a problem for public health and should be combated by crackdowns. This common understanding was initiated from the IMPACT and will be discussed in Chap. 6 of this book. However, we need to be careful not to make early conclusions on whether or not the situation in which influential international organizations of the world facing one direction represents a correct understanding of a problem.

2.6 Discussion

The international organizations including WHO and the administrative authorities as well as research-based pharmaceutical companies in developed countries (in particular, Japan-United States-EU trilateral world) have expressed that they have the common understanding that counterfeit medicines constitute a problem of public health and should primarily be combated by crackdowns. This common understanding was initiated under the initiative of WHO/IMPACT discussed in Chap. 6. Prior to concluding that the common understanding by the developed world and the influential international organizations is based on justifiable rationale, the factors listed below should be taken into account.

Firstly, the common understanding is shared among the developed world and international organizations, but is not always shared by the emerging/developing world (see Chap. 6). The reasons for or background behind the absence of sharing need to be further discussed. Secondly, the WHO's definition that initiated the common understanding should be focused on. The definition was based on type classification and had an essential defect. Nonetheless, the developed world and international organizations accepted the WHO's definition as it was. This involves several problems as described below.

The first problem is to what extent counterfeiting can be identified. Quality control units of large-scale pharmaceutical companies admit that counterfeiting ranges from cases in which visual inspection can easily identify it to cases in which even scientific analysis cannot easily detect it.

The second problem is cracking down represented by INTERPOL and seized drugs as a result of the crackdown. INTERPOL cracks down illegal online pharmacies and whether or not it is confirmed that seized medicines are counterfeit is not fully clarified. This facilitates the easy creation of an impression that products available at illegal pharmacies would all be dangerous counterfeits.

Thirdly, the reliability of information published by the media should be considered. Medical and scientific reports are stained by commercialism (Caulfield 2004). Researchers demonstrated that only 57% of medical research news reported on front pages of major newspapers were based on reliable evidence (Yuk and Lane 2009). In many cases, our impression and understanding depend on the media.

Fourthly, stakeholders have their own concerns of interests. Large-scale research-based pharmaceutical companies have concerns on their own branded pharmaceuticals, many of which are originators protected by patents. On the other hand, there exist a lot of small-scale companies in emerging and developing countries which have a business model of manufacturing generics, and these companies cannot have the same level of concerns as those of the large-scale research-based pharmaceutical companies.

Both large-scale research-based pharmaceutical companies and INTERPOL have a special concern about the online market through the Internet, which suggests that counterfeit medicines are linked with the supply-demand characteristics of the online market; the online market is characterized by supplying goods to customers who demand anonymity and convenience, and not providing supply to those who demand lifesaving and public health. Drugs to treat ED are one of the representative counterfeits available on the online market. The argument that counterfeit medicines damage public health by referring to the counterfeit ED treatment drugs is unreasonable.

As discussed above, many factors are contained in the common understanding shared by the developed world and the international organizations, and therefore, the problem of poor quality pharmaceuticals gives an impression that the problem is strongly related to counterfeiting. At the same time, many stakeholders individually have dispatched information and offered their own arguments, which have complicated the problem. In his book entitled "More Dammed Lies and Statistics" (Best 2004), Best J explores the issues raised in connection with social statistics. He identifies five different sorts of numbers, i.e., missing numbers from statistics, confusing numbers, scary numbers, authoritative numbers, magical numbers, and contentious numbers. When the word "numbers" is replaced with the expression "argument using numbers," we might understand that we need to be careful to accept the arguments made on the problem of poor quality pharmaceuticals, at face value.

References

Almuzaini, Tariq, Imti Choonara, and Helen Sammons. 2013. Substandard and counterfeit medicines: a systematic review of literature. BMJ 3 (8). https://bmjopen.bmj.com/content/3/8/e002923. Accessed 6 June 2019.

Best, Joel. 2004. *More Dammed Lies and Statistics*. Trans. University of California Press.

Bogdanich, Walt, 2008. Heparin Find May Point to Chinese Counterfeiting. The New York Times. http://www.nytimes.com/2008/03/20/health/20heparin.html. Accessed 8 Dec 2016.

Caudron, J.-M., et al. 2008. Substandard medicines in resource-poor settings: a problem that can be no longer be ignored. *Tropical Medicine & International Health* 13 (8): 1062–1072.

Caulfield, T. 2004. The Commercialisation of Medical and Scientific Reporting. PLoS Med 1 (3): e38. https://doi.org/10.1371/journal.pmed.0010038. Accessed 2 Sept 2018.

EMA. Falsified medicines. http://www.ema.europa.eu/ema/index.jsp?curl=pages/special_topics/general/general_content_000186.jsp&mid=WC0b01ac058002d4e8. Accessed 9 Sept 2016.

FDA. Counterfeit medicines. http://www.fda.gov/Drugs/ResourcesForYou/Consumers/BuyingUsingMedicineSafely/CounterfeitMedicine/default.htm. Accessed 9 Sept 2016.

Franco, A. 2007. A counterfeit contaminated drugs linked to Wan Guiping, shown with police officers after his arrest, killed at least 18 people in China. The New York Times. http://www.nytimes.com/2007/05/06/world/americas/06poison.html. Accessed 2 October 2016.

Frontier economics. The economic impact of counterfeiting and piracy. https://www.inta.org/communications/documents/2017_frontier_report.pdf#search=%27THE+ECONOMIC+IMPACT+OF+COUNTERFEITING+AND+PIRACY++Executive+Summary+2015%27. Accessed 9 Sept 2018.

IFPMA, PhRMA, EFPIA, et al. 2012. Intahnetto Hanbai to Anzen na Iyakuhin Akusesu ni kansuru IFPMA/PhRMA/EFPIA/JPM no Kyodo Seimei ni tsuite [Joint Announcement by IFPMA/PhRMA/EFPIA/JPMA on Internet Sales and Safe Access to Pharmaceutical Products]. Accessed 8 2016.

IMPACT Secretariat. 2011. IMPACT International Medical Products Anti-counterfeiting Taskforce The Handbook 2006–2010. http://apps.who.int/medicinedocs/documents/s20967en/s20967en.pdf. Accessed 10 Oct 2013.

Interpol. Pharmaceutical crime. http://www.interpol.int/News-andmedia/Publications2/Factsheets2. Accessed 9 Sept 2016.

JETRO Singapore Center. 2009. Indoneshia, Tai, Shingapohru ni okeru Mohoh-hin Ryutsu Jittai-chohsa Tokkyocho Itakujigyo [Surveillance on imitated products in the markets of Indonesia, Thailand and Singapore] Commissioned project by Japan Patent Office.

Johnston, A., and D.W. Holt. 2014. Substandard drugs: a potential crisis for public health. *British Journal of Clinical Pharmacology* 78 (2): 218–243. https://doi.org/10.1111/bcp.12298. https://www.ncbi.nlm.nih.gov/pubmed/24286459. Accessed 2 Sept 2018.

JPMA. 2012. Gizo Iyakuhin ni taisuru Torikumi [Countermeasures Against Counterfeit Pharmaceuticals]. http://www.jpma.or.jp/globalhealth/fake/. (In Japanese) Accessed 8 Sept 2016.

JPMA. http://www.jpma.or.jp/eventedia/release/pdf/120724_01_j.pdf. (In Japanese) Accessed 8 Sept 2016.

Kimura, Kazuko. 2009. Kauntafitto Yaku (Gizoiyakuhin) Hirogaru Osen, Ou Taisaku [Expanding pollution with counterfeit drugs, followed by delayed countermeasures]. Media Forum 9 June 2009. http://www.jpma.or.jp/event_media/forum/repo_20.html. (In Japanese) Accessed 3 Oct 2018.

Kimura, Kazuko. 2013. Chikyu Kibo no Mozoyaku (Kauntafitto Yaku) Man-en ni taisuru Kisei to Kenko Eikyo ni kansuru Chohsa Kenkyu [Survey Research on Regulatory Control Against Global Prevalence of Counterfeit drugs and Impact on Health]. http://mhlw-grants.niph.go.jp/niph/search/NIDD00.do?resrchNum=201203005A. (In Japanese) Accessed 13 Sept 2016.

McGinnis, M. 2013. Media Reports on Medicine Quality: Focusing on USAID-assisted Countries. United States Pharmacopeia. http://www.usp.org/sites/default/files/usp_pdf/EN/PQM/pqm-mediareports.pdf#search='1%29+Media+Reports+on+Medicine+Quality%3A+Focusing+on+USAIDassisted+Countries. Accessed 3 March 2016.

MHLW Japan. 2014. Gizo Iyakuhin oyobi Shitei Yakubutsu ni taisuru KohseiRohdohSyoh no Torikumi [MHLW's Countermeasures Against Counterfeit Medicines and Designated Drugs]. https://www.mhlw.go.jp/file/05-Shingikai-11121000-Iyakushokuhinkyoku-Soumuka/0000043360_1.pdf#search=%27%E5%8E%9A%E7%94%9F%E5%8A%B4%E5%83%8D%E7%9C%81%E5%8C%BB%E8%96%AC%E5%93%81%E9%A3%9F%E5%93%81%E5%B1%80+%E7%9B%A3%E6%9F%BB%E6%8C%87%E5%B0%8E%E3%83%BB%E9%BA%BB%E8%96%AC%E5%AF%BE%E7%AD%96%E8%AA%B2%2C+%E5%81%BD%E9%

80%A0%E5%8C%BB%E8%96%AC%E5%93%81%E5%8F%8A%E3%81%B3%E6%8C%
87%E5%AE%9A%E8%96%AC%E7%89%A9%E3%81%AB%E5%AF%BE%E3%81%99%
E3%82%8B%E5%8E%9A%E7%94%9F%E5%8A%B4%E5%83%8D%E7%9C%81%E3%
81%AE%E5%8F%96%E3%82%8A%E7%B5%84%E3%81%BF%27.

Moore, Thomas, David Lee, Niranjan Konduri, et al. 2012. Assuring the Quality of Essential Medicines Procured with Donor Funds. World Bank. Washington DC. https://openknowledge. worldbank.org/handle/10986/13577. Accessed 2 Sept 2018.

Nakao, Sasuke. 1992. *Bunrui no Hasso* [Concept of Classification]. Tokyo: Asahisensyo. (In Japanese).

OECD. 2007. The Economic Impact of Counterfeiting and Piracy Executive Summary. https:// www.oecd.org/sti/38707619.pdf. Accessed 3 June 2018.

OECD. 2008, The Economic Impact of Counterfeiting and Piracy. http://apps.who.int/ medicinedocs/documents/s19845en/s19845en.pdf#search=%27THE+ECONOMIC+IMPACT+ OF+COUNTERFEITING+AND+PIRACY+2008%27. Accessed 9 Sept 2018.

Pharmaceutical Security Institute. 2014. Counterfeit situation. http://www.psi-inc.org/ geographicDistributions.cfm. Accessed 3 April 2014.

Pharmaceutical Security Institute. 2016. Counterfeit Situation/Incident Trends. http://www.psi-inc. org/incidentTrends.cfm. Accessed 5 April 2016.

Suzuki, Atsushi. 2011. *Yudoku Manzu Wain Jiken* [The Affairs of Toxic-Manns Wines]. In Sengo Iryosi [Post War History of Medical Affairs] 368–370. Tokyo: Jiho. (In Japanese).

UNICRI. 2012. Counterfeit medicines and organised crime. http://www.unicri.it/topics/ counterfeiting/medicines/report/Ctf_medicines_and_oc_advance_unedited2013.pdf. Accessed 9 Sept 2016.

UNODC. Counterfeit Goods—A bargain or a costly mistake? https://www.unodc.org/documents/ toc/factsheets/TOC12_fs_counterfeit_EN_HIRES.pdf. Accessed 9 Sept 2016.

USP. Medicines Quality Database. http://www.usp.org/global-public-health/medicines-quality-database. Accessed 2 Sept 2018.

WHO. 1999. Counterfeit and Substandard Drugs in Myanmar and Viet Nam. http://apps.who.int/ medicinedocs/en/d/Js2276e/6.html. Accessed 6 March 2016.

WHO. 2011. Chan M, Director-General of the World Health Organization, Meeting on substandard/spurious/falsely-labeled/falsified/counterfeit medical products. http://www.who.int/ dg/speeches/2012/medical_products_20121119/en/. Accessed 14 Sept 2016.

WHO. 2017a. WHO Global Surveillance and Monitoring System for substandard and falsified medical products Reports and Executive summary. http://www.who.int/medicines/regulation/ssffc/ publications/gsms-report-sf/en/. Accessed 3 June 2018.

WHO. 2017b. A study on the public health and socioeconomic impact of substandard and falsified medical products. http://www.who.int/medicines/regulation/ssffc/publications/se-study-sf/en/. Accessed 3 June 2018.

WHO. 2018. Low quality healthcare is increasing the burden of illness and health cost globally. http://www.who.int/news-room/detail/05-07-2018-low-quality-healthcare-is-increasing-the-burden-of-illness-and-health-costs-globally. Accessed 11 Aug 2018.

WIPO. 2006. Factsheet (Revised November 2006). http://www.wipo.int/edocs/mdocs/enforcement/ en/third_global_congress/third_global_congress_ref_z3.pdf. Accessed 3 June 2018.

Yuk, W.Y., and T. Lane. 2009. Characteristics of Medical Research News Reported on Front Pages of Newspapers. PloS One. https://doi.org/10.1371/journal.pone.0006103. Accessed 2 Sept 2018.

Chapter 3
The World Health Organization

3.1 Mission and Constitution of WHO

The WHO was established by the inter-governmental agreement among the countries concerned, and is an independent international agency with its own initiative under the international law; this initiative is separate from that of the United Nations. The WHO is one of the agencies within the family of United Nations and is entrusted with improving and directing global public health as specified in its Constitution.

As of May 2016, 194 countries participate in the WHO. Each member state has the right to cast one vote. This means that at the World Health Assembly which is the supreme decision-making body for WHO, those arguments made by developing and emerging countries are relatively stronger.

The Constitution of WHO provides the rationale for its Charter 1 of the Constitution specifies a high objective for the WHO to achieve, i.e., to attain good health of all peoples, as indicated below.

Constitution of the World Health Organization

Chapter 1—Objective

Article 1
The objective of the World Health Organization (hereinafter called the Organization) shall be the attainment by all peoples of the highest possible level of health.

Chapter 2—Functions

Article 2
In order to achieve its objective, the functions of the Organization shall be:

(a) to act as the directing and coordinating authority on international health work;
(b) to establish and maintain effective collaboration with the United Nations, specialized agencies, governmental health administrations, professional groups and such other organizations as may be deemed appropriate;

© Springer Nature Singapore Pte Ltd. 2020
S. Kimura and Y. Nakamura, *Poor Quality Pharmaceuticals in Global Public Health*, Trust 5, https://doi.org/10.1007/978-981-15-2089-1_3

(c) to assist Governments, upon request, in strengthening health services;
(d) to furnish appropriate technical assistance and, in emergencies, necessary aid upon the request or acceptance of Governments;
(e) to provide or assist in providing, upon the request of the United Nations, health services and facilities to special groups, such as the peoples of trust territories;
(f) to establish and maintain such administrative and technical services as may be required, including epidemiological and statistical services;
(g) to stimulate and advance work to eradicate epidemic, endemic and other diseases;
(h) to promote, in co-operation with other specialized agencies where necessary, the prevention of accidental injuries;
(i) to promote, in co-operation with other specialized agencies where necessary, the improvement of nutrition, housing, sanitation, recreation, economic or working conditions and other aspects of environmental hygiene;
(j) to promote co-operation among scientific and professional groups which contribute to the advancement of health;
(k) to propose conventions, agreements and regulations, and make recommendations with respect to international health matters and to perform such duties as may be assigned thereby to the Organization and are consistent with its objective;
(l) to promote maternal and child health and welfare and to foster the ability to live harmoniously in a changing total environment;
(m) to foster activities in the field of mental health, especially those affecting the harmony of human relations;
(n) to promote and conduct research in the field of health;
(o) to promote improved standards of teaching and training in the health, medical and related professions;
(p) to study and report on, in co-operation with other specialized agencies where necessary, administrative and social techniques affecting public health and medical care from preventive and curative points of view, including hospital services and social security;
(q) to provide information, counsel and assistance in the field of health;
(r) to assist in developing an informed public opinion among all peoples on matters of health;
(s) to establish and revise as necessary international nomenclatures of diseases, of causes of death and of public health practices;
(t) to standardize diagnostic procedures as necessary;
(u) to develop, establish and promote international standards with respect to food, biological, pharmaceutical and similar products;
(v) generally to take all necessary action to attain the objective of the Organization.

Chapter 2 of the Constitution specifies the 22 functions necessary for the WHO to achieve the objective set in Chapter 1. These functions as described in Chapter 2 suggest that the attainment of good health is realized by an aggregate of nutrition, housing, sanitation, recreation, economy, working conditions, and other aspects of environmental hygiene. This was verified by the Declaration of Alma-Ata. In Chapter 2, health care is regarded as one of the pillars that are set to aim at promoting health work and health service from the viewpoint of public health, and medicines are considered as means to realize the promotion. The WHO is responsible for supporting the member states and collaborating with the other international agencies concerned.

Chapter 2 of the Constitution reflects how realistically the WHO tries to achieve its mission. Ideally, good health should be attained by the aggregate of nutrition, housing, sanitation, and other aspects of environmental hygiene. In reality, however, the actual situations of member states do not always allow them to improve all of these factors simultaneously as feasible challenges. Under these circumstances, health care is selected as a good cost-performance means to save lives directly and most quickly, and recover health. Consequently, the idea that the recovery and maintenance of health equals the prioritization of health care is created.

The WHO understands that healthcare contributes to public health. Since medicines are regarded as an effective means in health care, the WHO has formulated its policies in two directions; one is to provide vaccination and the other, to create a concept of essential medicines. As a whole, the mission of WHO also fostered an environment in which people have excessively depended on health care and medicines.

Box 6: SDG Target 3.b

The Sustainable Development Goals (SDGs) set the target described below in one of the Goals (United Nations).

Target 3.b in Goal 3: Support the research and development of vaccines and medicines for the communicable and non-communicable diseases that primarily affect developing countries, provide access to affordable essential medicines and vaccines, in accordance with the Doha Declaration on the TRIPS Agreement and Public Health, which affirms the right of developing countries to use to the full the provisions in the Agreement on Trade-Related Aspects of Intellectual Property Rights (TRIPS) regarding flexibilities to protect public health, and, in particular, provide access to medicines to all.

Indicator 3.b.1: Proportion of people who can obtain medicines at appropriate prices under sustainable conditions.

Indicator 3.b.2: Total net official development assistance (ODA) to medical research and basic health sectors.

Box 7: From MDGs to SDGs

One of the indicators set in the Millennium Development Goals (MDGs) was "a proportion of people who can obtain affordable medicines by negotiating with pharmaceutical companies" (United Nations Development Programme (UNDP)). When compared with this indicator, the above-stated target in the SDGs is more strategic, and protects, although using indirect expressions in the latter half of the Target, proactive use of compulsory licensing, which is the right included in the Doha Declaration (2001).

Despite the Doha Declaration, it does not seem that compulsory licensing has so far been used to the full. Even when compulsory licensing was to be used international conflicts occurred regarding interpretation of licensing terms and conditions. Compulsory licensing was perceived as no more than a kind of annoyance for global pharmaceutical companies.

The intention of the Doha Declaration is to secure access, from the viewpoint of public health to new medicines protected by intellectual property rights. The Executive Board of WHO verified its aims in 2009. This intention was reverified in the SDGs, with an aim of trying to prevent global pharmaceutical companies and developed countries from excessively claiming their intellectual property rights.

It is worth noting whether or not compulsory licensing through utilization of the SDG framework to try to enable improved access to newly developed medicines more than previously will actually work.

Through its healthcare policies, the WHO has played important roles in improving and directing global public health. In 1975, the WHO introduced the concept of essential medicines to identify the values of pharmaceutical products. In the Declaration of Alma-Ata in 1978, the WHO clearly positioned these essential medicines in public health. Consequently, international problems with medicines are directly related to the significance of the WHO, as specified in the Constitution. Under these circumstances, it was quite natural for the WHO to lead the IMPACT.

3.2   WHO Definition of Health

In this section, the authors discuss the WHO definition of health because it is considered that it is one of the factors contributing to the spread of modern medicine across the globe. In 1948, the WHO defined health as follows: Health is "*a state of complete physical, mental and social well-being and not merely the absence of disease or infirmity.*" This definition has remained the core of the health concept since the end of World War II. A critical discussion about this definition has been published and is introduced below.

If the part of "complete physical, mental well-being" in the definition were read as "normal (good) state," there would be no cases representing "the normal state." On the other hand, there exist cases representing the abnormal state, e.g., bleeding, fever, and high blood glucose levels, and these abnormalities are easily understandable by ordinary people who are not specialists.

In other words, health means "a state with no abnormalities" and whether or not a person is healthy is determined on the basis of whether or not there is any abnormality. This may lead to a belief that if a person tries to reach better health, he/she has to continue to find out an abnormality and to eliminate it endlessly. The definition of health and the way to realize the defined health depends on the process of elimination. Namely, health does not indicate any real state.

Using the adjective "complete" may lead to a notion that improving health is an unending challenge and therefore, people should seek out a better health endlessly. This means that the state of "being well" changes in nature into the belief of aiming at "a state with no abnormalities" (Iijima 2009). In addition, the adjective "complete" separates "the people who are not well" from those who are well. The state of health greatly varies depending on individuals and there certainly exist people who are in "incomplete" well-being. This definition may induce a discriminatory thought.

The definition of health implicitly labels people who are disabled or suffer from disease, as "being unhealthy" and in addition, makes people driven into a mindset in which they cannot accept the "unhealthy state" caused by aging and geriatric symptoms which no human being can avoid. Another related matter requiring investigation is the possibility that the concept of "healthy life expectancy" may intensify the mentality of trying to artificially manipulate the natural history of health.

What disrupts the environment inside and outside the body has adverse effects on health. Disturbing factors make people vulnerable to disease from short-, middle-, and long-term perspectives. However, many of the disturbing factors are related to society and are not easy to control. Direct intervention in a disease which is the outcome of disturbance, is the shortest way to address health-related problems when compared with elimination or correction of society-related disturbing factors. In this way, people admire medical intervention and strongly believe that the intervention is effective in recovering and maintaining health. In fact, modern medicine has provided many achievements sufficiently good enough for people to espouse the belief that modern medicine is an effective means of curing and mitigating disabilities and disorders. The WHO definition of health and this belief in medical intervention act on the mindset of people on one side, and on the other, are linked to the function of WHO to promote modern medicine, without any mutual contradiction. Modern medicine has not spread across the world only naturally.

Box 8: The Health Foods Market Exceeding the OTC Drugs Market

Uesugi has pointed out that modern medicine can stir up unnecessary anxiety in people around their health. This has created an increasing tendency toward reliance on health foods which modern medicine and health care do not see them to be beneficial (Uesugi 2002). The market for health foods, supplements, and healthcare foods in the fiscal year 2017 in Japan achieved 1 trillion and 562.4 billion Japanese Yen (Intage 2017).

People use health foods because of a wide range of reasons; they expect the effects of preventing/improving hypertension and decreasing blood glucose levels which can be mistaken for those of officially approved indications for medicines; and they expect effects in terms of weight reduction/figure slimming, cancer prevention, anti-oxidization/antiaging, and others which that are difficult to officially approve as indications for medicines.

On the contrary, despite its steady growth, the market for OTC drugs is estimated to achieve 671.5 billion Japanese Yen (in 2017) (Yano Research Institute 2018). In Japan, due to the increasing national medical spending, the central government has begun to officially recommend self-treatment with OTC drugs for mild diseases. Out-of-pocket expenses spent by patients to purchase OTC drugs are subject to tax deduction.

References

Iijima, Yuichi. 2009. *Kenko Fuan Shyakai wo Ikiru* [Living with Anxiety on Health]. Tokyo: Iwanami Shinsho. (In Japanese).

Intage. 2017. Kenko Shokuhin, Sapurimento+Herusu Kea Fuzu Shijo Jittai Haaku Repohto 2017 Nendoban [Market Report on Health Foods, Supplements and Health Care Foods FY2017]. https://www.intage.co.jp/news_events/news/2017/20171128_1.html. (In Japanese) Accessed 13 May 2018.

Uesugi, Masayuki. 2002. *Kenkobyo* [Health-oriented Disease]. Tokyo: Yosensha. (In Japanese).

United Nations. Sustainable Development Knowledge Platform. https://sustainabledevelopment.un.org/sdgs. Accessed 3 2018.

Yano Research Institute. 2018. 2017 Nen no OTC Shijo Kibo wa Zen-nenhi 1.0% Zoh no 8,280 Okuen [OTC Market in 2017 up to 828 Billion Yen, 1% increase from previous year]. https://www.yano.co.jp/press-release/show/press_id/1941. (In Japanese) Accessed 19 Sept 2018.

Chapter 4
Quality and Standardization for Globalization

4.1 What Is Quality?

Quality can be defined and viewed in many different ways. The International Organization for Standardization (ISO) defines quality as "degree to which a set of inherent characteristics fulfills requirement[1]." In the discipline of quality engineering, quality is defined as "loss imparted to society from the time the product is shipped, although losses caused by functions themselves are excluded" (Taguchi 1993).

Good Manufacturing Practice (GMP) is a technical idea originated in the US and born in the 1960s. The concept emphasizes that it is uneconomical to inspect quality at the final stage of production and therefore, quality should be built up in the process of manufacturing. This means that if works-in-process that happened to be nonconforming for some reason at any stage of manufacturing went through the process to the end, and at the final stage of production, were to be eliminated as nonconformance goods or requiring correction to be ready for sale, operations or tasks applied to such works after the time point at which they failed to conform to the relevant specification would bring about financial losses. The WHO has also adopted the concept of GMP and has formulated the WHO-GMP that fits the level of emerging countries. The view of "depending on the actual status of a country" is important when the quality of medicines is discussed on a global scale. This means that the WHO may not always require total uniformity in quality across the world.

However, some researchers have claimed different ideas from the above-stated concepts. P. Crosby argued that good or bad quality and high or low quality have no

---

[1]In the section "Introduction" of ICHQ6A, it is stated as follows: "A specification is defined as a list of tests, references to analytical procedures, and appropriate acceptance criteria, which are numerical limits, ranges, or other criteria for the tests described. 'Conformance to specifications' means that the drug substance and/or drug product, when tested according to the listed analytical procedures, will meet the listed acceptance criteria. Specifications are critical quality standards that are proposed and justified by the manufacturer and approved by regulatory authorities as conditions of approval."

© Springer Nature Singapore Pte Ltd. 2020
S. Kimura and Y. Nakamura, *Poor Quality Pharmaceuticals in Global Public Health*, Trust 5, https://doi.org/10.1007/978-981-15-2089-1_4

meaning as a concept but instead, quality is "conformance to requirement" (DIA-MOND Online 2008). In response to this argument, G. M. Weinberg proposed the idea that "statements regarding quality are all for somebody" and furthermore, asked the question: "Who is the somebody being behind that statement?" His answer was that "quality" is a relative thing and is valuable for somebody.

He further argued as follows: "quality is always defined politically and emotion-ally" and that "in most cases, the decision on the definition is put out of sight away even from the consciousness of people who make that decision," which further com-plicates matters (Weinberg 1992). This argument also applies to the controversies surrounding the definition of counterfeit medicines in the WHO/IMPACT. Below is the inside story of WHO relevant to this issue that was described by a person who was sent from a Japanese pharmaceutical company to the WHO.[2]

> At that time, India and Brazil strongly opposed the IMPACT. In African countries, many people died because of counterfeit medicines and they lived in difficult circumstances in which an illness should have been cured but actually was not due to counterfeits. On the other hand, there was an argument that there was no time to make the opposition like India and Brazil. This was an intense dispute in which individual countries expressed their opinions dependent upon their own honor.

> It cannot be considered that any individual working for drug regulatory authorities would be in favor of counterfeit medicines. Nonetheless, India and Brazil strongly asserted that the IMPACT system was unforgivable, and in addition, questioned the definition of counterfeits proposed by the WHO/IMPACT.

> Therefore, Dr. Margaret Chan interrupted the dispute saying, "We have no time to stick to the definition" and proposed the combination of substandard, falsified, and all other relevant medicines as one, which stopped the discussion concerning the definition. As a result of this, the term SSFFC (substandard/spurious/falsely-labeled/falsified/counterfeit) medical products was born.

> The abbreviation SSFFC was born for the purpose of discontinuing the discussion about the naming that did not seemed to reach an agreed conclusion. It was not true that the term "substandard" was forced to be included in the abbreviation. Nevertheless, Brazil and India did not accept the way of handling the term "counterfeit."

The above-stated story indicates that what is referred to as "quality" does not usually exist as a visible thing. At the same time, it means that who requires what and to which extent varies depending on stakeholders and because of this relativity, individual interests can exist. What is necessary is a means by which the abstract notion proposed by Crosby, i.e., conformance to requirement, can be understood as a specific notion. This means is "specification." Specification can be expressed with numerical values and words. Specification is a language to make the abstract notion visible. Conformance to specification is a surrogate parameter for quality and expresses quality with simplified wording.

---

[2]Interview conducted by the author 18 November 2014 in Tokyo.

4.2 Requirement of Compatibility Was the Foundation for the Concept of Specification

4.2.1 Emergence of the Concept of Compatibility

The concept of compatibility was born from the need to efficiently repair parts of musket guns used in the American War of Independence (1783). At that time, guns were individually made under craftsmanship; when a gun was broken, the broken parts were not replaced with those of another gun.

In other words, even the same parts were not identical to one another in terms of configuration and dimension, and they, therefore, were not regarded as the same ones within the range of allowable errors (although specification enables one to achieve the same configuration and dimension within the range of allowable errors). Muskets were invented in France and the idea of setting specification in the new world was something that brought about confrontation with the craftsmanship-based manufacturing in the old world (Hashimoto 2015).

4.2.2 The Idea of Specification that Enables Handling of Networking

Technology regarding compatibility began with a screw, which is a very basic component of machinery. Initially, in the UK, compatible screws were made within individual factories, although this did not achieve inter-factory compatibility. At that time, in the US in which mass production had already started, a new specification for screws was proposed, although this was different from one of the UK, and it subsequently became the national standard specification of the US (Hashimoto 2015).

> **Box 9: Emergence, Blooming, and Root-Taking of Technical Idea**
> In his book about the science history on "manufacturing," Hashimoto shed light on the fact that regarding the production of musket guns, there existed a confrontation between the traditional and innovative methods in France, and there was also a confrontation between the two powers related to the interests which those in favor of the individual methods owed.
>
> The power promoting the innovative method consisted of the elite engineers who received education and training at engineering school and were technical officers in artillery units. The power involved in the manufacturing and sales of traditional iron products and arms were craftsmen and merchants.
>
> In the end, a mass production method for standard model guns utilizing compatible parts was not established in France. Craftsmen placing importance

on traditional manufacturing methods and citizen labors did not accept the way according to which they were unreasonably expected to follow the imposed rationality of enlightenment at the level of manufacturing. It was Thomas Jefferson, who became the President of the US later, who brought the excellence of this technology into the U. The commissioned officer in technology who was stationed in France contributed to establishment of an American way of manufacturing method (Hashimoto 2015).

This history provides the following lessons: a series of development from emergence, blooming, and root-taking of a technical idea does not exist in a straight line but substantially involves the state of society and mindset of people; and manufacturing technology is not completed until techniques regarding each and every component used to compose a product are developed and these techniques are integrated into a complete system. These lessons are highly suggestive when we discuss technology transfer in the current international cooperation.

At a conference of the American Society of Mechanical Engineers held in 1889, Mr. James W. See listed more than 100 products appropriate for standardization, including, among others, gas pipes, water pipes, screws, gauges for railroad tracks, paper, envelops, and clips. These listed products are divided into the following three categories: (1) components that are combined with multiple components; (2) products to be purchased that are graded; and (3) rules for activities (Hashimoto 2015).

In all categories, the key was to secure consistency of activities through networking formed by goods and men. At this time point, specification arose from the idea that networking is useful in coping with globalization. In light of the above, it is understood that the concept of "compatibility" is based on "specification" and that adopting a certain specification as "standard" serves a function to make the world linked into one. When compatibility, specification, and standardization work together as a single entity, these three produce the highest effect. This does not only apply to manufacturing of components but also to the fields of technology, management, and services.

Specification reduced the need to rely on the personal skills of craftsmen. Specification has evolved to have a practical function as a common language in many fields. It can be said that specification has established the foundation for the current globalization.

At present, global rationalization requires "three types of product standardization," that is: (a) standardization of production, (b) standardization of products, and (c) standardization of technical specification (Hayashi and Furui 2012). Thus, specification has continued to expand its roles.

4.2.3 Benefits from Specification and Standardization that Enabled Mass Production

Technology for standardization facilitates standardization of machine tools and manufacturing methods, and provides an advantage that products of high uniformity can be mass-produced. World War I was a war of enormous attrition, and therefore, accelerated establishment of the technology for mass production. The economic growth and demand for improving standard of living as consumers in the developed world required mass consumption, which also boosted mass production.

As of today, thanks to benefits from the technology for mass production, medicines can also be mass-produced on a global scale. Extremely popular drug products referred to as blockbuster drugs[3] are born from a system which can supply a large quantity of uniform drug products. Blockbuster drugs have become a target of research and development-oriented pharmaceutical companies.

4.3 Setting Specifications and Standardization for Pharmaceutical Products

In the previous section, how the concept of compatibility has grown and expanded to realize specification-setting and standardization is overviewed. In this section, the roles and meanings that specification-setting and standardization have in the fields of pharmaceuticals and healthcare are discussed by reference to the concept proposed by P. Crosby.

4.3.1 "Specifications" of Medicines Embody Requirements of Patients

Pharmaceutical products are intended to enable, through their effects, treatment (e.g., radical treatment, remission/maintenance, prevention of exacerbation, improvement of QOL, prevention) of patients. Patient safety is as important as drug effectiveness. What patients require is that a medicine is highly effective and safe, which corresponds to the concept of standard for quality proposed by Crosby and Weinberg.

As described below, however, an indicator with which therapeutic effectiveness is assessed (which is referred to as an endpoint) is not decided in such a way as allowing only one interpretation. The endpoint is relative in that it is based on the objective of treatment. Safety is also relative in that it varies depending on the genetic makeup,

---

[3]In the pharmaceutical industry in Japan, it is understood by custom that blockbuster drugs are those that generate total global annual sales of at least 100 billion Japanese Yen a year for the pharmaceutical companies that sell them.

predisposition to an illness, past medical history, complications, disease condition, and many other relevant factors of the patient. The extent of conformance to patient requirements (which Crosby refers to as "quality") cannot be determined uniformly or automatically.

What is necessary to enable understanding (measurement) of the extent of conformance to patient requirements while taking into account the above-described relativity is to set criteria for patient requirements. Specifications set for medicines must incorporate the requirements of patients, and must be specific and measurable. This first requires disease specification, which is discussed in the subsection later.

4.3.2   Approval for Pharmaceutical Products and Setting Specifications for Drug Therapies

A pharmaceutical product is a specific substance and at the same time, must have information about how it should be used in which type of disease (i.e., information about indication(s), dosage and administration, and precautions for use). A medicine will not be manufactured (imported) or sold until the national government approves the substance and information concerned. A disease for which the use of a certain medicine is indicated as the recommended form of treatment is a matter for approval as the indication (that is also referred to as "Label Claim") of that medicine.

For the use of a medicine, the dosage and administration for the medicine must be specified, which is also a matter for approval. The disease and the medicine used for treatment of the disease are both strictly specified. As a result of this, the act of conducting medical care with a medicine (i.e., a drug therapy) is also specified.

The indication(s) and dosage/administration of a pharmaceutical product are specified, which then specifies pharmacotherapies. In this way, interchangeability of drug regimens becomes viable. Treatment interchangeability means the situation in which a similar therapeutic effect can be achieved irrespective of differences between healthcare professionals engaged in treatment, medical institutions, and manufacturers of the medicines concerned, provided that the responses of individuals to the same medicine remain within a certain allowable range. In other words, setting specifications for pharmaceutical products has enabled systematization and interchangeability of drug regimens.

4.3.3   Extraction of Disease Concept from Disease Conditions and Symptoms, and Setting Specifications for Diseases

When the Industrial Revolution was advancing (in the 1760s to the 1830s), an increasing number of labors came to cities and many of them fell ill. Hospitals were built to accommodate these patients, who were divided into groups depending on symptoms and were treated.

On the basis of clinical management of these accommodated patients, Dr. Bright reported, in 1827, 24 patients who presented all of the following 3 symptoms: swelling, proteinuria, and organic lesion (found by autopsy) of the kidney. This condition was referred to as Bright's disease, a disease of the kidneys. His report first discovered a "disease" from symptoms presented by patients (Tadara and Takizawa 2011). Dr. Bright recognized the existence of "disease" as the state where a patient was suffering an illness. In other words, he organized the states of being ill and created a specification concept of disease. This specified disease concept is currently referred to as an "indication" of pharmaceutical products.

4.4 Newly Developed Medicines and Generic Medicines

4.4.1 Newly Developed Medicines (Originators) and Generics

Generics are required to exert clinical effectiveness equivalent to that of originator brand products (i.e., clinical (=therapeutic) equivalence). How to assure this clinical equivalence is determined by the development capacity of a generic manufacturer. Pharmaceutical products are not composed of active ingredients (also referred to as active pharmaceutical ingredients or drug substances) alone but also include necessary excipients or additives.

Box 10: Definition of Generic Medicines

The terms "generic drugs/medicines or generics" are commonly used, although there exist no international definitions for these terms. In the developed world, it is recognized that generic drugs must meet the following conditions: (a) the active ingredient contained in a generic is the same substance as that used for its counterpart originator; and (b) a generic is biologically equivalent to the originator.[4]

The WHO states as follows: "a pharmaceutical product usually intended to be interchangeable with the originator brand product, manufactured without a license from the originator manufacturer and marketed after the expiry of patent or other exclusivity rights. Generic medicines are marketed either under a nonproprietary name, for example diazepam or occasionally another approved name, rather than under a proprietary or brand name. However, they are also

---

[4]Strictly speaking, clinical studies to compare a generic with its counterpart originator are necessary to verify the clinical equivalence between the two. However, there are criticisms that implementation of such clinical comparative studies waste medical resources, i.e., patients, and imposes too much economic burden to generic manufacturers that have to strive against many competitors.

quite frequently marketed under brand names, often called 'branded generics'. Many different branded generic products of the same medicine can be on the market in a country along with the originator brand product" (GaBI 2012).

As described above, generics are dogged by problems resulting from the following two issues: termination of the period in which an originator is protected by the relevant intellectual property right; and equivalence to the originator in terms of how the pharmaceutical product should act. The second issue is related to the national pharmaceutical regulations of individual countries, and accordingly, each country may have its own definition for a fake drug. There can be cases in which drugs containing smaller quantities of active ingredients and drugs which are unlikely to dissolve in the body are not regarded as fake drugs (Yamane 2008).

The quality standard for a generic is that the newly developed originator brand product that has already been commercially available in the market. A pharmaceutical company which has developed the originator has no legal obligation to disclose the know-how regarding formulation design. Generic manufacturers by themselves design a formulation (i.e., set specifications) for a generic that will be equivalent to the originator. Specifications required for generics to be equivalent to originator brands are outlined below.

The premise is that clinical equivalence between generics and originators is not assured until the three types of equivalences described below are all secured (Ogata 2013). Official approval of generics only requires, as a general-rule evidence for equivalence to originators; this substantially reduces the total cost necessary for the development of generics when compared with originators. Consequently, generics are made less expensive than originators in the market, and are of social and economic significance in that they contribute to the wider availability of pharmaceutical products and to reduction of healthcare costs. This is a major reason why the WHO Model List of Essential Medicines primarily consists of generics.

Chemical equivalence: This means that a generic contains the active ingredient equivalent to that of the originator, and this equivalence is verified by quantitative and qualitative tests.

Pharmaceutical equivalence: This is extremely important because it especially involves formulation design and is the key for a generic to exert its therapeutic efficacy as expected. For tablets taken as an example, a tablet must dissolve in the intestinal tract within a certain period of time after oral administration: if it does not, then of course, the drug is not absorbed correctly in the body and, therefore, is not expected to exert its clinical effectiveness.

Enteric-coated tablets are designed not to dissolve in the stomach and not to dissolve and be absorbed until they reach the intestinal tract (this is a pharmaceutical strategy intended to bypass the stomach for cases in which active ingredients easily lose activity when exposed to gastric acid). This equivalence is verified by dissolution, release, permeation, and disintegration tests.

Bioequivalence: This refers to equivalence in concentration of a drug at a site where the drug exerts its effect. This is verified in many cases by blood drug concentration and drug disposition. Usually, a bioequivalence verification test is conducted in a group-comparative manner to administer a generic and the originator to several dozens of healthy male volunteers.

Bioequivalence is the most important condition that must be met to assure clinical equivalence. The acceptable range for bioequivalence is usually between 80 and 125%, as described below.

The 90% confidence interval for the ratio of a generic to its branded counterpart in terms of blood drug concentrations (Cmax and AUC) exists in the rage of 0.80–1.25. Here, Cmax means the maximum drug concentration a drug reaches when administered and Area Under Curve (AUC), the area under the concentration-time curve as the blood concentration changes over time after its administration. An allowable range is set for specification as described above because blood drug concentrations may vary for the reasons listed below.

Differences between pharmaceutical products (i.e., between a generic and its branded counterpart) note that the objective of bioequivalence studies is to determine whether these differences exist or not and in addition, to the following variability.

Variability in the following factors:

a. Variability in the quantity of an active ingredient of the dosage form to be administered (note that the actually contained quantity of an active ingredient is usually set at the range of 95–105% of the designed quantity)
b. Variability in measured blood concentrations which is usually within the range of 10–20%
c. Intraindividual variability in pharmacokinetics which is usually within the range of 10–20%.

As described above, specification is a process to put something that by nature varies into a certain range. The allowable range for specification depends on the extent of quality requirements, a possibility that manufactured products may meet such requirements, costs, and other relevant matters, and therefore, cannot be determined uniformly.

Furthermore, quantitative, qualitative, release, dissolution, permeation, and disintegration tests are available as specification tests, and an applicant for official approval for a generic medicine (which is a pharmaceutical company) selects which tests should be performed. Based on test results derived from actually measured data, the applicant sets specification values (together with allowable ranges). The applicant submits the specification values and results of pharmacokinetic parameters (Cmax and AUC) to the regulatory authorities, which then review the data. When the regulatory authorities determine that the data is appropriate, the generic medicine is officially approved. In other words, the specification tests selected by an applicant and the specification values (and allowable ranges) set by the applicant have a direct impact on the design quality of a generic medicine. The capability of the administrative agency to assess these matters assures the quality of a generic medicine to be commercially viable or not. A very basic duty of drug regulatory authorities is that they are able to adequately review submitted data and make a correct decision on approval.

4.4.2 Intellectual Property Rights and Business Model of Pharmaceutical Companies

Intellectual property rights cover a wide range of rights including, among others, patent rights, trademark rights, and registered design rights. Patent rights in the field of pharmaceutical products are unique in nature, when compared with those in other fields because the central concept exists in substance patents, which protect the active ingredients within the medicine.

The term of protection for substance patents in Japan and the United States is 20 years since the filing date. A long period of time is necessary for development of a pharmaceutical product, and the period during which the product is protected by the patent after it becomes commercially available to the market is only a length of time left until the expiration of protection. Development of a new medicine requires results from both preclinical and clinical studies, and needs a large sum of investment and a long-term period. Consequently, many newly developed medicines are actually protected by intellectual property rights for limited periods, from several years to 10 at the longest.

Research and development-oriented pharmaceutical companies usually adopt a business model of high risk and high return. They face difficulties due to the huge amount of investment required, a long-term period necessary for development, and a high hurdle to traverse in the discovery of a novel compound, whereas they can obtain large profits once their new drug products become blockbusters. When they launch a new medicine, they start corporate activities to maximize their sales before the expiration of protection period by intellectual property rights. The pipeline for newly developed compounds affects short- and medium-term sales forecasts of companies and there is a great deal of interests toward mergers and acquisitions (M&A).

In the market, competition for prescribing physicians becomes ever more severe. Research and development-driven pharmaceutical companies recognize that development of more effective drug regimens is their social mission, which is described in the slogan, "We deliver excellent medicines to people of the world as quickly as possible." However, "people of the world" means those who can pay for the medicines.

On the other hand, generic manufacturers employ a business model of producing and selling many different types of products in small quantities. When the protection period for a new medicine by the relevant intellectual property rights expires, the knowledge and information about an active ingredient of the new medicine come into the public domain and, therefore, study results which applicants for generic medicines have to submit to drug regulatory authorities are substantially reduced.

Consequently, generic medicines are significantly (by 50–70%) less expensive than their branded counterparts, which leads to easier access to generics than originator brand products. Generally speaking, the market share of an originator is decreased by more than 90% in a short period of time after the generic(s) of their counterpart originator is (are) launched into the market. For a single active ingredient, many pharmaceutical companies make applications for approval for generic medicines and sell them, which increases competition in the market, e.g., they are severely competing for acquisition of accounts at medical institutions. On the contrary, the quantities of production and sale for one company are small, which makes one wonder if a continuous supply of generics is stable.

Another challenge related to production of many different types of products in small quantities is that it can be difficult for a single company to be engaged in the whole manufacturing process from procurement of raw materials to production of final drug products. Generic manufacturers, therefore, rely on manufacturers of raw materials both inside and outside their mother nations from which they procure necessary raw materials. This means that due to a long and complicated route of procurement, it becomes more difficult to secure the required quality and in addition, there are increasing opportunities to prioritize prices when procuring raw materials.

As described above, research and development-oriented pharmaceutical companies differ from generic manufacturers in the social roles they play. This gap is generated by the difference between the two in earning structure attributable to intellectual property rights protecting originator brand products.

Under the current circumstances in which national governments of individual countries promote their policies to suppress national medical expenditures, the period of 2011 through 2020 in which many originator brand medicines lose their patent protection is referred to as a "patent cliff." During this period, originators are losing $200 billion sales across the world, which provides extensive business opportunities to generic manufacturers. This situation has generated financial resources and market influence, which helps generic manufacturers transiting from fringe players into what can be called the "New Big Pharma" industry (Nasdaq 2016). In response to this transition, research and development-oriented pharmaceutical companies are entering into the generic market. It is predicted that the conflicting and competing situation between generics and their branded counterparts that have existed in traditional branded medicines would also occur in the category of biosimilars.

4.4.3 International Agreement on Intellectual Property Rights

The first international agreement on the rules regarding intellectual property rights is the Paris Convention for the Protection of Industrial Property (to be referred to as the "Paris Convention") adopted in 1883. The three principles of the Paris Convention are (a) national treatment for nationals of countries of the Union, (b) the right of priority, and (c) independence of industrial property rights obtained for the same invention in different countries. These principles allow each country to be independent from the others in protecting their national intellectual property rights under their national laws.

Consequently, countries began to reorganize relations between and among relevant national systems, and to cause frictions with other countries because of their intention to prioritize their own national systems. In response to the first move, the World Intellectual Property Organization (WIPO) was established in 1967. As of 2018, the WIPO has 116 member countries. Japan participated in the Organization in 1975. WIPO is responsible for promoting protection of intellectual property rights on a global scale on the basis of the conventions regarding protection of intellectual property rights, harmonizing national systems of individual countries, regulating and administering international registration of intellectual property rights, and resolving disputes.

The Paris Convention prescribes the protection of intellectual property, although there are no provisions on enforcement procedures. The Agreement on Trade-Related Aspects of Intellectual Property Rights (TRIPS), that has an enforcement mechanism, was negotiated at the Uruguay Round of the General Agreement on Tariffs and Trade (GATT) and came into force in 1995, as a separate framework from the WIPO.

4.4.4 TRIPS Agreement Regarding Access to Pharmaceutical Products

4.4.4.1 Compulsory Licensing

The TRIPS Agreement imposes an obligation on Member States to introduce a patent system for pharmaceutical products. Researchers and specialists in relevant fields have pointed out that the existence of this patent system has increased prices of patented medicines, which has made developing countries become unable to freely import these medicines, which in turn has led to the propagation or outbreak of infectious diseases such as acquired immunodeficiency syndrome, malaria, and tuberculosis in the developing world.

For addressing the above-described problem, the TRIPS Agreement prescribes in Article 31 that under certain conditions, compulsory licensing is permitted, although

Article 31 (f) stipulates that use of compulsory licensing "shall be authorized predominantly for the supply of the domestic market of the Member authorizing such use." For countries with insufficient or no manufacturing capacities in the pharmaceutical sector (which are primarily least-developed countries (LDCs)), it is meaningless to grant compulsory licenses in their own countries.

On the other hand, if countries with pharmaceutical production capacities should produce drug products granted patents in their own countries, for the purpose of exporting such drug products to the countries which have insufficient or no capacities to manufacture medicines on their own, then this production would violate the TRIPS Agreement. This means that as far as the Agreement is observed supply of medicines for the purpose of contributing to public health is disturbed. After the World Trade Organization (WTO) was established in 1995, for the purpose of addressing this problem, the Doha Declaration on the TRIPS Agreement and Public Health was adopted by the 4th WTO Ministerial Conference held in Doha in 2001.

The Declaration is outlined below.

The extreme seriousness of the public health problems afflicting many developing and least-developed countries, especially those resulting from HIV/AIDS, tuberculosis, malaria, and other infectious diseases is recognized.

The need for the TRIPS Agreement to be part of the action to address these problems is emphasized.

The importance of intellectual property protection for the development of new medicines is recognized. The concerns about its effects on prices are also recognized.

It is agreed that the TRIPS Agreement does not and should not prevent members from taking measures to protect public health. It is affirmed that the Agreement can and should be interpreted and implemented in a manner supportive of WTO members' right to protect public health and, in particular, to promote access to medicines for all.

While maintaining our commitments in the TRIPS Agreement, it is recognized that the flexibilities of the Agreement include the following:

a. The TRIPS Agreement shall be interpreted by reference to the customary rules of international law and the objectives of the TRIPS Agreement.
b. Each member has the right to grant compulsory licenses and the freedom to determine the ground upon which such licenses are granted.
c. Each member has the right to determine what constitutes a national emergency, and HIV/AIDS, tuberculosis, malaria, and other infection diseases can be regarded as a national emergency.
d. Each member can establish their own regime for exhaustion of intellectual property rights without being sued.

The Council for TRIPS will discuss the problem that WTO members with insufficient or no manufacturing capacities in the pharmaceutical sector have difficulties in making effective use of compulsory licensing, find solutions to this problem, and report to the General Council before the end of 2002.

The promotion of technology transfer to least-developed country members is reaffirmed. With respect to pharmaceutical products, the transition period for the least-developed country members is extended to January 2016, without prejudice to the right of these members to seek other extensions of the transition periods pursuant to Article 66.1 of the TRIPS Agreement.

The establishment of compulsory licensing rules is intended to prevent abuse of intellectual property rights with respect to, in particular, objectives of public health. However, the international pharmaceutical industry, including Japan, is not comfortable with these rules.[5]

4.4.4.2 Data Protection

The Trans-Pacific Strategic Economic Partnership Agreement (TPP) imposes an obligation to Member States to protect undisclosed information also as intellectual property. When medicines utilize newly developed chemical substances which are new agricultural chemical products approved with a condition for granting marketing approval, that undisclosed test or other data for such products are protected, and that data regarding such medicines submitted to drug regulatory authorities are not disclosed. This rule is different from substance patents, and accordingly, double protection applies to intellectual property of newly developed medicines.

The TRIPS Agreement does not specify a period for data protection. In 2018, the TPP prescribes that the period for data protection is 5 years at shortest for newly developed medicines and 8 years at shortest for biopharmaceuticals.

The period for data protection starts to be counted when an approval is granted.

4.4.4.3 Confrontation Between the Emerging World and the Developed World Regarding Substance Patents

As prescribed by the TRIPS Agreement, each Member State is allowed to establish its own patent system. As of today, the patent system of each Member State is reaching much closer, although not completely yet, to a common platform. In the past, however, great disparities existed, in particular, with regard to substance patents. The representative case was the Indian patent system. Emerging countries such as India tried to avoid, as much as possible, interference with patents for newly developed medicines, or they issued compulsory licenses, for the purpose of promoting growth of its own national pharmaceutical industry and providing its people with affordable

---

[5]The Japan Pharmaceutical Manufacturers Association (JPMA) states in its website as follows: "The problem with access to medicines cannot be resolved only by issuing compulsory licenses. If an issuance of compulsory licenses lacks rationality and transparency, then it may raise concerns over difficulties in making adequate investment for research and development. We will continue to have dialogues with governments of other countries for the purpose of enhancing sustainable access to medicines.".

generic medicines (Minato 2007). When a generic drug made in India was seized by the Dutch customs (see Chapter 6.5), developed countries authorized substance patents, whereas India authorized patents for manufacturing methods or processes but did not adopt substance patents.

In other words, the world patent system was not adequately harmonized on a global scale, which enabled each Member State to give priority to its own interpretation of patents based on its position. Emerging countries including India took a stance of prioritizing its interpretation according to national laws, whereas developed countries followed international rules. Thus, conflicts in intellectual property rights were created between newly developed medicines and generics, and the conflicts became overlapping confrontations between the developed and developing worlds. In 2005, India introduced substance patents, interpretation, and administration of which was not at the same level as those in developed countries. Even after the introduction of substance patents, lawsuits were filed between India and developed countries.

4.5 Standardization of Pharmaceutical Products in the International Society

4.5.1 WHO Activities Regarding the GMP

The Good Manufacturing Practice (GMP) was a legally systematized set of regulations first promulgated in the United States in 1963 under the Federal Food, Drug and Cosmetic Act, and provides standards for both production and quality control for pharmaceutical products, etc. The underlying concept of GMP is that quality assurance relying on quality testing alone is insufficient and that quality assurance requires systematic management involving all processes from receipt of raw materials, packaging, quality testing, through release of final products (Hiyama 2010).

GMP is a concept of requiring manufacturers to do what they must do. GMP requires manufacturers "to design a GMP system" that minimizes human errors, protects drugs from contamination, and assures high quality. The WHO took over this idea and developed WHO-GMP. What the WHO claims with regard to GMP is summarized below (WHO).

> Quality is built up in the process of manufacturing. After the completion of manufacturing process for a product (i.e., after release of a product), the product cannot be examined for quality. The GMP prevents human errors which cannot be eliminated by quality control of final products. Poor quality products do not result in economic savings. From a long-term perspective, finding poor quality products after manufacturing is more costly than preventing production of poor quality products at the starting point.

The United States emphasizes "the limitation of relying on quality testing" and the WHO stresses that "quality is built up (in a product) during the process of manufacturing." The two have the same concept, although they use difference expressions.

The WHO determined to adopt GMP in 1968 and at the World Health Assembly in 1969, recommended Member States to introduce WHO-GMP. In 1975, the WHO revised the WHO-GMP guidelines by incorporating opinions of Members, and in 1975, recommended again Member States to introduce WHO-GMP.

In Japan, the "Project Team Committee for Investigations of GMPs" was organized in the Ministry of Health and Welfare (MHW, that is currently the Ministry of Health, Labour and Welfare) in 1972 and GMP was enshrined in the MHW Ordinance No. 3 entitled "Regulations for Manufacturing Control and Quality Control of Drugs" in 1994 (Takechi 2011). GMP has become a requirement for granting approval for each product item, which has required GMP auditing and then has an integrated GMP compliance inspection in the review process for registration dossiers.

4.5.2 PIC/S Aiming at Improving GMP and Quality Control System

PIC/S is an abbreviation used to describe both the Pharmaceutical Inspection Convention (PIC) and the Pharmaceutical Inspection Co-operation Scheme (PIC Scheme), which are international organizations with the intention to make arrangements between Member States and medicinal products-auditing authorities (JPMA 2010). These two operate together in parallel to achieve proactive and constructive cooperation in the field of GMP.

The mission of PIC/S is to lead the international development, implementation, and maintenance of GMP standards and quality systems. Their mission is to be achieved by developing and promoting harmonized GMP standards and guidance; that is, training competent authorities, in particular, inspectors and GMP inspecting agencies, and facilitating cooperation and networking for authorities and international organizations. Forty-eight regulatory authorities across the world participate in the PIC/S, whereas those of Brazil, Russia, India, and China do not (as of the end of 2015). These nonmembers are newly emerging countries that have huge populations and economic powers, and in addition, are eager to produce medicines and supply them to world markets. This means that adequate global harmonization has not yet been achieved in the efforts to improve the quality of generic medicines in particular.

4.5.3 Standardization of Quality Guidelines that Is Promoted by the ICH

The International Council for Harmonization of Technical Requirements of Pharmaceuticals for Human Use (ICH) is intended to promote international sharing of data used for approval for newly developed medicines and mutual acceptance of data. Specifically, ICH has developed harmonized guidelines in four categories, i.e., quality, safety, efficacy, and multidisciplinary.

The benefits of ICH for the regulatory authorities that conduct review and grant approval include increased efficiency and speeding-up of review as well as improving review quality. The benefits of ICH for companies developing new medicines are that they can avoid the overlapping of studies necessary for development, make application for approval simultaneously in major countries across the world (which minimizes opportunity losses), and prepare registration dossiers acceptable across the world. Consequently, companies can save costs, time periods, and medical resources necessary for development, and have become able to "deliver excellent medicines to patients more quickly."

On the other hand, the GMP has been successful for the past 30 years, although its negative regulatory consequences have also been taken into account. Under these circumstances, the Japanese Ministry of Health, Labour and Welfare proposed, at the ICH-GMP Workshop in 2003, to establish a quality assurance system incorporating new items such as management responsibilities and technology transfer. This proposal was adopted as a vision entitled "a harmonized pharmaceutical quality system applicable across the life cycle of the product (i.e., from development to post-marketing) emphasizing an integrated approach to quality risk management and science" (Hiyama 2010). This quality vision led to the ICH Guidelines Q8, Q9, and Q10,[6] indicating an evolutionary history of quality-related guidelines.

4.6 Discussion

Reasons, why pharmaceutical products have spread throughout the world and become dominant therapeutic means have so far been explained by the superiority of modern medicine over traditional medicine. Part of this superiority is attributable to the contribution by Robert Koch, Louis Pasteur, Shibasaburo Kitazato, and other relevant bacteriologists to the bacteriological theory (Miichi et al. 2001). In other words, the key was the remarkable effectiveness of medicines in treatment of infectious diseases. In this chapter, the roles of specification and standardization in globalization of pharmaceutical products are discussed as described below.

First of all, specification enabled quality to be visible.

Secondly, it enabled manufacturing of generic medicines based on their branded counterparts, which led to the assumption that if a drug meets the specifications of a newly developed medicine already available in the market, then it is assured that the safety and efficacy of the drug will be the same as those of the new medicine. In addition to the manufacturing of generics based on their originator counterparts, interchangeability between generics and their branded counterparts was also assured.

---

[6]The titles of quality-related ICH Guidelines Q8 through Q10 are as follows: Q8: Pharmaceutical Development; Q9: Quality Risk Management; and Q10: Pharmaceutical Quality System.

Thirdly, specification grew to have a practical function as a common language in the field of technology, which facilitated technology transfer from developed countries to developing and emerging countries. As technology transfer spread across the world, complying with specification enabled drug regimens to be interchangeable in a given therapeutic system on a global scale.

Fourthly, complying with specification enabled mass production. Pharmaceutical products became industrial products, which made it possible to respond to mass consumption of drug products.

On the other hand, setting specifications for pharmaceutical products became closely related to disease specification, and thus made it possible to promote systematization of disease concept and treatment methodology so as to enable sharing of the systematization among people beyond the borders of different countries, ethnic groups, and cultures. This means: the universality of that modern medicine which is called "Biomedicine" is based on the biological idea, and is endorsed by specification, which is the technical idea.

The discussion from the viewpoint of "specification" indicates that what is described above was a driving force to secure the superiority of modern medicine over traditional medicine and to promote the spread of modern medicine across the world.

Nowadays, international (especially tripartite, referring to EU, USA, and Japan) harmonization and standardization of drug regulatory authorities for pharmaceutical products are advancing. This is a process of attempting global harmonization of the healthcare field including pharmaceutical products under the norms of the developed world. However, India, China, and other developing countries remain observers for the club consisting of developed countries and do not fully follow the move of the developed world. This is one of the causes creating a gap between the developed countries and the developing and emerging countries regarding the norms of quality. A pharmaceutical product is a small item but contains an extremely advanced system of technical basis and ideas. Nevertheless, introduction of technology has made it relatively more easy to copy the appearances of a drug product, i.e., to just try to comply with a given set of prescribed specifications, so as to produce an equivalent product.

Some countries have succeeded in technology transfer in a true sense, whereas others have been somewhat successful in the transfer but have not fully utilized it yet, or remain even at the beginning of the process of transfer. The idea of specification was born in Europe but the technical aspect of the idea came into bloom in the United States when that was a developing country. This was deeply related to the absence of guild system for craftsmen in the United States, which fostered a free and open society (Hashimoto 2015). It should, therefore, be considered that the spread, root-taking, and further development of technical ideas associated with technology transfer do not occur automatically nor autonomously, but instead are determined by social conditions or the historical background of the country concerned.

Consequently, design quality, manufacturing quality, and management quality for pharmaceutical products are not uniform among countries. Poor quality products which do not meet prescribed specifications may be generated by the lack of uniformity in technical and social systems among countries. The concept of specification built the foundation for technology transfer, although whether or not technology transfer is successful is affected by the actual situation of society and culture in the country concerned.

In accordance with its Constitution, the WHO has endeavored to establish global standards for the quality of pharmaceutical products that form the fundamentals of public health system across the world. This was the reason why the WHO led the IMPACT. It can be interpreted that the WHO regards drugs which do not meet appropriate specifications as "substandard" medicines, based on the thought that if the interchangeability of drug regimens across the world should be damaged, then the system that has been built by the WHO would also be damaged.

Based on its view of access to medicines, the WHO claims that the quality of "essential medicines" should be acceptable. This means that the quality should not unreasonably increase costs nor require unlimited improvement of management methods. It should be understood that the quality which the WHO considers appropriate is adequate for assuring safety and clinical efficacy, provided that the amounts of manufacturing and quality management costs necessary to achieve the appropriate quality should be rational.

The WHO proposed WHO-GMP to achieve the above-stated appropriate quality. WHO-GMP is based on the premise that lowering prices of medicines to reasonable levels will improve access to medicines. This is because under the healthcare circumstances in emerging and developing countries, rates of patient's co-payments are greater. The WHO claims that a point of compromise between the pursuit of quality of medicines and the access to medicines must be sought so that the pursuit will not inhibit the access. However, the technology and concept for quality control in the developed world continue to advance, and medicines exported from the developing world to the developed world need to satisfy those requirements that are more stringent than those of WHO-GMP.

It is unavoidable that medicines supplied to the developed world need to satisfy the quality control requirements that are the same level as those specified by the PIC/S. As far as medicines are used only within the domestic markets of emerging and developing countries, these medicines do not need to meet the requirements of PIC/S, on the basis of the above-stated premise regarding the relationship between prices of and access to medicines. However, taking into account the facts that pharmaceutical products easily cross borders and are the goods that influence life and public health, the logic and argument raised by the developed world are that the quality level should be the same as that in the developing world is given priority.

Miichi has focused on the following point while quoting the opinion of Kunits (Miichi et al. 2001):

> In the discipline of modern Western medical science, it is understood that 'barriers of countries or cultures' must not 'disturb' business activities to eradicate the disease, from the viewpoint that 'individual illnesses are the same everywhere in the world.' It is also understood that 'human beings are all identical biologically and science can be applied everywhere.'

Consequently, Western medical science is administered as a specific cure across the world in a single uniform way (Kunits 1988).

The point of Miichi and the perspective of this chapter are on the same trajectory in that the logic of the developed world is made uniformly accepted by the emerging and developing world. This is an aspect of globalization. As far as modern medicine is regarded as the global standard, it is essential that setting specifications for pharmaceutical products and complying with the specifications are also regarded as the global standards.

References

Diamond Online. 2008. Phillip Crosby ZD (Kekkan Zero) Undo [Phllip Crosby ZD (Zero Defect Campaign)]. http://diamond.jp/ articles/-/3273. (In Japanese) Accessed 13 September 2016.

GaBI. 2012. Definitions of generics. http://gabionline.net/Generics/General/WHO-definitions-of-generics. Accessed 24 June 2018.

Hashimoto, Takehiko. 2015. *Monozukuri no Kagakusi -Sekai wo Kaeta Hyojun Kakumei -* [Science History on Manufacturing - Revolution of Standardization Which Has Changed the World-]. Tokyo: Kodansha Gakujutsubunko. (In Japanese).

Hayashi, Takabumi, and Furui, Hitoshi. 2012. *Takokuseki Kigyo to Gurohbaru Bijinesu* [Multinational Enterprises and Global Business]. Tokyo: Zeimu Keiri Kyokai. (In Japanese).

Hiyama, Yukio. 2010. Iyakuhin no Hinshitsu Kakuho to GMP [Pharmaceutical Product Quality Control and Good Manufacturing Practices]. *Bulletin of National Institute of Health Sciences* 128: 1–16. http://www.nihs.go.jp/library/eikenhoukoku/2010/001-016.pdf#search=%27%E6% AA%9C%E5%B1%B1%E8%A1%8C%E9%9B%84+%282010%29%2C+%E5%8C%BB% E8%96%AC%E5%93%81%E3%81%AE%E5%93%81%E8%B3%AA%E7%A2%BA%E4% BF%9D%E3%81%A8GMP%2C%27. (In Japanese) Accessed 1 Sept 2018.

JPMA. 2010. PIC/S no Gaiyo ni Tsuite [Overview on PIC/S]. http://www.who.int/about/agenda/en/. (In Japanese) Accessed 14 September.

Kunits, S.J. 1988. Hookworm and Pellagra. *Journal of Health and Social Behavior* 29.

Miichi, Masatoshi, Saito Osamu, and Wakimura Kohei. 2001. *Shippei, Kaihatsu, Teikokuiryo—Ajia ni okeru Byoki to Iryo no Rekishigaku* [Diseases, Development and Imperial Medication—History on Diseases and Medication in Asia]. Tokyo: Tokyo University Press. (In Japanese).

Minato, Kazuki. 2007. Indo Seiyaku Sangyo -Hatten no Seidoteki Haikei to TRIPS Kyoteigo no Henka [Pharmaceutical Industry in India: The Institutional Background of Development and Changes after TRIPS Agreement]. ed. Kubo Keisuke, 21–54. In *Nihon no Jenerikku Iyakuhin Shijo to Indo, Chugoku no Seiyakusangyo* [Generic Drug Market in Japan and Pharmaceutical Industry in India and China]. Chiba: IDE-JETRO. (In Japanese).

Nasdaq. 2016. Generic Drugs: Revolutionary Change in the Global Pharmaceutical Industry. https://www.nasdaq.com/article/generic-drugs-revolutionary-change-in-the-global-pharmaceutical-industry-cm576603. Accessed 14 Aug 2018.

Ogata, Hiroyasu. 2013. Jenerikku Iyakuhin no Seibutsugakuteki Dohtohsei ni Tsuite no Kangaekata [Bio-equivalency of Generic Medicines]. Central Social Insurance Medical Council. https://www.mhlw.go.jp/file/05-Shingikai-12404000-Hokenkyoku-Iryouka/0000013714.pdf#search= %27%E3%82%B8%E3%82%A7%E3%83%8D%E3%83%AA%E3%83%83%E3%82%AF% E5%8C%BB%E8%96%AC%E5%93%81%E3%81%AE%E7%94%9F%E7%89%A9%E5% AD%A6%E7%9A%84%E5%90%8C%E7%AD%89%E6%80%A7%E3%81%AB%E3%81% A4%E3%81%84%E3%81%A6%E3%81%AE%E8%80%83%E3%81%88%27.   Accessed   1 Sept 2018.

Tadara, Kozo, and Toshiyuki Takizawa. 2011. *Koshu Eisei* [Public Health]. Tokyo: Foundation for the Promotion of the Open University of Japan. (In Japanese).

Taguchi, Gen-ichi. 1993. Hinshu to Hinshitsu [Species and Quality]. *Quality Engineering Forum* 1 (4): 2–6. https://www.jstage.jst.go.jp/article/qes/1/4/1_2/_pdf. (In Japanese) Accessed 24 June 2018.

Takechi, Kyozo. 2011. GMP no Hoseika to Naraken Seiyaku Sangyoh –Kigyohsha Shiteki Siten kara- [Legislation of GMP and the Pharmaceutical Industry in Nara Prefecture: From Viewpoint of Entrepreneurial History]. *Journal of Business Studies* 57(3): 59–126. Kindai University Academic Resource Repository. https://kindai.repo.nii.ac.jp/?action=pages_view_main&active_action=repository_view_main_item_detail&item_id=11778&item_no=1&page_id=13&block_id=21. (In Japanese) Accessed 1 Sept 2018.

Weinberg, G.M. 1992. *Quality Software Management: Volume 1 Systems thinking*. Trans. New York: Dorset House Publishing.

WHO. GMP Question and Answers. http://www.who.int/medicines/areas/quality_safety/quality_assurance/gmp/en/. Accessed 2 October 2016.

Yamane, Hiroko. 2008. *Chiteki Zaisanken no Gurohbaruka -Iyakuhin Akusesu to TRIPS Kyotei-* [Globalization of Intellectual Property Rights -Access to Medicines and TRIPS Agreement-]. Tokyo: Iwanami Shoten. (In Japanese).

Chapter 5
Global Rising Tides Associated with Pharmaceuticals

5.1 The Times of Globalization

Some researchers argue or consider that globalization began during the Age of Discovery or even before that. In this chapter, our discussion is based on the data available through the Google Ngram Viewer.[1]

Momentum for globalization passed an inflection point in the mid of the 1980s and reached a peak in 2008 (Fig. 5.1).

In 1985, the WHO raised the problem of poor quality drugs. In 2006, the International Medical Products Anti-Counterfeiting Taskforce (IMPACT) was established as an international organization to address the problem. Namely, the period during which the problem of poor quality drugs so massively expanded that they became recognized as international issues coincided with the period during which globalization rapidly progressed. Some of the international changes and tides that occurred during this period became entangled with the phenomenon involving poor quality drugs.

The definition of globalization is controversial. M. B. Steger simply defined it as follows: "Globalization means expansion and intensification of social relations and consciousness through world time and world space" (Steger 2009). Defining brings about a risk where generalization due to defining may make individual circumstances invisible. What globalization gave to the quality of pharmaceutical products and how this effect was generated will be discussed.

---

[1]Erez Aiden and Jean-Baptiste Michel hit upon an idea of creating a set of records on all words and phrases that appear in English written books, using a means of regarding one word as one gram, based on the Google's Archive of Books. The Google Ngram Viewer is a system to make a graph showing the frequency of appearance of a certain word or phrase against a chronological axis (Uncharted: Big Data as a Lens on Human Culture by Erez Aiden and Jean-Baptiste Michel). In this chapter, the authors used American English and viewed data until 2008.

© Springer Nature Singapore Pte Ltd. 2020
S. Kimura and Y. Nakamura, *Poor Quality Pharmaceuticals in Global Public Health*, Trust 5, https://doi.org/10.1007/978-981-15-2089-1_5

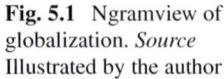

Fig. 5.1 Ngramview of
globalization. *Source*
Illustrated by the author

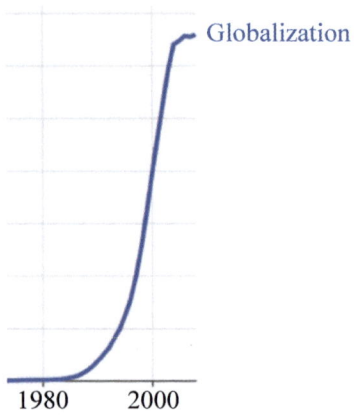

In this chapter, the authors utilize the concept of network loop[2] to demonstrate that the intrinsic nature of globalization is to produce unexpected effects and to make a certain event complicated.

5.2 Growth of Pharmaceutical Industry in Emerging Countries

Emerging countries that have achieved enormous economic development during the period of globalization are collectively referred to as BRICs. They have rapidly gained power starting in the 2000s (Fig. 5.2).

This group consists of Brazil, Russia, India, and China. Among them, India and China, both of which are major powers in Asia, have attracted attention because of the remarkable development of their pharmaceutical industries, including manufacturing of raw materials for generics and even end products.

India has succeeded in achieving import substitution industrialization for generic medicines and, in addition, is currently a major supplier of high-quality final products to the US and other high-income countries.

The pharmaceutical industry of China has a presence as a supply source of not final products but raw materials. Japanese generic manufacturers import raw materials from China. As of today, global relationships are being achieved regarding the supply and demand for raw materials and final products of pharmaceuticals.

The reasons why the global supply and demand relationship is achieved for raw materials include the following: manufacturing of low-molecular active ingredients

---

[2]In the computer model used for the research on "The Limits to Growth" that was entrusted by the Club of Rome, the method of system dynamics was used. The phenomenon in which even limited factors make a system produce unexpected behavior through a network loop is suggestive to the authors when investigating globalization. (Meadows et al. (2004), LIMITS TO GROWTH The 30-Year Update.)

Fig. 5.2 Ngramview of
BRICs. *Source* Illustrated by
the author

BRICs

1980   2000

is relatively easy; and generic manufacturers aim at supplying a wider variety of pharmaceutical product items and, therefore, purchasing from outside sources is more beneficial in terms of cost than self-manufacturing. At the present time, the emerging and developed worlds play complementary roles and at the same time, there exists a tension and confrontation between the two. The fact that these conflicting relations make the problem of poor quality drugs further complicated will be discussed.

5.3 Intellectual Property Rights and Substance Patents

The US was the first country that tried to hold a global leading position in the field of intellectual property rights. In the latter half of the 1970s, the US suffered from a trade deficit of 30 billion dollars per year and turned into a country with a persistent deficit-prone nature. In 1979, President Jimmy Carter submitted the State of the Union regarding "original policy to uplift America's competitive power and entrepreneur spirit" to the Congress.

In the State of the Union, the relaxation of the antitrust law (Anti-Monopoly Act) and intensified protection of intellectual property rights attracted attention. In 1983, President Ronald Reagan established the "President's Commission on Industrial Competitiveness." Facing the reality that Japan and West Germany had caught up with the US in the field of high technology and stood at an advantage over the US in terms of productivity enhancement, the Commission issued recommendations on how to improve the US industrial ability to compete (Mori 1994). Namely, in the 1980s during which neoliberalism, which is regarded as an ideology for globalization, was gaining power, inclination to intellectual property rights began (Fig. 5.3).

Fig. 5.3 Ngramview of
Intellectual property rights.
Source Illustrated by the
author

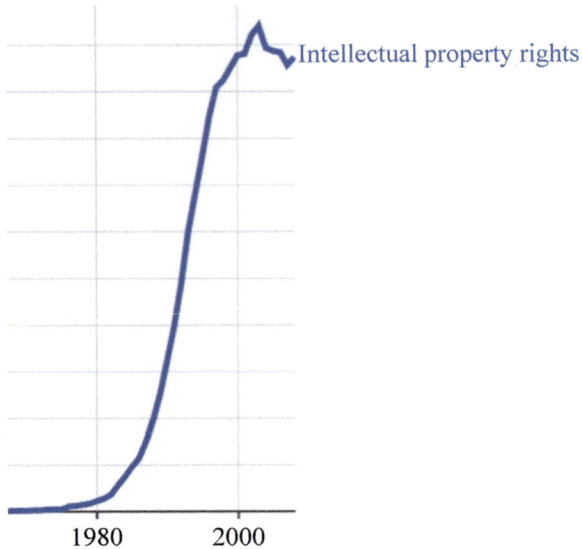

Intellectual property rights

1980   2000

For research and development-driven pharmaceutical companies, which have adopted a business model of developing and marketing originator products, intellectual property rights and substance patents constitute a fundamental lifeline. Pharmaceutical companies holding a business model of focusing on original products have to prepare their next product before the patents for the existing ones expire, and try to maximize the sales of existing original products while they are protected by patents. Monopolizing control of intellectual property rights is the most effective method for maximizing sales.

Continual efforts have been made to build an international consensus regarding intellectual property rights. Patent systems are basically administered within the range of discretion of the sovereignty of each state. That is why international conflicts of interests have occurred with regard to intellectual property rights. Among intellectual property rights, substance patents are especially important in the field of pharmaceutical products, in which the nature of substance patents is different from that in other fields.

5.4 HIV/AIDS that Has Become a Challenge in Public Health

HIV/AIDS emerged at the end of the twentieth century and rapidly spread for 10 years since the 1980s (Fig. 5.4).

Fig. 5.4 Ngramview of
AIDs. *Source* Illustrated by
the author

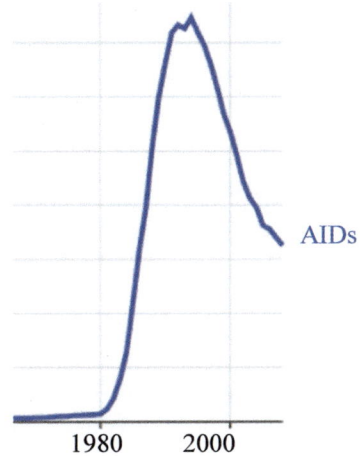

The first effective anti-HIV drug, zidovudin, was developed in 1985. Since then, more than 20 anti-HIV/AIDS drugs to prevent and treat HIV/AIDS have been developed. HIV/AIDS is no longer a fatal disease, although it is not completely curable.

HIV/AIDS has become a challenge in global public health because anti-HIV/AIDS drugs were protected by patents and low- to medium-income countries were not able to use them at affordable prices. The WHO recognized that this was a great problem in global public health.

At a public hearing of the Commission on Intellectual Property Rights, Innovation and Public Health (CIPIH) held at the WHO Headquarters in May 2005, the AIDS patient groups appealed to international public opinion, saying that "We are not robbers of intellectual property rights. We have a right to manufacture anti-HIV/AIDS drugs in our own countries." In response to the appeal, the representative of the International Federation of Pharmaceutical Manufacturers and Associations (IFPMA) counter-argued, saying that "It is not reasonable to discuss access to medicines and national manufacturing on an equal footing" (Yamane 2008).

The core issue at the WTO Ministerial Conference held in Doha in 2001 was how to balance protection of pharmaceuticals-related patent rights with protection of public health, that is, how to keep a balance between the interests of rights holders and social benefits (Kato 2003). As a measure to keep this balance, the right to grant compulsory licenses was included in the Doha Declaration. Developed countries have accumulated dissatisfaction with the establishment of compulsory licensing rules.

At this Ministerial Conference, the developed world insisted on intellectual property rights until the very end of the discussion. Japan was one of the developed countries that opposed production of affordable anti-HIV/AIDS generics (Africa Japan Forum 2003). This attitude of Japan was a good example indicating what the developed world was interested in. The developed world stubbornly insisted on intellectual property rights and this attitude caused low- to medium-income countries to have a growing antipathy against the developed world.

5.5   Acceleration of M&A and Reorganization
of Pharmaceutical Industry in Developed Countries

In these times of globalization, mergers and acquisitions (M&A) have been accelerated (Fig. 5.5). Advantages of M&A included intensifying financial strength, increasing sales, and strengthening pipelines. The pharmaceutical industry is globally active and is not an exception to this move. Since the beginning of the twentieth century, the pharmaceutical industry as a whole has continued to grow constantly, although it has experienced ups and downs in its growth. Over a period from the beginning of the 1970s to 2000, in particular, large-scale pharmaceutical companies were reorganized through a global scale of M&A (see Sect. 1.5.5).

This reorganization enabled the global pharmaceutical industry to have a great influence on the WHO, which was partly reflected in the fact that they were exclusive players in the management organization of IMPACT (see Sect. 6.3.1).

In addition the reason, which IMPACT particularly emphasized, among the problems related to poor quality drugs, counterfeit drugs which substantially affect the pharmaceutical industry was because they recognized the above-stated great influence of the global pharmaceutical industry.

Fig. 5.5 Ngramview of
M&A. *Source* Illustrated by
the author

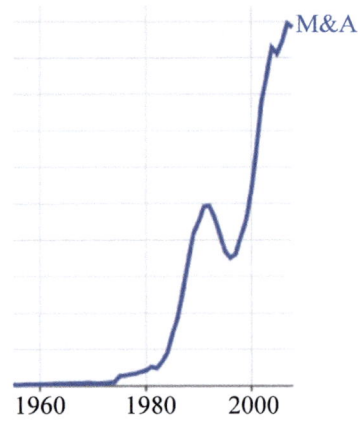

Fig. 5.6 Ngramview of
wealth gap. *Source*
Illustrated by the author

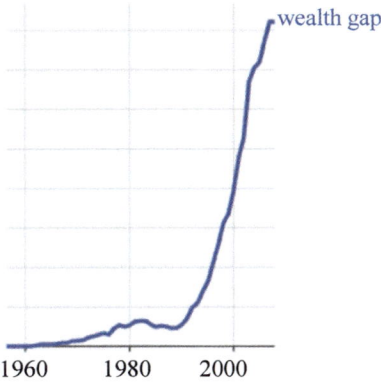

5.6 Expanding Wealth Gap Between Poor and Rich, and Reproduction of Poverty

The benefits of globalization have been trumpeted by the trickle-down theory of economics. However, many researchers have pointed out that in the era of globalization, the wealth gap between poor and rich has expanded.[3] This gap began to rapidly expand in around 1990 and the expansion appears to continue even now (Fig. 5.6).

In developing countries, contracting a disease is the second largest risk, following natural disasters, imposed on household budgets (World Bank 2014). Statistics on global poverty rates reveal a reduction in the East Asia and Pacific Region from 88% in 1990 to 40% in 2010.

When a cutoff line at which households are likely to fall into poverty is set at 10 dollars a day, some 92% of the population in the Region still remains vulnerable to poverty. In the regions of South Asia and Sub-Saharan Africa, 98% of the population lives on less than 10 dollars a day (World Bank 2014).

In the US, with the world's highest healthcare costs, contracting an illness on only occasion often leads to the victim become bankrupt (Tsutsumi 2008). Namely, the possibility of becoming trapped in poverty cannot be determined by the cutoff line in income distribution but instead depends on what safety net exists within society.

Teshigawara conducted a case study on agricultural communities in the Philippines. On the basis of his analysis of structural arrangements and globalization related ideologies such as the TRIPS Agreement, and through his interview with village people, he shed light on the fact that the "access to healthcare services" that policy-makers, those engaged in "healthcare services," and NGOs involved in healthcare have tried to improve, have actually served to collapse the foundations of livelihood of low-income earners (Teshigawara 2013). In other words, globalization has

---

[3] Many researchers have pointed out that globalization has expanded the wealth gap between poor and rich. In his authored book entitled "Making Globalization Work," J. E. Stiglitz discusses individuals who pay little attention to inequality but attach special importance to economic efficiency, and "winners" and "losers" produced by unfair rules.

remained more unforgiving to the people in middle or lower classes in society, and in particular, to the poorest.

Healthcare services can make the people in middle classes fall into poverty, and cause the poorest to become trapped into more severe poverty. This is nothing else but the reproduction of poverty. It is an ironic phenomenon in which the demand by poor people for healthcare services and medicines continues to constitute a part of the mechanism of reproducing such poverty. Those concerned on the supply side will not have any incentive to improve quality since poor people have no financial leeway to pay for quality, which is an added value.

In developing countries, the proportion of out-of-pocket healthcare expenses in the total household budgets is the second highest, following food expenses. It is estimated that healthcare expenses cause 150 million people a year to revert to poverty (Bremmer 2016). The World Bank highlights the fact that the risk management including health exceeds, in many cases, cost-benefits (World Bank 2014), and intends to promote awareness reform among those who formulate public policies and make policy decision. It has to be said that the current healthcare system has an aspect of promoting the reproduction of poverty.

Poor people should not blame themselves for the words from the Bible; "For everyone who has will be given more, and he will have abundance. Whoever does not have, even what he has will be taken from him." (Matthew 25:29). It is politics that is responsible for this.

5.7 Asymmetry of Information

Individuals on the supply side have an advantage over consumers, which is epitomized by information asymmetry. An American theoretical economist Kenneth Joseph Arrow first drew attention to this asymmetry of information.

In his paper entitled "Uncertainty and the Welfare Economics of Medical Care" presented in an American economic journal "American Economic Review" in 1963, Kenneth J. Arrow pointed out a phenomenon in which the presence of information asymmetry between medical doctors and patients impedes efficient administration of medical insurance programs (Wikipedia).

As of today, in developed countries, the requirement of implementing an informed consent process has mitigated this information asymmetry, although only partially, when compared with the past. Nevertheless, a great asymmetry of information about pharmaceutical products still exists between pharmaceutical companies, medical doctors, and patients. Concerns about information asymmetry started to grow over the past decades (Fig. 5.7). The increased information asymmetry increases transaction costs. The poor and needy who cannot afford to pay high transaction costs have no option but to access medicines which are available within their reach in the easiest manner.

Unfortunately, information asymmetry noted in markets of low- and middle-income countries are even greater. This asymmetry is amplified by lack of medicines,

Fig. 5.7 Ngramview of information asymmetry. *Source* Illustrated by the author

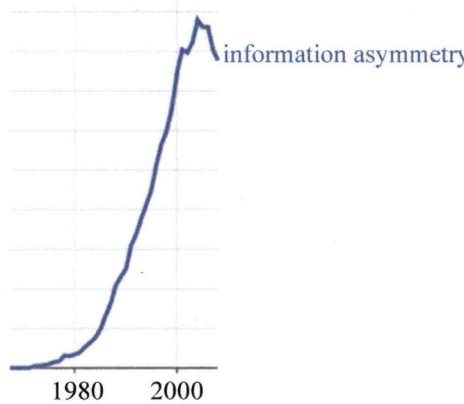

co-payments, economic strength of patients, and other relevant factors. It is only several decades ago when a great impact of information asymmetry on economic activities began to be recognized.

Feedback from markets (consumers) takes a stand against the asymmetry. Whether or not an increasing number of individuals understand and accept the idea that the costs necessary for quality control and creating long-term profits, depends on how the current market can be reshaped into an ideal one, remains to be seen.

References

Africa Japan Forum. 2003. Koheizuyaku he no Akusesu [Access to Anti-HIV Drugs]. https://www.google.com/search?hl=ja&hq=inurl%3Awww.ajf.gr.jp&ie=Shift_JIS&oe=Shift_JIS&filter=0&q=TRIPs&submit.x=8&submit.y=9. (In Japanese) Accessed 22 March 2014.

Aiden, Erez and Jean-Baptiste Michel. 2013. *Uncharted: Big Data as a Lens on Human Culture*. Trans. Erez Lieberman Aiden and Jean-Baptiste Michel.

Bremmer, I. 2016. Tojokoku mo Manseibyo Taisaku ga Kyumu [Urgent Action Needed for Chronic Diseases in Developing Countries]. Nihon Keizai Shimbun, May 30. (In Japanese).

Kato, Akiko. 2003. WTO no TRIPs Kyotei ni okeru Iyakuhin Kanren Hatsumei Hogo Seido no Zanshinteki Hatten -Tokkyoken wo Chuhshin ni- [Step-by-step Development of Protection System for Medicine-related Inventions in the TRIPS Agreement of WTO]. http://www.iip.or.jp/summary/pdf/detail02j/14_19.pdf. (In Japanese). Accessed 4 Sept 2016.

Meadows, D., J. Randers, and D. Meadows. 2004. *Limits to Growth the 30-Year Update*. Trans. Earthscan.

Mori, Makoto. 1994. *Tokyo no Bunmeisi* [History of Patents from the Perspective of Civilization]. Tokyo: Shinchosya.

Steger, M.B. 2009. *Globalization: A Very Short Introduction*. Trans. Oxford: Oxford University Press.

Teshigawara, Kayoko. 2013. *Iryo Akusesu to Gurohbarizeshon –Firipin no Noson Chiiki wo Jirei to shite* [Access to Healthcare Services and Globalization -A Case Study on Agricultural Communities in the Philippines]. Tokyo: Akshi Shoten. (In Japanese).

Tsutsumi, Mika. 2008. *Rupo Hinkon Taikoku Amerika* [Reportage -USA: A Power in Poverty-]. Tokyo: Iwanami Shinsho. (In Japanese).

WHO. 2004. 11th International Conference of Drug Regulatory Authorities (Madrid, 16–19 February 2004. http://www.who.int/medicines/publications/druginformation/ICDRA11_proceedings. pdf?ua=1. Accessed 9 Nov 2014.

Wikipedia. Information asymmetry. https://ja.wikipedia.org/wiki/. Accessed 1 July 2018.

World Bank. 2014. *World Development Report 2014 Risk and Opportunity-Managing Risk for Development*. Trans. Washington, DC. https://openknowledge.worldbank.org/handle/10986/16092. Accessed 1 Sept 2018.

Yamane, Hiroko. 2008. *Chiteki Zaisanken no Gurobaruka -Iyakuhin Akusesu to TRIPS Kyotei-* [Globalization of Intellectual Property Rights -Access to Medicines and TRIPS Agreement-]. Tokyo: Iwanami Shoten. (In Japanese).

Chapter 6
A Dead End of IMPACT

6.1 Counterfeiting-Related Problems Became a Global Political Issue

The International Medical Products Anti-Counterfeiting Taskforce (IMPACT) started with a mission of combating counterfeit medicines on a global scale. However, the background behind the establishment of the Taskforce complicated the counterfeiting-related problems and in addition, the IMPACT itself had factors complicating these problems globally. Before discussing the main subject of this chapter, the authors would like to introduce the interview results obtained from a specialist[1] engaged in the counterfeiting-related problems in the WHO, to which he was sent from his Japanese pharmaceutical company. This is for the purpose of providing readers with an image of how wide and complicated these problems can be.

> The IMPACT was established under the initiative of WHO. From the beginning, some emerging countries strongly argued that pharmaceutical companies of developed countries took advantage of the IMPACT in favor of themselves; namely, they utilized the WHO so as to exclude generic medicines from the market.

> However, this is a big misunderstanding. The International Federation of Pharmaceutical Manufacturers & Associations (IFPMA) suffered huge damage as a result of counterfeiting branded medicines manufactured by its members, which were overwhelmed by the damage. In addition, under the circumstances in which counterfeit medicines attracted increasing attention in society, if a person should die of a counterfeit, then a pharmaceutical company manufacturing its originator medicine might be sued in a litigation on the basis of allegation that the company should have endeavored to protect itself against counterfeiting.

> In reality, such litigation has not yet been filed. However, if a company did not take any action to prevent counterfeiting, then it has to assume the possibility that the company may be pursued accountability for not taking such action. The pharmaceutical industry most feared the distribution of medicines through the internet because this channel accelerated sales of counterfeit medicines.

---

[1] Interview conducted by the author on May 4, 2014 in Tokyo.

© Springer Nature Singapore Pte Ltd. 2020
S. Kimura and Y. Nakamura, *Poor Quality Pharmaceuticals in Global Public Health*, Trust 5, https://doi.org/10.1007/978-981-15-2089-1_6

The IFPMA became a formal member of the IMPACT in order to give cooperation in resolving the counterfeiting-related problems. However, these problems remained the political issue until the end. Surveys revealed that large quantities of poor quality drugs and substandard medicines were commercially available in the market.

In some African countries where control laboratories check drug quality, it is said that problematic drugs, e.g., those containing active ingredients at lower or upper levels than those indicated in the specifications, or containing impurities, are circulated in large quantities in the national markets. However, many of them are not counterfeit drugs in a real sense but instead are substandard medicines of the products officially approved by governments (which are in some cases referred to as poor quality medicines).

In many developing countries, counterfeits and substandard medicines were frequently mixed up and were collectively regarded as counterfeit medicines because either ones might cause health damage in any way. This means that this was not what the WHO understood but the understanding of the national administrative authorities of the countries concerned.

Consequently, some African countries having a certain level of quality checking technology, such as Kenya and Nigeria, were extremely afraid that these counterfeits flew into their countries. In other words, they noticed that although they used their national budgets to try to provide good medicines with people, drugs containing insufficient concentrations of active ingredients or containing a lot of impurities were circulated in their national markets. They therefore feared the inflow of counterfeits or substandard medicines.

On the other hand, the countries exporting medicines were afraid that the generics industry of emerging countries would be damaged if the crime of counterfeiting were confused with the quality problems associated with substandard medicines and both counterfeit and substandard medicines were cracked down at the same level. We have heard that in India, an influential generics association exists and put strong pressure on the government. In this way, counterfeiting-related problems became a political issue.

The International Criminal Police Organization referred to as INTERPOL also participated in the group responsible for cracking down on counterfeiting. Emerging countries were hostile to this participation. We have heard firsthand complaints that in India, that INTERPOL performed an unannounced inspection and because of this, the administrative agencies of Indian government that are responsible for pharmaceutical regulatory affairs and drug quality lost face completely. The police authorities are responsible for crackdowns and we assume that the police agency did not have prior discussions with the Indian Ministry of Health & Family Welfare. This means that the administration of the country suffered from internal divisions.

6.2   Background for Establishment of IMPACT

In 1985, the WHO convened the Conference of Experts on the Rational Use of Drugs at Nairobi, Kenya and issued the following recommendation regarding counterfeit medicines: "Governments should take the action necessary to prevent drug counterfeiting, which was characterized by several participants as a criminal act that all drug regulatory authorities must try to combat" (WHO 1985, 2011).

At the World Health Assembly of WHO in 1988, the resolution on the rational use of drugs was adopted. In this resolution, the Health Assembly requested the Director-General "to initiate programs for the prevention and detection of the export, import and smuggling of falsely labeled, spurious, counterfeit or substandard pharmaceutical preparations" (WHO 2011). Here, in addition to counterfeits, substandard medicines attracted attention.

At the World Health Assembly of WHO in 1994, the Health Assembly requested the Director-General "to support Member States in their efforts to ensure that available drugs are of good quality and in combating the use of counterfeit drugs" (WHO 2011). At the 11th International Conference of Drug Regulatory Authorities (ICDRA) in 2004, the conference at its satellite meeting recommended that "the WHO in collaboration with other stakeholders, should develop a concept paper for an international convention on counterfeit drugs before the next ICDRA" (WHO 2004).

In February 2006, the WHO convened, with the support provided by the Italian Medicines Agency and the International Federation of Pharmaceutical Manufacturers & Associations (IFPMA), an international conference entitled "Combating Counterfeit Drugs: Building Effective International Collaboration" and announced the "Declaration of Rome" (IMPACT Secretariat 2011). On the basis of this declaration, the IMPACT with a mission to combat counterfeit medical products was established.

6.3   Concept Paper Providing the Base for Establishment of IMPACT and the Declaration of Rome

The major points of the Concept Paper that provided the base for establishment of the IMPACT (WHO 2006a) are outlined below. The proposals of the Concept Paper determined the nature of IMPACT.

6.3.1 The Optimistic Proposal of the Concept Paper

The quality of pharmaceuticals has been a concern of the WHO since its inception in 1946. The WHO began to collect data on counterfeit drugs in 1982 and since then, many unofficial research studies have reported that the percentage of the total pharmaceutical market that counterfeit drugs represent greatly ranges from 1% to 50%. This great amplitude of prevalence of counterfeits indicates that the situation substantially differs depending on Member States. The Concept Paper is outlined below.

There are three reasons why an international framework convention to combat counterfeit drugs is necessary.

Measures currently in place by Member States are insufficient to meet all the challenges counterfeit drugs present.

Trade in counterfeit medicines is not only a domestic problem in Member States but also an international problem.

Because of the above-described nature of counterfeits-related problems, formation of an international framework convention requires international agreements.

Experience with other framework conventions has shown that the development of this type of international agreement requires a long time and financial resources. However, immediate actions should be taken to handle counterfeiting-related problems. If we wait for establishment of an international framework convention, then achievement of the necessary international cooperation may be delayed.

For the purpose of combating counterfeits, unlike the Framework Convention on Tobacco Control, a simpler mechanism such as an international taskforce would be. Thirdly, the establishment of an international framework convention on counterfeit medicines requires political will and consensus of WHO Member States. The consensus is not yet achieved. Through the experience gained from the work of an international taskforce, however, the need for such an international consensus may be more widely recognized.

Because of the above-stated reasons, the WHO is advancing the proposal of establishing an International Medical Products Anti-Counterfeiting Taskforce (IMPACT) as an immediate response to the need for urgent internationally coordinated action to combat counterfeit medicines. This proposal was to be discussed at the international conference "Combating Counterfeit Drugs: Building Effective International Collaboration" to be held in Rome, Italy from February 16 to 18, 2006.

This Concept Paper had a problem in that an organization was to be immediately established for the purpose of taking urgent action without forming an international consensus for the establishment. In other words, the idea of this paper was to start with whatever issue that could be addressed and to believe that an international consensus could be formed as the Taskforce would accumulate its achievements. The IMPACT was established without obtaining approval at the Health Assembly of WHO and therefore, lacked legitimacy, which was one of the signs that foreshadowed a dead end of IMPACT within subsequent years.

The Concept Paper included the statement that "a simpler mechanism such as an international taskforce could suffice," which was far too optimistic.

6.3.2   Declaration of Rome

As stated in the Concept Paper, the Declaration of Rome entitled "Conclusions and Recommendations of the WHO International Conference on Combating Counterfeit Medicines" was issued on February 18, 2006 (WHO 2006b). The Declaration of Rome is introduced below.

Counterfeiting medicines, including the entire range of activities from manufacturing to providing them to patients, is a vile and serious criminal offense that puts human lives at risk and undermines the credibility of health systems.

Because of its direct impact on health, counterfeiting medicines should be combated and punished accordingly.

Combating counterfeit medicines requires the coordinated effort of all the different public and private stakeholders that are affected and are competent in addressing the different aspects of the problem. Counterfeiting medicines is widespread and has escalated to such an extent that effective coordination and cooperation at an international level are necessary for regional and national strategies to be more effective.

National, regional, and international strategies aimed at combating counterfeit medicines should be based on the following:

(a) Political will, adequate legal framework, and implementation commensurate to the impact of this type of counterfeiting on public health, and providing the necessary tools for a coordinated and effective law enforcement.
(b) Intersection based on written procedures, clearly defined roles, adequate resources, and effective administrative and operational tools.
(c) Creating an awareness about the severity of the problem among all stakeholders and providing information to all levels of the health system and the public.
(d) Development of technical competence and skills in all required areas.
(e) Appropriate mechanisms for ensuring vigilance and input from healthcare professionals and the public.

The WHO should lead the establishment of an International Medical Products Anti-Counterfeiting Taskforce (IMPACT) of governmental, nongovernmental, and international institutions aimed at

(a) Raising awareness among international organizations and other stakeholders at the international level in order to improve cooperation in combating counterfeit medicines, taking into account its global dimensions.
(b) Raising awareness among national authorities and decision-makers and calling for effective legislative measures in order to combat counterfeit medicines.
(c) Establishing effective exchange of information and providing assistance on specific issues that concern the combating of counterfeit medicines.
(d) Developing technical and administrative tools to support the establishment or strengthening of international, regional, and national strategies.
(e) Encouraging coordination among different anti-counterfeiting initiatives.

The IMPACT shall function on the basis of existing structures/institutions and will in the long term explore further mechanisms, including an international convention, for strengthening international action against counterfeit medicines. As this declaration indicates, the IMPACT tried to obtain cooperation from all levels of the international society as widely as possible and for the time being, aimed to raise awareness among people and provide support by utilizing the existing organizations, for the purpose of "combating" counterfeit medicines. The IMPACT formulated a policy to make the government and policy-makers of each Member State be the main body of anti-counterfeiting initiatives and assume the primary responsibility for these initiatives.

This policy is reasonable given the fact that the pharmaceutical regulatory system of each Member State exerts its authority within the scope to which sovereignty of a State covers, and that each Member State has its own situation. At the same time, the IMPACT cannot avoid having a disadvantage in that the extent of international collaboration is determined by the discretion of each Member State.

6.4   Management Organization of IMPACT that Is Occupied by Developed Countries, and Its Strategies

6.4.1   Management Organization of IMPACT

The IMPACT was organized by the governments, organizations, institutions, associations, and any other relevant entities of Member States on the basis of a voluntary will to participate in the Taskforce. In addition to Member States, 24 structures and institutions who are members of international organizations including the WHO, World Bank, World Trade Organization (WTO), International Federation of Pharmaceutical Manufacturers & Associations (IFPMA), and World Intellectual Property Organization (WIPO) participated in the IMPACT (IMPACT Secretariat 2011). Thus, the IMPACT was a gigantic structure.

In the IMPACT, five working groups were established: a Working Group on Legislative and Regulatory Infrastructure (chaired by a person from the Federal Ministry of Health, Germany), a Working Group on Regulatory Implementation (chaired by a person from the Food and Drug Administration (FDA), USA), a Working Group on Communication (chaired by a person from the Fédération Internationale Pharmaceutique (FIP) or International Pharmaceutical Federation in English), a Working Group on Technologies (chaired by a person from the IFPMA), and a Working Group on Enforcement (chaired by a person from the International Criminal Police Organization referred to as INTERPOL and the Australian administrative authorities) (IMPACT Secretariat 2011). The management of IMPACT was practically driven by the administrative authorities and pharmaceutical industries of developed countries and INTERPOL.

The WHO chaired general meetings of IMPACT which were annually convened, functioned as the secretariat of IMPACT, and chaired most of the planning meetings. At the same time, the WHO, as a technical partner for IMPACT, participated in the Working Group on Legislative and Regulatory Infrastructure and also on Regulatory Implementation (IMPACT Secretariat 2011).

6.4.2   Strategies of IMPACT

The IMPACT formulated the strategic policies described below (IMPACT Secretariat 2011).

Communication Strategy: The vision was to eradicate all counterfeit medicines from supply chains of the developed world and reduce counterfeits to one-third in the developing world by 2020. A communications campaign was required to create awareness of the risk, support program policy objectives, and increase commitment from those who can influence change. The target groups of the campaign were patients, general public, media, healthcare professionals, the pharmaceutical supply chains, enforcement officers, and governments.

Working Group on Enforcement: By working with INTERPOL, WTO, and the Permanent Forum on International Pharmaceutical Crime, the IMPACT aimed at improving coordination of operations and rapid exchange of information among Member States. The IMPACT was also expected to be a platform for enforcement officers to establish communications with health authorities and other stakeholders (including industry and healthcare professionals).

Specifically, in 2008, eight countries (Australia, Canada, Ireland, Israel, Singapore, Switzerland, the United Kingdom, and the United States of America) participated in Operation Pangea, which was a platform for combating international pharmaceutical crimes, within the WHO-led framework of IMPACT, with support of INTERPOL. This operation was taken over by Operation Pangea II, which focused on a crackdown of the three essential components that were required to trade illicit and counterfeit medicines through illegal websites: Internet service provider, electronic payment system, and mail delivery service. Clamping down on illegal pharmacies in the Internet market was continued thereafter.

Working Group on Regulatory Implementation: This Working Group promoted the implementation of the Good Manufacturing Practice (GMP), Good Distribution Practice (GDP), and Good Pharmacy Practice (GPP) guidelines and quality assurance systems to ensure supply chain integrity. It developed training materials aimed at improving quality assurance within the distribution network. It developed guidance on the role of quality control laboratories in combating counterfeit drugs, and devised other pharmaceutical regulatory measures.

Working Group of Technologies: This Working Group assessed technologies to combat counterfeit products, taking into account specific country needs and situations in drug regulatory authorities of each Member State, and facilitated the exchange of information on technologies and their implementation. It also disseminated information on the merits and limitations of technologies.

As described above, the strategies of IMPACT indicated that it was characterized by a strong function of guiding authorities of Member States (e.g., facilitating information exchange and developing guidelines). The exception was that INTERPOL was practically responsible for cracking down on illegal transactions; the target being illegal Internet websites through collaboration with police agencies of Member States.

6.5   A Case as a Trigger to a Dead End of IMPACT

In December 2008, a case raised a question about the structure and administration of IMPACT. The case was a seizure by the Dutch customs of a generic drug made in India to be exported to Brazil, and the seizure was based on an allegation of the infringement of intellectual property rights in the country of transit (Third World Network 2009).

The governments of India and Brazil criticized this seizure by the Dutch customs arguing that research and development-oriented pharmaceutical companies in developed countries exercised their patent rights under the pretext of cracking down on fake drugs. At a meeting of the Executive Board of WHO held in February 2009, the next year, this case invited criticisms against the WHO and IMPACT.

6.6   Criticisms Against IMPACT/WHO at a Meeting of the Executive Board of WHO

At a meeting of the Executive Board of WHO held about 2 months after the case of a seizure described above had occurred, discussion about the seizure case triggered a lot of criticism focusing on the WHO and IMPACT. Major criticisms are outlined below (WHO 2009).

Brazil criticized the seizure by the Dutch customs of the generic drug in the previous year arguing that the case represented the developed world holding down the pharmaceutical industry of developing countries under the pretext of IMPACT.

> The WHO was the proper forum to discuss methodologies to protect public health and promote access to medicines but not to discuss the enforcement of intellectual property rights. The previous day, a shipment of the generic drug was seized by the Dutch customs, en route from India to Brazil. This medicine was not protected by patents in either country. This seizure was a blow to universal access to medicines, a distortion of the international intellectual property system, and a setback to the spirit and provisions of the "Doha Declaration on the TRIPS (Trade-Related Aspects of Intellectual Property Rights) Agreement and Public Health" (WTO 2001). The IMPACT had sought to amend WHO's position on generic medicines on the pretext of combating counterfeit medicines, in an attempt to impede legitimate trade in generics.

Indonesia raised questions about the legitimacy of IMPACT and its representation led by developed countries.

> The IMPACT was set up in 2006 pursuant to the Declaration of Rome in order to combat counterfeiting. However, this Declaration did not appear to have been discussed or endorsed by the Executive Board. In fact, the Taskforce appeared to be composed mainly of representatives of developed countries and the pharmaceutical industry, with an inadequate representation of developing countries.

Bangladesh pointed out that no verified data were available, and expressed its concern about the structure that police agencies, which lack understanding of medicines, were allowed to take initiatives under the IMPACT.

The term "counterfeit" most often referred to violations of intellectual property and should not be dealt with by WHO. A better understanding of the impact of counterfeit medical products on public health was needed. Without independently verified data, it was premature for WHO to address the issue. National drug regulatory agencies were losing their authority on the issue in favor of law enforcement agencies, which lacked understanding of matters relating to the quality, safety, and efficacy of medical products; their decisions could affect the supply of medicines.

The United Arab Emirates pointed out again the actual status in which generics and counterfeit medicines were tangled together, despite the definition proposed by the IMPACT.

A distinction should be made between counterfeiting and any issue relating to infringement of intellectual property. Generic medicines should not be considered counterfeit, nor should substandard batches of legitimate products.

Iran expressed concern over the term "counterfeiting" itself and made reference to the fact that the IMPACT had not been legitimately entrusted by the Health Assembly of WHO.

The given definition of counterfeit medical products would prevent developing countries from gaining access to medicines and from gaining self-sufficiency in the manufacturing of pharmaceutical preparations, neither of which was acceptable. "Counterfeit" was a term used in trade agreements and was not a matter for WHO. The WHO should focus instead on falsely labeled, spurious, and substandard medicines. The IMPACT had not been established by Member States or mandated by the Health Assembly to conduct discussions on counterfeit medical products.

Egypt pointed out that although the problems with substandard medicines are far greater and much more serious than those with counterfeits from the viewpoint of public health, the WHO confused these two issues. Egypt also expressed concerns about conflicts of interest which existed inside the IMPACT led by the developed world, and about distorted objectivity of data related to counterfeiting.

Substandard medicines were a far greater threat to public health than counterfeit medical products, and the two subjects must not be confused, above all at WHO. With regard to the Taskforce, Egypt expressed concern about representation, conflicts of interest, and objectivity of data.

The statement given by *Malawi* appealed to the international society concerning the fact that many medicines African countries relied upon through imports were of poor quality.

Counterfeit products remained a major public health problem. Africa was the dumping ground for such products.

Niger, like Malawi, spoke on behalf of the Member States of the African Region. The statement given by Niger appealed to the international society due to their concern about the absence or weakness of basic pharmaceutical affairs-related infrastructures to eradicate poor quality drugs.

A counterfeit medical product was an area of grave concern for African countries, particularly given their lack of control laboratories. The magnitude of the problem was difficult to estimate; however, a lack of appropriate legislation, the absence or weakness of national pharmaceutical regulatory authorities, and weak enforcement of laws and sanctions all contributed to the existence of counterfeit medical products.

In response to these criticisms, the WHO Secretariat "recognized the need to identify the concerns about public health and focus on what the Secretariat was doing to support Member States in strengthening their drug regulatory authorities in that regard" and at the same time, showed an understanding of "the misgivings about transparency and legitimacy of IMPACT that Member States had." On the basis of these understandings, the Secretariat expressed its commitment "to explore a way of setting up a group for comprehensive discussions" (WHO 2009).

At this time point, the IMPACT actually came to a dead end. After the above-described discussion made at the meeting of Executive Board of WHO, the main body to address the challenge of anti-counterfeiting was transferred to a new structure, i.e., the Member State mechanism (WHO 2013a).

6.7   Discussion

The seizure by the Dutch customs of the generic drug directly triggered the subsequent dead end of IMPACT. Even before that, however, there had been multiple factors unfavorably affecting the prospects of IMPACT.

The IMPACT was established without obtaining approval at the Health Assembly of WHO, which aroused antipathy among Member States, especially developing and emerging countries, toward this apparent lack of legitimacy. The antipathy had been developed by the background consisting of multiple, important, multilayered matters.

6.7.1   Internal Structure of IMPACT and Leadership

The Management Organization of IMPACT consisted of the international institutions representing the interests of developed countries and pharmaceutical industries in these countries. These participating institutions were basically independent in terms of specialty and speculation of interest. INTERPOL assumed the responsibility for cracking down on crimes. Research and development-driven pharmaceutical companies wanted to protect their brand name products and monopolize their patent rights. The WTO aimed at optimizing international supply chains. Thus, individual stakeholders had their own interests and concerns. The counterfeiting-related problems thus became more and more complicated as the number of stakeholders increased.[2] The complexity of these problems was doubled by the environment surrounding them.

On the other hand, developing countries were excluded from the management organization of IMPACT and questioned the legitimacy of IMPACT because the Taskforce was not formally approved by the Health Assembly of WHO. Complicated partnerships with the WHO and confrontations of interests between the developed world and the developing and emerging world made the developing world have further negative emotions against the developed world and WHO. From the beginning, the IMPACT had internal structural weaknesses. In addition, the WHO itself accepted an external review that the Organization "is only one of the participants in the IMPACT and its role has been limited" (WHO 2011), which suggests that the leadership of WHO was not strong enough to make up for the structural weakness of IMPACT.

6.7.2 Intellectual Property Right and Counterfeiting as a New Attribute Given to Generics

Intellectual property rights for pharmaceutical products have brought about conflicts of interests between research and development-oriented companies and generic manufacturers even within a single country. Furthermore, the rights have resulted in conflicts of interest between the developed world and the emerging and developing world. In these conflicts, arguments made by developed countries have so far outweighed those of the developing world. However, these arguments should be closely examined to determine if they can be taken at face value.

Intellectual property rights involve both national management and the interests of the pharmaceutical industry. An act deviated from the international procedures and interpretations of intellectual property rights is regarded as a counterfeiting act. Although the WHO has emphasized that legitimate generics have nothing to do with counterfeiting, the confrontation between emerging and developed countries regarding intellectual property rights has developed a feeling of distrust of generics among developed countries, which has added a new attribute, i.e., "counterfeiting," to generic medicines.

The WHO defines counterfeit medicines as products whose true identity and source are unknown or hidden, which means that counterfeits are drug products manufactured and distributed by those who are not legally licensed. As far as developed countries determine that generics manufactured by infringing intellectual property rights are not regarded as legitimate medicines, those generics manufactured in emerging and developing countries are lumped together with counterfeits as the same group. What the term "legitimate" means differs between the developed world and the emerging and developing world. The confrontation between these two worlds

---

[2]The game theory indicates that when there are multiple actors among whom their interests conflict, it is extremely cumbersome to specify an optimal, reasonable act in that situation (Simon 1996).

about substance patents constituted the background for the above-stated aggregation and needs to be understood. As intellectual property rights attracted increasing attention and conflicts of interests became more severe, the concern about the impact of the quality of medicines on treatment and public health became relatively decreased.

6.7.3   Limitations of IMPACT

The mission of IMPACT was to "combat/fight" counterfeit medicines. This wording was stated in documents of the IMPACT and WHO and in addition, frequently used in scientific publications and other relevant reports.

In response to this, an opinion that "attempts to fight fake drugs are as much a risk to access to the real medicines as the fakes themselves" was introduced in a news medium and this article was began with the following sentence: "Are counterfeit products first and foremost a threat to human health and safety or is provoking anxiety just a clever way for wealthy nations to create sympathy for increased protection of their intellectual property rights?" (Kaitlin 2010). This opinion questions the understanding of and actions by the IMPACT. The author of this article has misgivings about the fact that the initiatives are taken by the developed world distract attention from more important issues. He made this comment while keeping in his mind the situation in which emerging countries have become important players in the procurement of medicines and raw materials, and the presence of problems with poor people's access to medicines.

The WHO used the term SSFFC (substandard/spurious/falsely labeled/falsified/counterfeit) medical products to refer to counterfeits, which caused confusion between substandard and counterfeit medicines, and intensified an image that these two should be handled similarly. This consequence was surely unpleasant to emerging and developing countries because there might have existed an implicit understanding that substandard medicines were derived from generic manufacturers: research and development-oriented originator manufacturers are unlikely to distribute out-of-specification medical products of their own newly developed drugs and in addition, are in the position of being a victim in terms of counterfeiting.

The developing world had a feeling that the IMPACT was managed to meet the interests of developed countries and large-scale pharmaceutical companies, which caused the confrontation between the two worlds in the management of IMPACT. At the first meeting of the Member State mechanism, a successor of the IMPACT, the Secretary-General of WHO highlighted that this mechanism had legitimacy on the basis of the resolution adopted by the World Health Assembly and that its work plans included, among others, strengthening national pharmaceutical regulatory capabilities of Member States, intensifying supply chains, and taking relevant actions from a public health perspective (WHO 2012). This statement served to indicate that the WHO admitted the existence of several important issues which the IMPACT approached inappropriately, and at the same time, implied that at the starting point of IMPACT, interests among the stakeholders were not adequately understood.

6.7.4 Technical Support to Developing and Emerging Countries

The WHO has a great concern about the quality of generics including essential medicines, and has formulated several policies such as the prequalification programme[3] which in particular it deems to be effective. It allows administrative officers of developing countries to be involved in evaluating and auditing activities, through which they receive some training on the relevant matters, and these training-endorsed activities are expected to end up facilitating technology transfer to developing countries.

On the other hand, guidelines prepared by the WHO are unlikely to be greatly effective. It has been pointed out that as far as they are just posted as a document on the website, no one is encouraged to observe them because there exist no incentives to do so (Caudron et al. 2008).

The types of incentives given to developing and emerging countries so as to provoke intrinsic development are the key to success for technology transfer. In addition, the intensity of crisis awareness of developing and emerging countries determines if technology transfer is successful or not. They need to get out of the passive attitude whereby they always wait until guidelines and know-how are given to them by developed countries.

6.7.5 Governance in Medicine Exporting Countries

A medicine is a highly advanced knowledge-intensive product, and requires pharmaceutical and regulatory systems, infrastructure, and human resources commensurate with that product. When exporting medicines to countries lacking these prerequisites, the administrative agencies and technocrats of the exporting country as a responsible member of international society must be responsible for the impact of those products they export. India has grown up to become a great exporter of generics and exports the generics even to the US, a country that performs stringent auditing.

On the contrary, the news media reported the investigation result indicating that the quality of generics exported from India to African countries is inferior to that exported to the other regions (Edney 2014). The Indian company concerned refused

---

[3]This is a global quality assurance program for medicines and is commissioned by the United Nations to the WHO (2013b). In this program, on the basis of an Expression of Interest (EOI) submitted by a company, document-based review on the product concerned and auditing to determine whether the manufacturing plant complies with WHO-GMP or not will be performed.

to make a comment to the press. For this type of case, those concerned should be accountable from the global viewpoint. Although each country tends to prioritize its own national pharmaceutical regulatory system, given the fact that medicines are actually global public goods nowadays, getting out of the present situation and establishing global governance is necessary for countries exporting medicines.

The level of technology transfer in developing and emerging countries has not yet reached an expected maturity. Technical support given by the WHO to these countries has limitations. The Declaration of Rome stated that each Member State by itself should be responsible for taking initiatives in addressing the challenges related to the quality of and access to medicines. In reality, however, developing and emerging countries cannot adequately handle this recommendation, which makes it difficult to resolve the problems with counterfeiting.

The interests involved in the problems with counterfeit medicines are multi-layered. Predominant arguments and logics presented regarding these problems are held by developed countries. There exist conflicts of interests and emotional confrontations between the developed world and the developing and emerging world.

Box 11: Data on Counterfeit Medicines

The criticism raised at the meeting of the Executive Board of WHO was the absence of data regarding counterfeit medicines. Multifaceted discussion is necessary to explore the real intention of this criticism. It at least points out the unavailability of countermeasures based on robust data and analysis.

Figure 6.1 shows the results of the authors' retrieval using the database of "Web of Science" for the purpose of trying to find when reports on research on counterfeit medicines were begun to be published.

Fig. 6.1 Trend in number of reports on poor quality drug. *Source* Illustrated by the author

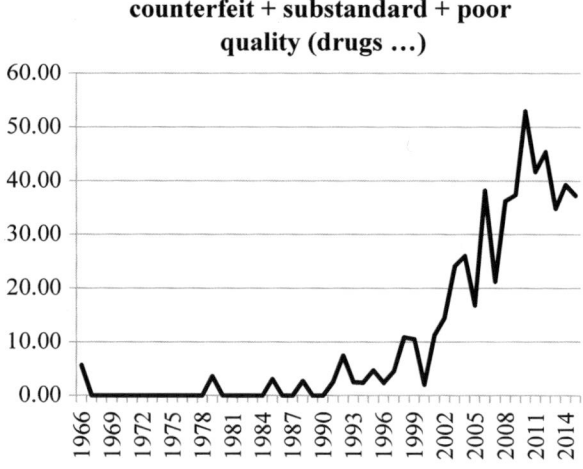

The key words used for the retrieval were Counterfeit + Substandard + Poor Quality drug. The frequency on a vertical axis indicates the number of reports per million articles. The number of reports on poor quality drugs showed a tendency toward an increase starting in the 1990s. The relative number of reports reached a peak in 2010, which indicates that the concern about the counterfeiting-related problems has increased for the past two decades. Generally, reports are included in the database up to several years since publication. It is presumed that these surveys and researches might have started in the latter half of 1985. The WHO's raising of the counterfeiting-related problems triggered the commencement of these studies.

Part of this chapter was published by the Bulletin of Global Human Sciences, Graduate School of Osaka University.

Kimura, S. (2015), Discussion on the Limitation of IMPACT on the Issue of Counterfeit Medicines 8: 87–101, Bulletin of Global Human Sciences, Graduate School of Osaka University.

References

Caudron, J.M., N. Ford, M. Henkens, et al. 2008. Substandard medicines in resource-poor settings: a problem that can be no longer be ignored, *Tropical Medicine and International Health* 13 (8): 1062–1072. 10.1111/j.1365-3156.2008.02106.x. https://www.ncbi.nlm.nih.gov/pubmed/18631318. Accessed 1 Sept 2018.

Edney, A. 2014. India's Poor Quality Drugs End Up in Africa, Study Finds. http://www.bloomberg.com/news/articles/2014-09-17/india-s-poor-quality-drugs-end-up-in-africa-study-finds. Accessed 16 Feb 2015.

IMPACT Secretariat. 2011. IMPACT International Medical Products Anti-Counterfeiting Taskforce the Handbook 2006–2010. http://apps.who.int/medicinedocs/documents/s20967en/s20967en.pdf. Accessed 10 Oct 2013.

Kaitlin, M. 2010. Coverage of Anti-Counterfeit Policy Debate Varies Widely Across Global Media. Intellectual Property Watch. http://wwwip-watch.org/2010/08/02/coverage-of-anti-counterfeit-policy-debate-varies-widely-across-global-media/. Accessed 11 July 2014.

Simon, H.A. 1996. *The Sciences of the Artificial*. Trans. Massachusetts Institute of Technology.

Third World Network. 2009. Developing countries attack Dutch seizure of generic medicines. https://www.twn.my/title2/health.info/2009/twnhealthinfo20090202.htm. Accessed 3 Feb 2019.

WHO. 1985. The rational use of drugs Report of the Conference of Experts Nairobi, 25–29 November 1985. http://apps.who.int/iris/bitstream/10665/162006/1/WHA39_12-Part-1_eng.pdf. Accessed 8 Oct 2014.

WHO. 2004. 11th International Conference of Drug Regulatory Authorities (Madrid, 16–19 February 2004. http://www.who.int/medicines/publications/druginformation/ICDRA11_proceedings.pdf?ua=1. Accessed 9 Nov 2014.

WHO. 2006a. Combating Counterfeit Drugs: A Concept Paper for Effective International Cooperation. http://www.who.int/medicines/events/FINALBACKPAPER.pdf?ua=1. Accessed 11 Oct 2016.

WHO.   2006b.   Declaration   of   Rome.   http://www.who.int/medicines/services/counterfeit/
RomeDeclaration.pdf?ua=1. Accessed 11 Oct 2016.
WHO. 2009. EB124/2009/REC/2. Ninth Meeting. http://apps.who.int/gb/ebwha/pdf_files/EB124-
REC2/B124_REC2-en-Meeting9.pdf. Accessed 18 Sept 2014.
WHO. 2011. WHO's relationship with the International Medical Products Anti-Counterfeiting Task-
force, A/SSFFC/WG/4. http://apps.who.int/gb/ssffc/pdf_files/A_SSFFC_WG4-en.pdf. Accessed
5 Nov 2014.
WHO. 2012. Meeting of substandard/ spurious/falsely-labeled/ falsified/counterfeit medical prod-
ucts. http://www.who.int/dg/speeches/2012/medical_products_20121119/en/. Accessed 23 Nov
2014.
WHO. 2013a. Sixty-six World Health Assembly Provision agenda item 17.1: A66/22, 17 May 2013.
http://apps.who.int/gb/ebwha/pdf_files/WHA66/A66_22-en.pdf. Accessed 5 Nov 2014.
WHO. 2013b. Prequalification program of medicines by WHO. https://www.who.int/news-room/
fact-sheets/detail/prequalification-of-medicines-by-who. Accessed 10 Jan 2019.
WTO. 2001. Declaration on the TRIPS agreement and public health. https://www.wto.org/english/
thewto_e/minist_e/min01_e/mindecl_trips_e.htm. Accessed 10 Sept 2015.

Part II
Market and Access in Local Aspects

Part II focuses on local case studies in the WHO member states. A medicine has two aspects, i.e., one common to the world and the other determined under each country-specific condition. The case studies were conducted in Indonesia and India, which are emerging powers, as well as in Japan, a developed country.

The problems with counterfeit medicines consist of aspects common to the world and those related to country-specific conditions, and these two are entangled. The author compares these three case studies so as to get closer to a more accurate picture of problems associated with poor quality drugs.

Chapter 7
A Case Study in Indonesia: Self-medication and Limited Access

7.1 Self-medication Across the World

Prior to the discussion on self-medication in Indonesia, the author overviews self-medication in various countries across the world, particularly in developing and emerging countries.

In developing and emerging countries, their rapidly growing economics have contributed to the development of healthcare infrastructures. However, the availability of healthcare professionals, improvement or expansion of medical institutions, accessibility to medicinal products, the establishment of systems to supply these products, and coverage of healthcare insurance schemes have not yet been sufficient enough to meet medical needs, resulting in suboptimal access to healthcare services.

Treatment with medicines is one of the most cost-effective medical interventions. Drug costs account for 10–20% of national budgets in developed countries, as compared with the corresponding figures of 20–40% in developing countries in which people depend more on medicines (The World Council of Church 2006).

Developing and emerging countries have implemented inadequate regulations on sales of prescription drugs, which have resulted in a high prevalence of self-treatment with antibiotics in particular. This is related to the structure of diseases in developing and emerging countries, i.e., infectious diseases which are predominant. Selling antibiotics without a physician's prescription is a deviation from the appropriate use of medicines and in addition, the overuse of antibiotics leads to increased antibiotic resistance. The development of antibiotic-resistant bacteria is a major problem in the field of public health (WHO 2016).

The WHO regards self-treatment with prescription drugs as inappropriate or non-rational use of drugs. Fifty percent of medicines over the world are inappropriately prescribed, dispensed, or sold, and antibiotics epitomize this inappropriateness (The World Council of Church 2006). The WHO first published its model list of essential drugs in 1977 and established the concept of rational use of drugs in 1985. Furthermore, in 1989, the WHO started its research on international intervention to promote the rational use of drugs. The research outcome was reviewed at the International

© Springer Nature Singapore Pte Ltd. 2020
S. Kimura and Y. Nakamura, *Poor Quality Pharmaceuticals in Global Public Health*, Trust 5, https://doi.org/10.1007/978-981-15-2089-1_7

Conference on Improving Use of Medicines in 1997, 2004, and 2011, respectively. In the 2011 review, it was concluded that in spite of large investments made over the past 10 years to promote appropriate access to drugs, inappropriate use of antibiotics still persists, resulting in increased antibiotic resistance (WHO 2011).

The actual status of self-medication has been reported in developing and emerging countries. Inappropriate self-medication has been found in the following countries where antibiotics are particularly overused: Indonesia (Puspitasari et al. 2011; Hadi et al. 2010; Widayati et al. 2011); Vietnam (Le et al. 2011); Mongolia (Togoobaatar et al. 2010); China (Pan et al. 2012); India (Badiger et al. 2012); Brazil (Padoveze et al. 2012); Peru (Mini et al. 2012); Nigeria (Auta et al. 2012); Iran (Sarahroodi et al. 2012); and Saudi Arabia (Bin et al. 2011).

Implementation of more strict pharmaceutical regulations and intensifying their effectiveness, improvement of pharmacies' responses, and patient education on the rational use of medicines have been pointed out as actions to reduce inappropriate self-medication. Pharmacies are supply sources of antibiotics to be used for self-medication and at the same time, sources of information given to patients. Researchers have demonstrated that pharmacies provide neither a desirable level of knowledge nor adequate information for patients (Mini et al. 2012; Bin et al. 2011). Self-medication noted in developing and emerging countries is described as a deviation from pharmaceutical regulations and also from appropriate or rational use of drugs. This description does not imply the actual circumstances that force people to choose their behavior among the limited options.

The field survey described in this chapter was conducted in 2012, that is, prior to the introduction of the National Social Health Insurance Scheme in Indonesia (year 2014).

7.2   Research Methods

7.2.1   Rationale and Method for Selection of the Survey Target Area

The primary criteria for selecting a target area for the survey included accessibility to people who live in medium or lower living standards and good accessibility to pharmacies, which increased survey efficacy. On the basis of preliminary survey results, Ciputat District, South Tangerang City, Province of Banten which is in the vicinity of Jakarta City (Fig. 7.1) was selected after it was confirmed that in this district, many people are in the middle class, and that community pharmacies and pharmacists to be surveyed are easily accessible.

The main industries in Ciputat District are woodworking, food industry, and textile manufacturing. It has a population of about 16,500 and functions as a commuter town for people who work in Jakarta City. Its level of education is high : 59% are graduates

Fig. 7.1 Survey area. *Source* streetdirectory.com

from high school or higher educational institutions, and the rate of literacy is almost 100%. There are nine community pharmacies and two public health clinics called Puskesmas (Indonesian: Pusat Kesehatan Masyrakat) (Bappeda 2010).

7.2.2 Survey Subjects

7.2.2.1 Questionnaire Survey at Pharmacy Exit

Six of the 9 community pharmacies in Ciputat District gave their consent to cooperate in this survey. Among the patients who visited the six pharmacies, those who came to the shops to buy antibiotics on the day of interview and those for whom it was confirmed within one month of purchasing that they had visited the shops and bought antibiotics, that is, 200 in total, were subject to the exit survey using the structured questionnaire. The sample size was calculated with an error of 5, a confidence level of 90%, a standard deviation of 30, and with assumptions that 50% of people take out health insurance and that 50% of people perform self-medication. The calculation of sample size was done using a programme provided on the Internet by BellCurve (BellCurve 2019), and the calculation result was 99. However, the sample size was increased to 200 in total because it was intended to analyze customers' behaviors and pharmacists' responses individually for those who take out health insurance and those who perform self-medication. Customers who bought antibiotics at pharmacies without a physicians' prescriptions are regarded as "patients who choose self-medication" (hereinafter referred to as "self-medication performers").

This survey targets antibiotics firstly because the above-stated prior research reports have demonstrated that antibiotics are particularly overused for self-medication and secondly because antibiotics are commonly used for self-medication due to the disease structures in emerging and developing countries.

7.2.2.2 Interview Survey on Pharmacists and Assistant Pharmacists

The interview survey included pharmacists and assistant pharmacists, seven in total, who work for the pharmacies that gave their cooperation in conducting the pharmacy exit interview, and one owner of the pharmacy. Table 7.1 shows the structured questionnaire.

7.2.2.3 Other Interview Survey

In addition to the above-stated questionnaire survey at the pharmacy exit and interview survey, the author interviewed a freelance reporter for the Jakarta Globe, an English language newspaper in Indonesia. Our survey was also conducted in a market area (called Pramuka) in Jakarta City which is a cluster of wholesalers of drugs and medical devices, as well as drugstores and extremely small-scale grocery stores (called "Warung" in Indonesian) in Ciputat District, because it is said that counterfeit drugs are sold in the market or these stores.

7.2.3 Survey Methods

7.2.3.1 Questionnaire Survey at Pharmacy Exit

The entire survey period was set between May 25, 2012 and July 3, 2012. For this survey, the author hired one student at the faculty of public health, Universitas Islam Indonesia and one graduate of the same university, both on a contract basis. The author communicated with the two collaborators in English. The questionnaire survey at the pharmacy exit was conducted in the time frame from 10 a.m. to 4 p.m. per day for a total of 6 days.

The questionnaire (Table 7.1) was newly drafted by the author in Japanese, translated into English, and then, translated into Indonesian by the lecturer at the faculty of public health, Universitas Islam Indonesia who understands English. Thus, reliability was confirmed before use. Regarding validity, the author did not conduct a full-scale test. However the author partially modified the questionnaire due to the results obtained in the preliminary test period.

Table 7.1 Questionnaire for pharmacy exit survey

I am Kimura, a Japanese researcher. I am conducting a survey on the actual status of customers (patients and/or their family members) who buy antibiotics at pharmacies and drugstores. I am asking for your cooperation in this survey and to answer the questions. I will ask you relating to this survey. If you have any question about this survey, I will answer it. I can assure you that your personal information will be handled appropriately to protect your privacy throughout the course of this study.	
Date of Interview: <u>Month Day, 2012</u> Place. Interviewer:. Oral explanation given and informed consent obtained (Check the box.) ☐	
Q1: Do you buy any antibiotic, today?	☐ Yes ☐ No (If the answer is "No," continue to ask the following questions only when the interviewee bought antibiotics within the past 1 month.)
Q2: Do you have a prescription for the antibiotic, today?	☐ Yes ☐ No
Q3: What made you select the antibiotic you bought today? (Select a single answer.)	☐ In accordance with a prescription ☐ Recommendation by pharmacist ☐ Recommendation by family, friend, etc. ☐ TV, magazines, advertisements, etc. ☐ Information available on the Internet ☐ Drug sample leftover from the past ☐ Others
Q4: When you bought antibiotics today, did you receive any question about your disease condition, etc.?	☐ Yes, sufficiently ☐ Yes, to some extent ☐ Yes, slightly ☐ No, not at all
Q5: Did the pharmacist instruct you to use up the antibiotic today?	☐ Yes ☐ No
Q6: Did the pharmacist instruct you on how to use the antibiotic you bought today?	☐ Yes, sufficiently ☐ Yes, to some extent ☐ Yes, slightly ☐ No, not at all
Q7: Did the pharmacist give you warnings or explanation about the possibility that the antibiotic you bought today may cause you any health hazards?	☐ Yes, sufficiently ☐ Yes, to some extent ☐ Yes, slightly ☐ No, not at all

(continued)

Table 7.1 (continued)

Q8: When you suffer from a disease (infectious disease) requiring antibiotics, do you always consult a medical doctor?	☐ Always ☐ Often ☐ Sometimes ☐ Not at all
Q9: Where do you usually buy antibiotics? (Select a single answer.)	☐ Pharmacy ☐ Drugstore ☐ Drug market (street shop) ☐ Others ()
Q10: What is the greatest reason for you to buy antibiotics there? (Select a single answer.)	☐ Reliable ☐ Convenient in terms of physical access ☐ Cheap ☐ Can buy them separately ☐ Have relationship with shop persons ☐ Recommendation by family, friend, or other persons around me ☐ Information from media ☐ Others ()
Q11: Finally, can you provide the following information, please?	Age: ☐ <20 years ☐ 20 to <30 years ☐ 30 to <40 years ☐ ≥50 years Occupation: ☐ Work for a private company ☐ Work for government ☐ Self-employed ☐ Informal sector ☐ Unemployed ☐ Others Health insurance: ☐ Take out ☐ Do not take out Educational background: ☐ Primary school ☐ Secondary school ☐ High school ☐ University (or higher) Personal computer: ☐ Can use it ☐ Cannot use it
Additional question: Are you a healthcare professional? In case of "Yes," is the antibiotic you bought is to be used for yourself or for your patient?	☐ Medical doctor ☐ Dentist ☐ Pharmacist ☐ Nurse ☐ Midwife ☐ Others ☐ For myself ☐ For my patient

Source This questionnaire was prepared by the author

7.2.3.2 Interview Survey on Pharmacists and Assistant Pharmacists

Pharmacists and assistant pharmacists were interviewed by two field workers on the basis of a semi-structured questionnaire in the presence of the author. Interview details were recorded in notes and with an IC recorder. After completion of each interview, its content was confirmed with the field workers. Table 7.2 shows the interview guide. Regarding the interview guide, reliability and validity were checked as in the questionnaire.

Table 7.2 Interview guide when interviewing pharmacists

Introduction at the start of the interview: · Explain the purpose of the interview (research) · The interviewee can ask the interviewer to rephrase a question whenever he/she does not understand its meaning · The interviewer promises to protect the interviewee's privacy. Obtain informed consent from the interviewee (who signs the consent form)
1. Questions about personal information Age, the length of career as a pharmacist, and function (responsibility)
2. How many customers visit your pharmacy per day?
3. Among those visiting your pharmacy per day, what proportion (how many customers) buy antibiotics?
4. Among those who buy antibiotics, how many customers do not have physicians' prescriptions? (*Note* Regarding the above Questions 2, 3, and 4, ask the interviewee to provide, if any, specific data per day, per month, or in the previous month)
5. What types of explanations or warnings do you give to customers who have physicians' prescriptions to buy antibiotics? (Ask the interviewee to provide specific examples)
6. What type of explanations or warnings do you give to customers who do not have physicians' prescriptions to buy antibiotics? (in contrast to Question 5)
7. If you have heard from others or have experienced by yourself that patients who are self-treated with prescription-only drugs buy without physicians' prescriptions are at risk, what types of risks do they face actually?
8. If you have heard from others or have experienced by yourself that counterfeit medicines or poor-quality drugs cause a health hazard, tell us about such cases
9. What do you think is important to prevent self-medication or distribution of poor-quality drugs?

Source This guide was prepared by the author

7.2.3.3   Other Interview Surveys

These surveys were not preplanned and all questions were made along with the flow of conversation.

7.2.4 Analytical Methods

Exit survey data were compiled by SPSS. Chi-square test was applied to analyze the proportions of participants with and without health insurance coverage, the proportions of interviewees with and without physicians' prescriptions when buying antibiotics, and the frequency of visiting medical institutions. The significance level was set at $p = 0.05$.

Two field workers cross-checked the recorded interviews and transcribed the interview texts in Indonesian. The transcription was translated from Indonesian into English by a professional Indonesian–English translator, and then, translated by the author into Japanese. The author asked the lecturer at the faculty of public health, Universitas Islam Indonesia to give us her opinion about the validity of our interview data. KJ method was used to analyze the transcription.

7.2.5   Ethical Consideration

This research was approved by the Research Ethics Committee at Global Human Study, Faculty of Human Sciences, Graduate School of Human Sciences, Osaka University. When conducting the pharmacy exit questionnaire survey, the author explained, both in writing and orally, the purpose of this survey prior to asking interviewees to answer the questions, and documented in the questionnaire form that orally informed consent was obtained from the interviewee concerned. The author made a documented request to pharmacies for their cooperation in this survey. When interviewing pharmacists and assistant pharmacists working for the collaborating pharmacies, the author gave again written and oral explanation and obtained written informed consent from them.

7.3   Survey Results

7.3.1   Questionnaire Survey at Pharmacy Exit

7.3.1.1   Demographic Characteristics of Survey Subjects

The demographic characteristics of 200 subjects of the pharmacy exit questionnaire survey are shown in Table 7.3. There are slightly more men, as indicated by 54.5% (109/200), than women. Age-group-specific analysis reveals increasing proportions of older interviewees.

Evaluation of occupation reveals that many interviewees are unemployed (34.0%). This may be explained by the fact that there are many housewives.

The second largest segment in the category of occupation is those who work for private companies (28.5%), followed by those who are self-employed (19.5%). Evaluation of education background reveals that 80.5% (161/200) of interviewees graduated from high school or higher educational institutions. In addition, 43.5% (87/200) of interviewees take out health insurance and 32.5% (65/200) access the Internet.

Table 7.3 Demographic characteristics of pharmacy exit survey subjects (n = 200)

Gender	No. of applicable subjects (%)
Men	109 (54.5)
Women	91 (45.5)
Total	**200 (100.0)**
Age-group	**No. of applicable subjects (%)**
>20 years	6 (3.0)
20–29 years	33 (16.5)
30–39 years	56 (28.0)
40–49 years	21 (10.5)
≥50 years	84 (42.0)
Total	**200 (100.0)**
Occupation	**No. of applicable subjects (%)**
Work for a private company	57 (28.5)
Work for government	15 (7.5)
Self-employed	39 (19.5)
Informal sector	10 (5.0)
Unemployed	68 (34.0)
Student	11 (5.5)
Total	**200 (100.0)**
Educational background (graduated from)	**No. of applicable subjects (%)**
Primary school	16 (8.0)
Secondary school	20 (10.0)
High school	94 (47.0)
University (or higher)	67 (33.5)
None	3 (1.5)
Total	**200 (100.0)**
Health insurance	**No. of applicable subjects (%)**
Covered	87 (43.5)
Not covered	113 (56.5)
Total	**200 (100.0)**
Access to the Internet	**No. of applicable subjects (%)**
Yes	65 (32.5)
No	135 (67.5)
Total	**200 (100.0)**

7.3.1.2   Treatment Choosing Behavior of Survey Subjects

Selection of treatment. When purchasing antibiotics, 48.5% (97/200) of interviewees did not have physicians' prescriptions (i.e., self-medication performers). No significant correlation was noted between the status of remaining with or without health insurance coverage and the status of having or not having physicians' prescriptions (Table 7.4) (p = 0.138).

When contracting an infectious disease, 45.5% (91/200) of interviewees responded that they always consult medical doctors, whereas 23.5% (47/200) do not do so at all. Combining these two categories constitutes a group of "those who always choose the same behavior when contracting infection" and this group accounts for 69.0%. No significant correlation was noted between the status of remaining with or without health insurance coverage and the frequency of consulting medical doctors (Table 7.5) (p = 0.964).

Reasons for selection of antibiotics by survey subjects. Among the population of self-medication performers who do not have physicians' prescriptions when purchasing antibiotics (n = 104), the proportion of those who answered that they selected their antibiotics on the basis of leftover drug samples was significantly highest, as indicated by 51.9% (54/104) (p < 0.001). The second highest proportion is found for the category of recommendation by family members or friends, as indicated by 16.3% (17/104), which is higher than that of the category of recommendation by pharmacists, i.e., 8.7% (9/104) (Table 7.6) (p = 0.334).

Table 7.4 Relationship between the status of taking out or not taking out health insurance and the status of having or not having physicians' prescriptions

Physicians' prescriptions	No. of subjects who take out health insurance (%)		
	Take out	Do not take out	Total
Have	50 (57.6)	53 (46.9)	103 (51.5)
Do not have	37 (42.5)	60 (53.1)	97 (48.5)
Total	**87 (100.0)**	**113 (100.0)**	**200 (100.0)**
	(p = 0.138)		

Table 7.5 Relationship between the status of taking out or not taking out health insurance and the frequency of consulting medical doctors

Frequency of consulting medical doctors	No. of subjects who take out health insurance (%)		
	Take out	Do not take out	Total
Always	42 (48.3)	49 (43.4)	91 (45.5)
Often	7 (8.0)	8 (7.1)	15 (7.5)
Sometimes	17 (19.5)	30 (26.5)	47 (23.5)
Not at all	21 (24.1)	26 (23.0)	47 (23.5)
Total	**87 (100.0)**	**113 (100.0)**	**200 (100.0)**
	(p = 0.964)		

Table 7.6 Relationship between the selection of antibiotics other than that "in accordance with prescription" and the status of taking out or not taking out health insurance

Factors which made interviewees select antibiotics, other than "in accordance with prescription"	No. of subjects who take out health insurance (%)		
	Take out	Do not take out	Total
Recommendation by pharmacist	6 (15.8)	3 (4.5)	9 (8.7)
Recommendation by family or friends	6 (15.8)	11 (16.7)	17 (16.3)
Leftover drug sample	14 (36.8)	40 (60.6)	54 (51.9)
Others	12 (31.5)	12 (18.2)	24 (23.1)
Total	**38 (100.0)**	**66 (100.0)**	**104 (100.0)**
	(p = 0.334)		

Details of "Others" are unknown. The pharmacist interviews revealed that some customers receive advice from midwives or other relevant healthcare professionals. No significant correlation was noted between the factors making interviewees select antibiotics, including that of "in accordance with prescription," and the educational background.

7.3.2 Interview Survey on Pharmacists and Assistant Pharmacists

7.3.2.1 Demographic Characteristics of Survey Subjects

The author interviewed 8 survey subjects, consisting of 5 pharmacists and 2 assistant pharmacists, who are all women, and one pharmacy owner who is a man. Their ages ranged from 25 to 43 years.

7.3.2.2 Customers' Mindset and Behavior in Terms of Accessing Drugs

The interview survey revealed that half the customers who want antibiotics do not have physicians' prescriptions. This finding agrees with the results of the pharmacy exit questionnaire survey. The interviewees pointed out that one of the reasons for choosing self-medication is the high expenditure necessary for consultation with medical doctors. Self-medication performers considered that for symptoms which are similar to those they experienced in the past, consulting medical doctors are unnecessary and taking drugs they get used to using is sufficient.

It was pointed out that these self-medication performers tend to be overconfident in their words and deeds and in addition, try to buy antibiotics even if their symptoms do not require these drugs. The pharmacists described patients' behavior as follows.

Half the patients who want to buy antibiotics do not have physicians' prescriptions. They easily take antibiotics when they get sick. A patient wanted to buy antibiotics for a bruise. They want antibiotics even for influenza.

Patients who perform self-medication come to pharmacies with left-over drug samples they took in the past. This phenomenon is noted only for antibiotics. They are not brave enough to willingly try a new drug. Patients say with full confidence that they get used to taking this particular drug or that the disease they currently suffer from is the same as that in the past and consultation with medical doctors is unnecessary.

Patients come to consult pharmacists because consulting medical doctors is expensive. This is the sole reason in almost all cases. On the other hand, patients strongly want antibiotics not only because of economic reasons. Even though they pay a lot of money to consult medical doctors, they receive physicians' prescriptions for similar medicines in almost all cases. A patient says: "Even if I go to the doctor, the drug prescribed is just the same as that I got before."

7.3.2.3   Pharmacists' Views About Self-care Performers

The pharmacists recognize the importance of pharmaceutical regulations implemented by the government. They have concerns about the development of allergy and antibiotic resistance in those who conduct self-medication because self-medication performers tend to readily use antibiotics and in addition, they do not take drugs appropriately.

Drugs are not something we may use thoughtlessly. Each drug has its own instructions for use. That is why the government regulates drugs. If you take a pain killer, you do not need to take it anymore when your pain disappears. On the contrary, you should take antibiotics in an adequate manner for 3 days and take the entire antibiotic dispensed. Conversely, a middle-aged woman consulted a medical doctor for a minor thing as if paranoia, causing her to take many different types of antibiotics. She has developed antibiotic resistance and when she gets sick, she has to receive more potent antibiotics by injection. Self-treatment with antibiotics causes a risk of allergy development because some of the antibiotics they are going to take were never taken by them in the past.

7.3.2.4   Responsive Actions Taken by Pharmacists

It was found that the pharmacists ask those who choose self-medication about their conditions and determine if antibiotic treatment is appropriate for the patient concerned. Self-medication performers usually do not take drugs appropriately and therefore, the pharmacists instruct them to take all of the antibiotics they bought and explain the reason why they need to do so. The pharmacists consider that patient education is necessary, and in addition to their everyday duties of giving instructions on how to take drugs and receiving consultations from customers, they approach the community to raise the standard of public education.

To a patient who chooses self-medication, I ask what type of disease he/she suffers from. If the disease requires a medical doctor's diagnosis, then I will never give any drug. When I judge that it is a less problematic case to dispense a drug to the patient, I explain the effectiveness of the drug and how to use it. For patients who do not have physicians' prescriptions, I advise them to take all of the antibiotics they bought. I always instruct them that if they take the drugs only inadequately and leave over a significant portion of them, antibiotic resistance will develop. I tell them that not taking drugs at all is even better than taking drugs inadequately.

On the wall of our pharmacy, "Medical Consultation" is posted. Since the opening of this pharmacy, we have provided free medical consultation. Our mission is to provide medical information for our customers, by promoting transfer from the product-oriented attitude that existed in the past to the customer-oriented mindset. By making the best use of blood donation opportunities and free medical events held once or twice annually in the community, we provide public education. We have confirmed that our message has reached people in this community.

7.3.2.5 Pharmacists' Awareness of the Responsibilities of Their Profession

The pharmacists recognize the actual situation in which they have to decide to sell antibiotics, against their original will, to those who do not have physicians' prescriptions, and are aware, because of their profession, that they try to minimize the harmful effects of self-treatment with antibiotics. The pharmacists take pains to keep a balance between the medical doctor's authority and expertise which they respect and the demands of the poor and needy.

At our pharmacy, we have not experienced risks imposed on patients who are self-medicating. To patients with renal or cardiac diseases requiring antibiotics, we sell the antibiotics even though they do not have physicians' prescriptions, provided that they usually take them. They are regular customers and we therefore can tell their situations. On the contrary, we ask many questions to new customers or patients who visit us from outside the community. In the case of renal disease or other comparable diseases for which we pharmacists cannot even determine any relevant parameters, we do not give them any drug and recommend they see a doctor.

I do not want to recommend a drug that a patient should take. It is within the scope of doctors' responsibilities. I do not want to assume any risk. It is outside my authority. What I can do is to give them advice. If patients take drugs for which pharmacists know and understand the rationale for taking them, then the absence of physicians' prescriptions would not be a problem. However, hormone drugs or psychotropic drugs definitely require physicians' prescriptions. Some patients overtly ask, "I want a drug for abortion. Which drug is effective?" Other patients try to use psychotropic drugs to achieve sedation.

7.3.2.6 Actual Status of Accessing Drugs

The pharmacists understand what problems actually exist in relation to peoples' access to drugs. They are faced with the dilemma between what is required by law or regulations and people's needs as well as their economic strength, and feel impatient as the reality is not an ideal situation. What pharmacists can do is to expect that the government's regulations will be intensified and to voluntarily educate patients.

In Indonesia, the regulations require that antibiotics are dispensed only in the presence of physicians' prescriptions. In reality, however, you can buy patented drugs and generic drugs without physicians' prescriptions.

It is necessary to balance the government's regulations with the reality, including on-site circumstances and pharmacies' needs. Here, no ideal pharmacies exist. I myself want to sell drugs in accordance with physicians' prescriptions. When considering our business achievement, however, we have to reach our customers. All people do not have financial leeway. We always tell them to see a doctor, whereas they say that they do not have enough money to go to a doctor.

Many people in this district do not take out health insurance. The majority are included in the lower-category of middle class. People in the upper-category of middle class usually remain with insurance coverage.

Kiosks are not legally allowed to sell antibiotics. Drugstores are not, either. In reality, however, many drugstores sell antibiotics. The government needs to regulate the sales of antibiotics more strictly.

Healthcare professionals need to provide regular consultation services for people in the community. This may prevent them from taking drugs thoughtlessly or in an unplanned manner through their self-medication. These regular consultation services should be given in collaboration with medical doctors. All medical institutions including Puskesmas should give their cooperation in providing these services.

Many patients come to our pharmacies for the sole purpose of consulting us about illness or a request for drugs. Doctors do not give them sufficient explanation about drugs or merely issue prescriptions without any explanation. Patients want to ask doctors about drugs but cannot do so; they have no time for questioning because the hospital is so crowded. That's why patients come to pharmacies.

7.3.2.7 Counterfeit Medicines and Pharmacies' Measures to Avoid Them

The community pharmacies always try to procure drugs from reliable distribution channels for the purpose of avoiding counterfeits and substandard medicines. The interviewees said that counterfeit medicines are not a problem at pharmacies. They have heard that other distribution channels have caused problems due to counterfeits and therefore, instruct people to buy drugs at pharmacies.

There still exist lots of fake drugs. Many of them are for acne or are whitening creams. The frequently told episode is that inflammation occurs on the face, which causes reddening of the skin or blackening of pustules. Some customers ask us that "I have bought this drug at another shop but my symptom has never improved. If I had bought a drug at a pharmacy, would my symptom have improved?"

A certain customer came to the pharmacy for consultation saying that "yesterday, my father bought the drug we are familiar with, at warung. When we unpacked it, differently than usual, there was neither stamp nor logo." I unpacked the same drug we have at our pharmacy and showed what was inside. The customer told me that "Oh, this is a real thing and totally different from what he bought at warung." It is quite difficult to differentiate a fake product from a genuine one, only on the basis of packaging.

There exist various types of counterfeit medicines. If you take fake antibiotics, recovery requires a longer time than you expect. For example, an allegedly labeled 500 mg tablet only contains an active ingredient of 100 mg and the remaining is flour. Fake tablets easily collapse. Genuine ones do not easily collapse. Packaging also tells you if it is a genuine or fake product. If it is a genuine product, its packaging should have the logo and the hologram is shining or bright. If it is a fake product, the hologram does not usually shine. It's true that the expiration date is erased with alcohol and rewritten. At unreliable shops, products with rewritten expiration dates are made available for sale.

We have heard that at Pramuka,[1] expired drugs are sold. We do our best to avoid counterfeit medicines. We never purchase drugs from Pramuka. We always procure drugs from officially certified shops. Accordingly, at this pharmacy, we have never faced any problem related to counterfeit medicines. We recommend our customers to buy drugs only at pharmacies so that they can avoid poor quality or counterfeit products. Drugs sold at drugstores or kiosks are sometimes fake ones.

7.3.3 Other Survey Results

7.3.3.1 Interview with a Reporter for an English Language Newspaper in Indonesia

A freelance reporter working for the Jakarta Globe, an English language newspaper (with its headquarters in Jakarta City), was interviewed. She is in her 30s and is responsible for healthcare-related articles in this daily newspaper. How she sees the problems with medicines and patients in Indonesia is outlined below.

The problems with counterfeit medicines are very sensitive. Many things that are ashamed of in Indonesia lurk behind these problems. Some of them include, among others, corruption, insufficient education, and crime.

Historically, people have lived under the influence of social stigma and discrimination such as prejudice against Hansen's disease and disadvantages imposed on the handicapped. This situation still exists as of today. The conditions for living such as accessibility to safe drinking water and hygiene are not yet satisfied. We have to overcome many challenges involving society as a whole. They include accessibility to adequate information, education, and public enlightenment. People have enough knowledge and educational background. However, they lack management skills with which they can utilize the knowledge and educational background to improve the quality of their lives or daily living activities.

Indonesia has good laws but they are not adequately enforced. The effectiveness of these laws is sometimes damaged by corruption's or briberies. People live in traditional cultures such as folk remedies or shamans' cultures.

Counterfeit medicines constitute the enemy of business for the pharmaceutical industry. Pramuka is not that bad. In Roxy District in the central Jakarta, counterfeit medicines are sold in some places, which make ordinary people, needless to say, and even journalists, feel in danger.

---

[1] The Indonesian term "Pramuka" refers to a market in Jakarta City which is a cluster of wholesalers selling drugs and medical devices. The author met a medical doctor who came to Pramuka from Sumatra Island for the purpose of purchasing a large quantity of antibiotics for her clinic. She personally came all the way to Jakarta because distribution channels are not adequately established.

In addition to the underclass, people in the middle and upper classes come to drugstores to buy drugs. This is primarily because penetration of health insurance is insufficient.

The government is currently making its efforts to achieve universal health insurance coverage, but such a system will not be enforced in near future. Even if it is attained, things will not change overnight. Some hospitals do not welcome this system because it will put a limitation on medical service fees.

7.3.3.2   Interview at Pharmaceutical Wholesalers

Employees at pharmaceutical wholesalers, which have adjoining pharmacies, were interviewed. This interview is outlined below.

The PBF (Pedagang Basar Farmasi) collectively refers to a cluster of officially certified distributing wholesalers for medicines (i.e. wholesalers with distributing function), and consists of many dealers. The PBF procure medicinal products directly from pharmaceutical companies. The PBF supplies these medicines to pharmacies including large-scale ones.

Large-scale pharmacies function also as secondary wholesalers, and supply medicines to small-scale pharmacies, hospitals, clinics, and Puskesmas. The PBF is not supposed to supply medicines to these end users, but in reality, it does so.

Large-scale pharmacies also supply medicines to drugstores and warung. These retailers do not obtain marketing authorization to sell prescription-only medicines from the Ministry of Health but sell these drugs to customers who do not have physicians' prescriptions. They escape from audits or crackdowns by the Ministry of Health. In areas surrounding this Ciputat District, however, almost no warung stores sell prescription-only medicines, maybe at about one per 100 warung stores does so.

The PBF is responsible for handling complaints from pharmacies: the PBF will replace a damaged product with a new one. Expired drugs are handled as follows: pharmacies inform the PBF of expiration of a certain drug product 3 months earlier than its date of expiration; and the PBF takes back expired drugs and return them to relevant pharmaceutical companies.

At Puskesmas located in regions with high population densities, medical doctors, pharmacies, midwives, and nurses work. This is not true for rural regions, in which nurses and midwives dispense drugs to patients.

7.3.3.3   Survey Through Purchasing Drugs at Warung

The interview at pharmaceutical wholesalers described in the previous subsection revealed that at about one per 100 warung stores sell antibiotics in the vicinity of the metropolitan area. The author tried to buy antibiotics at 10 warung stores (kiosks) in Ciputat District.

At 4 of the 10 warung stores, antibiotics were sold. When buying them, the author was neither asked about symptoms nor asked to show them the physician's prescription. What the author bought were amoxicillin and doxycycline. A shop master of a certain warung store indicated that he procures antibiotics from drugstores.

Almost all warung stores the author visited in Ciputat District are tiny retailers located inside buildings facing the streets. They only have small shop spaces of about 10 m² or so and sell beverages, processed foods, and households goods. Drugs constitute a type of products they are selling (Fig. 7.1). They may have no sense of selling drugs. At a certain warung, when the author told a shop master the name of a certain drug, the master handed over a small plastic box, saying "I do not know. Please look for it in this box" (Fig. 7.2).

That plastic box was similar in size to home medicine boxes and did not have a cover. Inside the box, there were PTP sheets containing tablets of several different types of drug products: PTP sheets were not contained in any outer packaging boxes and were disorderly put into the box. This constituted all drugs kept in stock at the warung.

As described above, it was found that at 4 of the 10 warung stores, prescription-only medicines were sold as part of groceries. Unlike the explanation given by the pharmaceutical wholesalers, the proportion of warung stores selling drugs is quite high.

Box 12: Warung

The Indonesian term "Warung" refers to a small family-owned business, e.g., a small grocery shop or a small restaurant. In some papers, this is translated into "kiosk." A warung (Fig. 7.2) faces an alley located at the back of the main street. At this warung, beverages, snacks, and other daily necessities are sold.

The photo (Fig. 7.3) shows all drugs kept in stock at a certain warung. The field worker is checking what is inside this plastic box. The drugs are packaged in PTP sheets although there are neither outer packaging boxes nor written instructions. Some tablets do not have logos on them, which did not enable us to tell their identity.

Fig. 7.2 Typical warung. *Source* Photo taken by the author

Fig. 7.3 How drugs are kept in stock at warung. Photo taken by the author

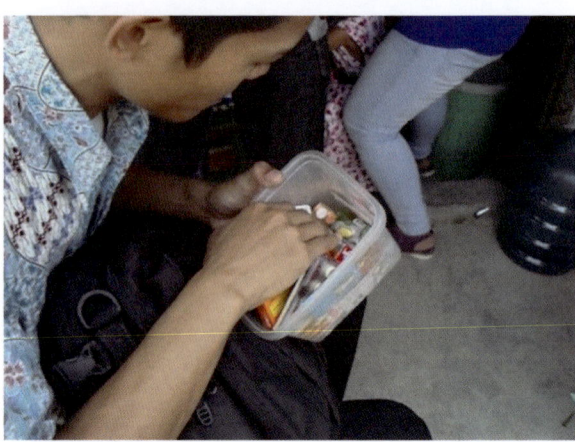

7.4   Challenges Found in On-Site Technology Transfer

Japan has provided technical support through the Japan International Cooperation Agency (JICA) with developing and emerging countries. In connection with our field survey, three specialists were interviewed about the challenges of international cooperation. These interviews contain episodes and input which are not documented in official records but involve both donor and recipient countries.

Interview 1: Mr. A worked for a Japanese pharmaceutical company. He was dispatched from the JICA to Indonesia and participated in an Indonesian–Japan joint project.[2]

> In whichever country we visit in the Southeast Asia, we have heard that we can buy prescription-only medicines without physicians' prescriptions. We do not think that the governmental agencies in these countries do not pay their attention to this fact. Unfortunately, however, we assume that in reality, they haven't gotten around to fighting against it. In Indonesia, the economic conditions have improved, although the standard of living and the situation of hygiene and healthcare have not yet caught up with the level of grown economy. The government's policies regarding hygiene and healthcare, social security, and any other related issues are left until last.

> The IMF rescue program for Indonesia to recover from the Asian Currency and Financial Crisis required the country to shift from centralization of administrative power to decentralization. As a result of this, the central government's power has reduced. Some criticize that this is because the decentralization went to the extremes. When the central government issues guidelines, the provincial governments cannot make them effective unless they have enough financial power to enforce them.

> Drug management was one of the targets of this Project executed in collaboration with the Indonesian Ministry of Health. The issues at the downstream of drug management include proper use of medicines in actual clinical settings, and inventory control. Taking antibiotics as an example, patients need to be instructed to take all of the medication prescribed. In rural areas, there are few pharmacists and midwives or nurses dispensing drugs. Even midwives or

---

[2]Interview conducted by the author on June 16, 2014 in Jakarta.

nurses do not know much about drugs. Patients have to take all of the antibiotics dispensed, but they discontinue taking them when they notice that their symptoms have improved. If the person responsible for dispensing drugs were aware of the reason why the medication dispensed should all be taken, he/she could instruct patients in this regard. In rural areas, those who are in the position of giving instructions lack knowledge.

Another issue to be improved was found for the mindset of persons responsible for dispensing drugs. As the Project progressed, those concerned became aware that drugs are not included in the category of general goods and require special handling in terms of usage and storage. However, they have low awareness of their duties to convey what they have learned to the other persons or successors. In the case of developing countries, information is regarded as a tool for promotion and they do not think that information should be shared. This can apply to not only Indonesia but also the other Southeast Asian countries. Consequently, they took it for granted that the textbooks provided by the Project were left at home and did not bring them to the clinical setting. Awareness reform about information sharing is one of the big barriers in developing countries. Now, their awareness has been raised.

This Project started at an issue of figuring out the best way to effectively use the limited budget. Someone did not know an effective way of using their budget and purchased drugs doubly or disposed of a lot of drugs. The first thing done under this Project was to ask the participants to record what a proper level of stock was and how they were able to procure the necessary amount of drugs, in their notebooks on a monthly basis. At the beginning, they did not know how much they used. At present, they have made progress when compared with the initial status.

In the above-described interview, the challenges that developing or emerging countries face on actual healthcare sites are condensed. At the same time, the essential issues related to the ideal way of providing assistance are raised.

Interview 2: Dr. B was dispatched by the JICA as a technical expert in quality of pharmaceutical products, from the Japanese National Institute of Health Sciences to the Indonesian National Institute of Health Research and Development (NIHRD). She described her experience as outlined below.[3]

I was dispatched by the JICA to Indonesia as a specialist at the Japanese National Institute of Health Sciences to give guidance on dissolution test. The Japanese Ministry of Foreign Affairs has had a strong tie with Indonesia and Japan has a long history of providing assistance to Indonesia. The programs prepared by Japan to assist Indonesia have continued since Japan's first giving guidance to prepare the Indonesian Pharmacopoeia. Individuals specialized in cracking down narcotics who are officials working for the Japanese Ministry of Health, Labour and Welfare (MHLW) go to Indonesia every year. Thus, the channels through which Japan assists Indonesia have been established.

However, what I felt on site was that the foundation to effectively receive assistance became unsettled and I wondered why the JICA could not take appropriate action to restore it. In other words, I thought that we had to guide them not on technology but instead more fundamental systems. We first needed to guide people on site regarding the very basics of the system. In the case of dissolution test as an example, we first trained them regarding what the standards were for conduct of dissolution test, and what information was the basis of dissolution test. Without training these basic matters, no matter how hard the procedures for dissolution test alone were explained, which was meaningless. Due to this experience, I decided not to go to Indonesia any more. It would just end in vain.

---

[3] Interview conducted by the author on February 20, 2015 in Osaka.

The JICA is the organization implementing public policies. Technical experts who are dispatched to foreign countries at a request of JICA may think that the JICA does not know the actual status. When experts write reports and explain what is going on to individuals dispatched from the Japanese MHLW, their opinions may be understood. However, it seems to me that they do not make efforts to resolve problems. To that extent, Japan cannot get into the recipient country, which is my thought. As such, the problems are not resolved and therefore, even though we give assistance or guidance, it seems to be useless. I hesitate to say this but I dare to mention that the Indonesian Pharmacopoeia that was prepared in the past with cooperation from Japan does not work at all, and I have heard that the Indonesian Pharmacopoeia will be revised by making an exact copy of the USP. The assistance is not effective.

We as technical experts directly contact Indonesian on-site staff who are responsible for testing. However, Japanese management staff who work on a full-time basis in Indonesia are made to keep distance from on-site staff. It seems to me that there have been circumstances in which the Indonesian side just wants Japanese management to purchase analyzers as part of assistance and does not want any more. On the other hand, Indonesian people can have close talks with us technical experts dispatched from Japan. As such, Japanese individuals dispatched from the Ministries just make arrangements for giving/receiving assistance but do not get into on-site workplaces. I do know if the situation has long continued in this way and I may consider that probably, this may be the current organizational culture of JICA.

Japanese individuals dispatched from the Ministries cannot talk about technology. They are dispatched to work as management. You cannot understand the actual status of assistance unless you get into on-site workplaces. Even I myself could not have noticed these things if I had not been engaged in guiding on-site staff regarding the quantitative test. I did find them since I actually witnessed their conducting dissolution test.

When considering the level of Japanese technology, it is natural that no deviations from specifications occur during quantitative testing. When considering the level of Indonesian technology, however, quantitative test is important. In Indonesia, national government-owned companies manufacture generic medicines and therefore, I do think that there are no problems with quantitative test. However, based on my experience in witnessing on-site dissolution test, it may be necessary to watch how quantitative test is conducted on site.

On the basis of my experience in conducting dissolution test for pharmaceutical preparations manufactured in Indonesia, the result was about 70% for those which were extremely excellent in solubility. This means that until the end, a tablet will not collapse and a tablet form will be maintained. If a tablet will properly collapse, then 80% of a tablet must be dissolved in 15 min. It seems to me that unfortunately, we have to accept the solubility of 70% as a good result for the level of Indonesian technology. This is the level of the formulation manufactured by the state-owned company. As of 2008, no companies in Indonesia developed new medicines.

There may be emotional confrontation between developing and developed countries. It seems to me that Indonesia may consider it enough to make developed countries purchase necessary equipment and machinery for Indonesian companies. It also seems to me that Indonesia expects to learn how to conduct tests, from technical experts in developed countries but does not want developed countries to be engaged in management of Indonesian companies.

By chance I found that on-site staff did not explain the rationale for selection of testing methods; I noticed this when we were to conduct tests after selecting relevant ones among many testing methods described in the USP. In the end, they said, "the Chinese Pharmacopoeia is good because it includes many pharmaceutical preparations and therefore includes many testing methods we can conduct."

It is meaningless to use the Chinese Pharmacopoeia in order to test drugs commercially available in Indonesia. It would be assumed that since they did not experience in making application for approval for newly developed medicines, they cannot understand the relationship between the testing methods described in registration dossiers and those described in pharmacopoeias. It also would be assumed that they may select halfheartedly the testing methods among those described in the USP when testing medicines imported from the US.

Generic medicines always follow their counterpart originators (which, for developing countries, are branded products manufactured by overseas countries). The specifications and testing methods for originators are not disclosed to the public and therefore, generic manufacturers who make application for approval for their generics have to independently develop and establish specifications and testing methods for the generics. At that time, it would be considered that they might carelessly use testing methods to be included in the application dossiers. The administrative agencies to grant approval might conduct test without referring to the application dossiers.

Interview 3: Dr. C is a specialist in pharmaceutical products at the Japanese National Institute of Health Sciences and has experienced in working in the management division. He has abundant experience in the area of international cooperation, including those in Indonesia.[4]

In the past, the Japanese National Institute of Health Sciences had a collaborative relationship with the JICA. I once wrote a report to JICA, indicating that the current way of giving assistance was meaningless. The JICA put importance on the allocation of funds as a state policy. After that, to what extent it gives assistance and cooperation is determined by the recipient country. If an adequate human relationship is established with the recipient country, then the assistance would be effective. However, if the recipient country only focuses on receiving assistance because Japanese responsible individuals do not stay long in the recipient country, then the assistance would not be so effective.

If an adequate and robust human relationship is established between the donor and recipient countries, then the donor could give advice to the recipient. Japanese administrative officials of the Ministries are relocated and consequently, they have limitations in establishing good human relationship in the area of international cooperation. The duty of bureaucrats is how to plan a project and from the perspective of their career, whether or not the project takes root and is useful in the recipient country is another issue. Their performance is assessed by whether or not they implemented a good-looking project.

In the above-described three interviews, the challenges that developing and emerging countries face on actual healthcare sites are condensed. At the same time, the essential issues related to the ideal way of providing assistance are raised.

7.5 Discussion

7.5.1 Health Insurance System and Self-care

The survey demonstrated, as prior research reports did, that in Indonesia, it is common practice to buy antibiotics without physicians' prescriptions so as to perform self-treatment with them, in spite of the pharmaceutical regulations implemented. The

---

[4]Interview conducted by the author on July 13, 2015 in Tokyo.

World Bank reported that among those who got ill in Indonesia (in 2007), 42% of them visited medical institutions, 45% chose self-treatment, and 13% chose to seek no treatment (Bank Dunia 2010). It cannot be said that all people included in this 45% segment of self-treatment did not suffer from infectious diseases requiring antibiotics. Taking into the fact that these regions show high prevalence rates of infections, however, it can be said that self-treatment with antibiotics has become a common practice.

In the survey, the status of taking out or not taking out health insurance was correlated with neither the status of having or not having physicians' prescriptions nor the frequency of consulting medical doctors. It is therefore considered that in addition to the status of remaining with or without coverage and economic factors that definitely influence people's selection of treatment, other factors may also have an impact on treatment selection. In particular, 24.1% (21/87) of those with coverage answered that they never consult medical doctors. When this category is combined with the category of those who answered that they sometimes visit medical institutions, i.e., 19.5% (17/87), it is demonstrated that 43.6% (38/87) of people do not adequately utilize the health insurance system.

Considering the fact that the majority of the insured are covered by the JAMKESMAS program that is available free of charge, there may be barriers to consultation with medical doctors other than the issue of high medical expenses. In a case study on the "Free Consultation Card" system in Indonesia, it is discussed that "people in the poor and needy hesitate to show their free consultation cards because this card is a symbol of poverty, and this hesitation is a psychological obstacle that can occur as a matter of course" (Shono et al. 2007).

The other barriers to consultation with medical doctors include little expectation on medical institutions or doctors (e.g., the drug prescribed is the same as the previous one and explanation is insufficient), and the fact that medical institutions are packed with patients. Above all, the reality that the way of supporting customers at pharmacies enables them to perform self-medication, and the social norms that have permitted self-medication have supported a practice of treating with antibiotics on their own judgment.

7.5.2 Behavioral Patterns and Mentality of Self-care Performers

Prior research has reported that patients who conduct self-treatment with antibiotics utilize drugs leftover from the past (Shono et al. 2007). The questionnaire survey at pharmacies present in this research revealed that the utilization of leftover drug samples was the most common answer among the factors making interviewees select antibiotics, other than "in accordance with prescription." This finding agrees with the pharmacists' responses that "self-medication performers do not try new drugs" and that "they always want the drugs that were prescribed by medical doctors in the past."

Their act of continuing the past successful experience may be endorsed by the fact that they have succeeded in their self-medication. It is not true that self-medication performers have no fear of risks such as adverse drug reactions (Badiger et al. 2012), but instead they may choose, among available options, safe ones to them in accordance with their own logic. This is a self-medication performers' own risk management. Self-medication performers have only limited knowledge and their knowledge is often wrong, but they are reported to be usually confident (Padoveze et al. 2012). Our interviewees said "our customers say with full of confidence that they get used to this particular drug or that the illness they currently suffer from is just the same as that they had previously and do not need to consult with medical doctors." Psychology has pointed out that people usually become overconfident when they intuitively make a judgment without reviewing the validity of limited experience or information (Kahneman 2011).

Researchers in a different treatment area than ours reported that more patients select topical drugs for their self-treatment in accordance with recommendations by their family members or friends than those who follow pharmacists' recommendations (Padoveze et al. 2012). In our research also, the proportion of interviewees who buy antibiotics based on recommendations by family members or friends was higher than that of those who followed pharmacists' recommendations. This indicates that self-medication performers put importance on information provided by those whom they are familiar with. This may be deeply related to the fact that Indonesia is a traditional society in which people value their ties, as the reporter for the local newspaper has pointed out.

7.5.3 Reasons Why Antibiotics Are Frequently Used for Self-treatment

The pharmacists interviewed in this research pointed out that the drug used for self-medication is limited to antibiotics. This is firstly because pharmacists allow their customers to buy antibiotics even in the absence of physicians' prescriptions and secondly because antibiotics are very effective for acute infections and in addition, the outcome of self-medication can clearly be confirmed in a short period of time.

This short-term feedback leads to a high learning effect. Antibiotics are indicated for multiple infections; there may be a case in which an antibiotic people experienced once in the past is effective and they use it at their own discretion on another occasion. This feature is advantageous for self-medication performers and their own successful experience may reinforce the behavior of conducting self-medication. In addition, people do not clearly understand the difference between bacterial infection and viral infection, which may be another factor supporting the abuse of antibiotics.

7.5.4 Pharmacists' Roles and Self-medication Determined by Society

The problems related to self-medication performers that involve pharmacists are as follows: they come to pharmacies to buy antibiotics even though the drugs are unnecessary; and their manner of taking the drugs is not correct. Under these circumstances, pharmacists consider it desirable that the pharmaceutical regulations are made stricter to inhibit self-medication; although in reality, to achieve this is difficult.

The pharmacists consider it essential to conduct patient education and provide pharmacists' advice for the purpose of minimizing the development of drug resistance and health hazards in individual patients. Our survey did not demonstrate a correlation between the selection of self-medication and the educational background. Researchers reported that higher education is associated with higher rates of self-medication (Grigoryan et al. 2006). It may be because the higher the education, the stronger is their confidence in their own judgment.

As the local pharmacists expect, if a patient's lack of knowledge is improved, this would change his or her behavior. This phenomenon is as described as the "Deficiency in Knowledge" model (Hirakawa et al. 2011); however, a lack of correlation between education and self-medication suggests that this model has its limitations. Medicines are accessible in a variety of forms and to various extents. When people buy prescription-only medications without physicians' prescriptions, this means that they are not incorporated in the official healthcare services system. People who live in medium or lower living standards are economically weak and have no choice but to choose self-medication in order to save healthcare expenses. This is a self-defense behavior for those to whom only limited options are available.

Non-legitimate distribution channels through drugstores or kiosks are complicated and enable the distribution of drugs for which quality is not assured. Access to non-legitimate distribution channels is associated with a risk of encountering non-quality assured drugs. Combination of self-medication with an illegal status of selling drugs has become an everyday practice, and this reflects structural disparities of society.

7.5.5 Sufficiency Rates of Medicines and Complicated Distribution Networks

The pharmacists interviewed in this survey indicated that pharmacies do business only with reliable distribution companies to avoid careless procurement of counterfeit medicines and therefore, they say that at their pharmacies, there are no problems with counterfeit medicines. They also mentioned that they have heard of quality-related problems or cases of health hazards, which are related to drug products sold at drugstores and warung stores or distributed through non-legitimate channels, which strongly suggests that counterfeit or substandard medicines are actually available on the market. The seriousness of problems with counterfeit medicines varies from minor cases in which the expiration date of the genuine drug product is erased and a fake date is overwritten to serious cases in which serious health hazards are caused.

The reporter for the local newspaper stated that there definitely exists the business of counterfeit medicines in Indonesia. As the pharmaceutical wholesalers pointed out, we see the gap, regarding the distribution of medicines in Indonesia, between what the regulations require and what is done in reality. In addition, the existing distribution routes are complicated. Medicines are not always distributed from upstream to downstream, nor from legally qualified companies to legally qualified wholesalers or retailers. The complicated and fragile distribution network facilitates the invasion of non-quality assured drugs into the market, which does not only apply to Indonesia.

Currently, the implementation of the Good Distribution Practice (GDP) is regarded as the main pillar of the countermeasures to combat counterfeit medicines. This is a strategy to prevent counterfeit medicines, if manufactured, from getting into the legitimate distribution channels. In Indonesia, a variety of distributors and non-legitimate distribution channels exist. GDP cannot effectively function unless medicines are sufficiently available to meet needs and their distribution channels are well established. However, there exist overwhelmingly great gaps between Jakarta and other cities as well as agricultural districts in terms of medical resources. The WHO's statistics regarding essential medicines indicate that the sufficiency rate in the Indonesian public sector is 65.5% (Suwa 2014).

The WHO promotes the introduction of universal health coverage with the aim of securing access to healthcare services. In January 2014, Indonesia started to promote a shift to the National Social Health Insurance Scheme in Indonesia (BPJS: Badan Penyelenggara Jaminan Sosial) over a 5-year period (Suwa 2014).

In the initial year of this shift, 72% of the total population, i.e., 177 million people, became insured. This is a public scheme which incorporated the existing health insurance systems, i.e., Jamkesmas, Askes, and Jamsostek, and the world's largest market of health insurance was born. When the basis for access to healthcare services is well established, people's selection behavior will change without fail.

Unfortunately, the annual medical spending per capita in the public sector, that is a major base for the BPJS, is as small as 84 dollars, whereas the annual medical spending per capita in the private sector, that is another base, is 660 dollars. The shift to the BPJS doubles the number of the insured, which in turn reduces the medical expenditure per capita (Suwa 2014). Indonesia still remains in the stage in which "quantity must be prioritized over quality" because the sufficiency rate of essential medicines is low and the circumstances of health care are not uniform over the nation. As the staff dispatched from the JICA pointed out, the improvement of quality of medicines may still be left until later.

The number of medical doctors per 10,000 population is 21 for Japan and one for Indonesia (Egami 2012). Even when the universal health insurance coverage is established, access to healthcare services may be unlikely to increase immediately in response to the establishment. Actually, access to healthcare services may become more difficult in the future because people who did not seek consultation at medical institutions will rush to these institutions subsequently.

In Indonesia, half the population self-medicates, which means that self-medication is a common practice. What is essential in order to change this behavior is to establish a social infrastructure functioning as a reservoir to accept those who are currently outside the social security system. People will not change their behavior unless they actually feel benefits from the reservoir and have an incentive to change their behavior. How people's behavior will change after the successful introduction of the universal health insurance coverage attracts our attention.

Part of this chapter was published by the Journal of the Japan Association for International Health.

Kimura, S., and Nakamura, Y. (2014), Self-treatment with antibiotics and pharmacists' responses to handle this issue—Cross-sectional research in the metropolitan area in Indonesia, Journal of the Japan Association for International Health 29(2), 81–90.

Box 13: Economic Growth in Indonesia

The nominal GDP increased from 179.5 billion dollars (in 2000) to 888.6 billion dollars (in 2014). The proportion of middle-income earners (with a household income of 5,000 to 34,999 dollars) increased from 29.9% (in 2000) to 60.6% (in 2014).

The number of hospitals increased from 1,632 (in 2010) to 2,228 (in 2013). The breakdown of the hospitals revealed that public hospitals showed a great increase and accounted for 70%. The number of beds increased from 163,680 (in 2009) to 235,983 (in 2014). The healthcare services market grew from 3.23 billion dollars (in 2000) to 26.64 billion dollars (in 2013). The import of medicines expanded from 200 million dollars (in 2009) to 450 million dollars (in 2014). Medicines are primarily imported from Germany, USA, France, Switzerland, and UK. The export of medicines expanded from 310 million dollars (in 2009) to 560 million dollars (in 2014). Medicines are primarily exported to India, Philippines, Japan, Thailand, and Nigeria (Ministry of Economy, Trade, and Industry of Japan 2016).

Box 14: Health Care in Indonesia

Health care in Indonesia has rapidly expanded although data on medical resources indicate that average values are not sufficient enough. The number of beds per population in Indonesia is three times smaller than that in Japan, and the number of medical doctors per population is twenty times smaller than that in Japan (in Indonesia, there are two medical doctors per 10,000 population). Furthermore, there exists a great gap between the rich and the poor, and there are big regional differences.

Medical resources are concentrated on Jakarta, whereas in rural areas such as Bali Island, neither medical doctors nor facilities are sufficient, and the situation is serious. Because of the introduction of the National Social Health Insurance Scheme in 2015, public medical institutions are extremely packed with patients. Prior to the introduction of the scheme, approximately half the population were not covered by public health insurance, and many of those without coverage belonged to the informal sector. On the other hand, private hospitals targeting wealthy people are built one after another in urban areas and some of them are equipped with state-of-the-art diagnostic devices. More wealthy people receive treatment in neighborhood countries such as Malaysia and Singapore. More than 100,000 people per year leave Indonesia for the purpose of receiving treatment or medical checkups. (Japanese Ministry of Foreign Affairs 2017)

References

Auta, A., S. Omale, T.J. Folorunsho, et al. 2012. Medicine vendors: self-medication practices and medicine knowledge. *North American Journal of Medical Sciences*. https://doi.org/10.4103/1947-2714.92899. https://www.ncbi.nlm.nih.gov/pubmed/22393544. Accessed 30 August 2018.

Badiger, S., R. Kundapur, A. Jain, et al. 2012. Self-medication patterns among medical students in South India. *The Australasian Medical Journal* 5(4):217–20. https://doi.org/10.4066/amj.2012.1007. https://www.ncbi.nlm.nih.gov/pubmed/22848313. Accessed 30 August 2018.

Bank Dunia. 2009. Indonesia's doctors, midwives and nursed: current stock, increasing needs, future challenges and options. The World Bank January 2009. http://documents.worldbank.org/curated/en/555011468039247466/pdf/477150WP0Indon1BOX0338925B01PUBLIC1.pdf. Accessed 30 August 2018.

Bappeda tangerang selatan (tangerang selatan local government planning board). 2010.

BellCurve. 2019. Boheikin no Kukan Suitei ni okeru Hitsuyo na Sanpuru Saizu no Keisan Fomu [Calculation form to calculate sample size in interval estimate of population mean]. https://bellcurve.jp/statistics/blog/15378.html#download. (In Japanese) Accessed 2 June 2019.

Bin Abdulhak, A.A., M.A. Altannir, M.A. Almansor, et al. 2011. Non prescribed sale of antibiotics in Riyadh, Saudi Arabia: a cross sectional study. *BMC Public Health* 11: 538. https://doi.org/10.1186/1471-2458-11-538. https://www.ncbi.nlm.nih.gov/pubmed/?term=Non+prescribed+sale+of+antibiotics+in+Riyadh%2C+Saudi+Arabia%3A+A+Cross+Sectional+Study. Accessed 30 August 2018.

Egami, Yuriko, Takashi, Yasukawa, Mitsue, Hirota, et al. 2012. Indonesia Kyowakoku no Hokeniryo no Genjo [Health Situation of the Republic of Indonesia]. *Journal of International Health* 27(2): 171–181. https://doi.org/10.11197/jaih.27.171. (In Japanese) Accessed 30 August 2018.

Grigoryan, L., F.M. Haaijer-Rauskamp, J.G.M. Burgerhof, et al. 2006. Self-medication with antimicrobial drugs in Europe. *Emerging Infectious Diseases* 12(3): 452–459. https://doi.org/10.3201/eid1205.050992. https://www.ncbi.nlm.nih.gov/pubmed/16704784. Accessed 30 August 2017.

Hadi, U, P. van den Broek, E.P. Kolopaking, et al. 2010. Cross sectional study of availability and pharmaceutical quality of antibiotics requested with or without prescription (over the counter) in Surabaya, Indonesia. *BMC Infectious Diseases* 10: 203–213. https://doi.org/10.1186/1471-2334-10-203. Accessed 30 August 2018.

Hirakawa, Hideyuki, Shoji, Tsuchida, and Tomoko, Tsuchida. 2011. Risuku Komyunikeshon Ron [Risk Communication Theory]. Osaka University Press, Osaka. (In Japanese).

Japanese Ministry of Economy, Trade and Industry. 2016. Iryo Kokusai Tenkai Kantori Repoto [Global Status of Healthcare Services: Country Report on Indonesia]. http://www.meti.go. jp/policy/mono_info_service/healthcare/kokusaika/27fy/27fy_countryreport_Indonesia.pdf# search =%27%E3%82%A4%E3%83%B3%E3%83%89%E3%83%8D%E3%82%B7%E3% 82%A2 +%E5%8C%BB%E7%99%82%E3%81%A8%E7%B5%8C%E6%B8%88%E7%99% BA%E5%B1%95%27. (In Japanese) Accessed 24 June 2018.

Japanese Ministry of Foreign Affairs. 2017. Sekai no Iryojijo [Health and Medical Care of the World—Indonesia]. https://www.mofa.go.jp/mofaj/toko/medi/asia/indonesia.html. (In Japanese) Accessed 24 June 2018.

Kahneman, Daniel. 2011. *Thinking, fast and slow*. USA: Farrar, Straus and Giroux.

Le, T.H., E. Ottosson, T.K. Nguyen, B.G. Kim, and P. Allebeck. 2011. Drug use and self-medication among children with respiratory illness or diarrhea in a rural district in Vietnam: a qualitative study. *Journal of Multidisciplinary Healthcare* 4, 329–336. https://doi.org/10.2147/jmdh.s22769. https://www.ncbi.nlm.nih.gov/pubmed/21966227. Accessed 30 August 2018.

Miní, E., R. Varas, Y. Vicuña, et al. 2012. Self-medication behavior among pregnant women user of the Instituto Nacional Materno Perinatal, Peru 2011. *Revista Peruana de Medicina Experimental y Salud Publica* 29(2): 212–217. https://www.ncbi.nlm.nih.gov/pubmed/?term=Self-medication+behavior+among+pregnant+women+user+of+the+Instituto+Nacional+Materno+ Perinatal%2C+Peru+2011. Accessed 30 August 2018.

Padoveze, E.H., L.F. Nascimento, F.R. Ferreira, and V.S. Neves. 2012. Cross-sectional descriptive study of topical self-medication in a hospital dermatology department in the state of São Pauro. *Anais Brasileiros de Dermatologia* 87(1): 163–165. https://www.ncbi.nlm.nih.gov/ pubmed/22481675. Accessed 30 August 2018.

Pan, H., B. Cui, D. Zhang, et al. 2012. Prior knowledge, older age, and higher allowance are risk factors for self-medication with antibiotics among university students in southern China. *PLoS One* 7(7): e41314. https://doi.org/10.1371/journal.pone.0041314. https://www.ncbi.nlm.nih.gov/ pubmed/22911779. Accessed 30 August 2018.

Puspitasari, H.P., A. Faturrohmah, and A. Hermansyah. 2011. Do Indonesian community pharmacy workers respond to antibiotics request appropriately? *Tropical Medicine and International Health* 16(7): 840–846. https://doi.org/10.1111/j.1365-3156.2011.02782.x. https://www. ncbi.nlm.nih.gov/pubmed/21545380. Accessed 30 August 2018.

Sarahroodi, S., A. Maleki-Jamshid, A.F. Sawalha, et al. 2012. Pattern of self-medication with analgesics among Iranian University students in central Iran. *Journal of Family and Community Medicine* 19(2): 125–129. https://doi.org/10.4103/2230-8229.98302. https://www.ncbi.nlm.nih. gov/pubmed/?term=Pattern+of+selfmedication+with+analgesics+among+Iranian+University+ students+in+central+Iran. Accessed 30 August 2018.

Shono, A., H. Omae, and M. Masuda. 2007. Indoneshia ni okeru Sefuteinetto Puroguramu no Hoken Iryo Bunya deno Genkai: Muryo Shinsatsu Kado wo Jirei toshite [The Difficulty with the Social Safety Net Health Sector Program in Indonesia: Case Study of Health Card Program]. *Journal of International Health* 22(2): 79–86. https://doi.org/10.11197/jaih.22.79. (In Japanese) Accessed 30 August 2018.

Streetdirectory.com. https://www.streetdirectory.com/indonesia/jakarta/zone/ciputat/. Accessed 11 Feburary 2019.

Suwa, Yoshihiro. 2014. Kokumin Kaihoken heto Ugokidashita Indonesia HerusuKea Sangyo no Miryoku to Otoshiana [Attractive Points and Pitfalls of Healthcare Industry in Indonesia Moving Towards Universal Health Insurance Coverage]. ITmedia Executive. http://mag.executive. itmedia.co.jp/executive/articles/1406/02/news014_4.html. (In Japanese) Accessed 1 September 2018.

Togoobaatar, Ganchimeg, Nayu, Ikeda, Moazzam, Ali, Munkhbayarlakh, Sonomjamts, Sarangerel, Dashdemberel, Rintaro, Mori, and Kenji, Shibuya. 2010. Survey of non-prescribed use of antibiotics for children in an urban community in Mongolia. *Bulletin of the World Health Organization* 88(12): 930–936. https://doi.org/10.2471/blt.10.079004. https://www.ncbi.nlm.nih.gov/pmc/ articles/PMC2995192/. Accessed 30 August 2018.

Widayati, A., S. Suryawati, C. de Crespigny, and J.E. Hiller. 2011. Self-medication with antibiotics in Yogyakarta City Indonesia: a cross sectional population-based survey. *BMC Research Notes* 4: 491. https://doi.org/10.1186/1756-0500-4-491.491. Accessed 30 August 2018.

WHO. 2011. Third international conference for improving use of medicines informed strategies, effective policies, lasting solutions. http://apps.who.int/medicinedocs/documents/s21782en/s21782en.pdf. Accessed 31 August 2013.

WHO. 2016. Global tuberculosis report 2016. http://apps.who.int/iris/bitstream/10665/250441/1/9789241565394-eng.pdf?ua=1. Accessed 13 December 2016.

World Council of Churches. 2006. Promoting Rational Use of Medicines: core components. Contact No. 183. http://apps.who.int/medicinedocs/documents/s19836en/s19836en.pdf#search=%27Contact+Promoting+rational+use+of+medicine%27. Accessed 30 August 201.

Chapter 8
A Case Study in India: Market as a Safety Net

8.1 Criticism Against Emerging Countries

India has succeeded in achieving import substitution industrialization for pharmaceutical products and in addition, is currently a big exporter of generic medicines. India supplies generics throughout the world including the United States (Kamiike and Sato 2006). The products exported from India have passed audits conducted by the regulatory authorities of developed countries and are evaluated to be high in quality. At the same time, India, together with China, is internationally criticized for distributing and exporting not a small number of poor quality drugs such as counterfeit and substandard drugs (Khan and Khar 2015). The Ministry of Health and Family Welfare of the Indian government posts information about counterfeits and substandard medicines such as relevant reports and data on its website. This indicates that the government of India has a great deal of concern about poor quality medicines. The government of India has published its survey results demonstrating that an extremely small number of counterfeit medicines are distributed in India so as to argue against the critical observation made by the international society or the media (CDSCO 2009).

These two-sided international observations may be explained by the presence of problems related to the structure of the Indian pharmaceutical industry. A study has reported that for some types of consumer products, the higher the sales prices, the higher the quality (Ueda 1999). In India, selling prices of medicines are kept low and can be an indicator of an estimation of quality. In India, there exists a huge section of underclass, and it was therefore presumed that actual sales prices of drugs could be related to low quality.

The World Health Organization (WHO) has focused on the illegality and criminality of counterfeit medicines. It is understood that substandard medicines are consequences of immature technologies of legally licensed manufacturers or failed control of random errors during manufacturing. Counterfeits and substandard medicines are mixed up because they are hardly distinguishable regarding the outcome of health hazards and the results of product analysis. Generic medicines support global public health in wealthy countries and low- and middle-income countries and consequently, substandard medicines of generics may constitute a more serious problem (Caudron et al. 2008).

In this chapter, the authors discuss, although in an exploratory manner, the social and structural issues related to the quality of medicines manufactured in India, on the basis of the results of our survey conducted in Delhi City and the adjacent state to the city to investigate selling prices of drugs at pharmacies and interview individuals engaged in the pharmaceutical industry.

8.2 Research Methods

8.2.1 Research Purpose

The research was designed to investigate selling prices of medicines in India and perform an interview survey on employees of pharmacies and individuals engaged in the distribution of drugs, for the purpose of discussing social and structural issues affecting the quality of medicines.

8.2.2 Survey Methods

8.2.2.1 Interview with Individuals Engaged in the Pharmaceutical Industry

The purpose of the interview survey was to explore the overall picture of the quality and distribution of medicines manufactured in India and make relevant any challenges needing to be addressed. The authors interviewed two persons living in Delhi City, i.e., a pharmacist who runs a pharmacy, and a president (Distributor/Consigner) of a distribution company for pharmaceutical products. The relatives of the pharmacy owner have served in important positions of the Association for Pharmacists in Delhi City. The president of the distribution company for pharmaceutical products has assumed the directorship of an association for Indian pharmacists. Both persons have profound knowledge and experience regarding the Indian pharmaceutical industry. The two persons were interviewed two times each in total, one at the beginning of our survey and the other at the end, in a semi-structured manner with the attendance of the guide. The initial interview focused on the overall status regarding the quality and distribution of pharmaceutical products in India. During the second interview, the questions raised from the survey through purchasing drugs and conducting interviews were discussed.

Before starting the interview, written informed consent was obtained from the two individuals. Interview details were recorded with an IC recorder. The interview was conducted in English, with occasional supplementary interpretation by the guide. The author transcribed an entire interview recorded on the IC recorder and the guide confirmed the transcription. The survey period was between January 20, 2015 and January 27, 2015. This survey was approved by the Research Ethics Committee at Faculty of Human Sciences, Graduate School of Human Sciences, Osaka University in Japan.

8.2.2.2 Survey Through Purchasing Drugs and Conducting Interviews at Pharmacies

The purpose of our survey was to determine a relationship between the confidence of pharmacies' employees on the quality of drugs and selling prices. The survey included full-time employees of pharmacies located in Delhi City and Uttar Pradesh State adjacent to the city in the Republic of India. For the purpose of conducting the survey, a dedicated guide engaged in healthcare survey jobs was hired. He is an Indian, and speaks Hindi as a mother language, as well as English and Japanese. The survey plan and informed consent form were sent to the guide in advance so as to help him understand the outline and purpose of the survey. At the same time, his experience was utilized to select target pharmacies so that they were accessed efficiently.

The target pharmacies were randomly selected in the areas around the Yellow Line and Blue Line subway stations in Delhi City (Fig. 8.1), and among those facing trunk roads in the areas from Delhi City to Uttar Pradesh State (Fig. 8.2).

The author first checked the shop front and observed from outside, the shop and the attitude of the shop workers. The survey was performed on pharmacies, which were judged by observation to be expected to give meaningful responses. Uttar Pradesh State was selected because it is adjacent to Delhi City, consisting of many agricultural areas, and having more underclass people than Delhi City does, which enabled a clear comparison and contrast to be made between the state and the city.

The guide accompanied our survey. Before conducting the survey, the purpose of the survey was explained and identified ourselves, and then, informed consent was obtained orally to participate in the survey. Following this, the interview in English was conducted with employees at pharmacies discussing the types of medicines sold at their pharmacies, a possibility that poor quality drugs (counterfeits, substandard medicines) may be distributed, prices, customer segments, and any other relevant questions. Here, the quality of medicines is defined as the attribute of being legally manufactured and distributed and in addition, meeting the relevant specifications.

At pharmacies open for business, over the counter, the author performed the interview survey and purchased drug products. Multiple employees responded to the interview one after the other, and many different interviewees were questioned during

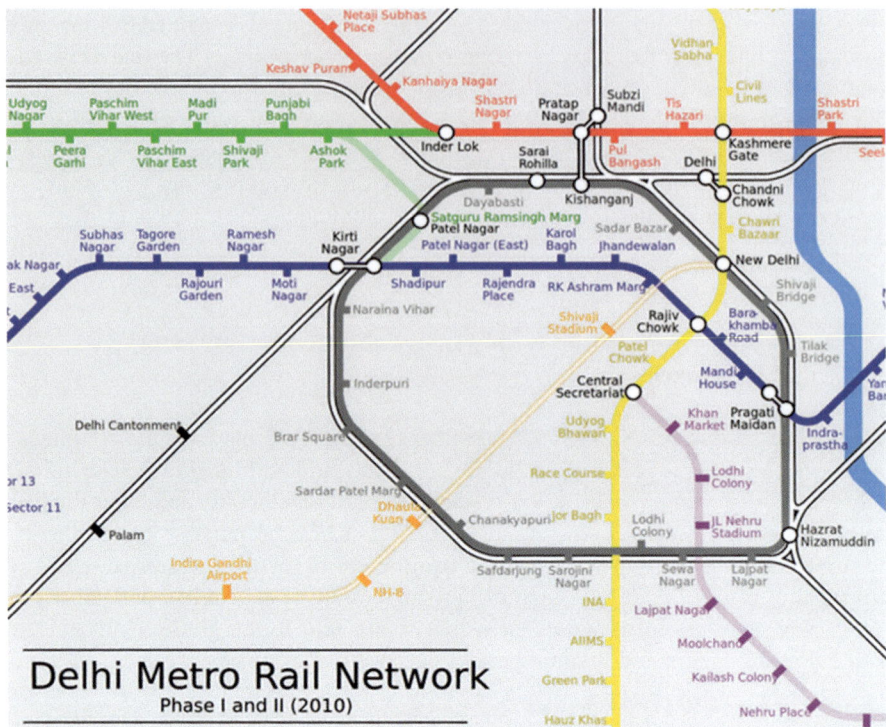

Fig. 8.1 Delhi metro rail network. *Source* Delhi Metro Rail Corporation Ltd.

the survey. Their qualifications or job career were not confirmed. The pharmacies were very crowded and the author did not want to make them feel against us, also the author did not obtain their written consent.

When a single pharmacy sold drugs, which have the same active ingredient and the same specification but are manufactured by different companies, the author purchased them in pairs for the purpose of investigating if there was any difference between list prices and market prices. If there was any difference, I asked the shop staff whether such difference was related to quality or not. At pharmacies where these kinds of paired products were not available, I decided not to purchase drugs and conduct the interview survey alone. When the shop staff did not speak English, the guide accompanying the author gave a supplementary explanation in Hindi. Interview details were recorded in notes without using an IC recorder. At the end of each survey day, I confirmed the survey content with the guide.

Fig. 8.2 Delhi city and Uttar Pradesh state. *Source* Google map

8.3 Survey Results

8.3.1 Survey Through Purchasing Drugs and Conducting Interviews in Delhi City

Among 15 pharmacies that were visited in Delhi City, we successfully achieved the two survey objectives, i.e., purchasing drugs and conducting interviews at 7 pharmacies. We performed an interview survey alone at one pharmacy. A total of 8 pharmacies were included in the survey. For the drug products purchased, the shop staff neither gave us relevant explanation nor handed over the written instructions for use. All purchased drug products but one were sold at list prices according to the maximum retail prices (MRPs).[1] The MRP was indicated on the entire reverse side of press-through package (PTP) sheet or on the outer box, together with the brand name, generic name, manufacturer's name and address, and any other relevant information.

---

[1]A maximum retail price (MRP) is a manufacturer calculated price that is the highest price that can be charged for a product sold in India and Bangladesh. However, retailers may choose to sell products for less than the MRP. MRP differs from systems using a recommended retail price because in those systems the price calculated by the manufacturer is only a recommendation, not enforceable by law. All retail products in India must be marked with MRP. Shops cannot charge customers over an MRP.

Table 8.1 compares the purchased drug products with the same active ingredient manufactured by different pharmaceutical companies. The MRP ratio for medicines with the same active ingredient and the same content ranges from 1.0 to 1.64 (Table 8.1). One drug product available at an exceptionally discounted price was Filgrastim injection 300 mg, for which the list price was 2,200 Rs (about 4,400 Japanese Yen) when manufactured by Roche (a Swiss-funded large-scale company), and was 2,249.9 Rs when manufactured by Dr. Reddy's, an Indian-capitalized large-scale pharmaceutical company. The list prices for this product manufactured by the two companies were within the same range.

However, the actual marketing price for Filgrastim injection 300 mg manufactured by the Indian company was 700 Rs (about 1,400 Japanese Yen), which was discounted to one-third of the list price. The injection requires refrigeration for storage. The drug products manufactured by both the companies were appropriately stored in refrigerators, and were dispensed in bags into which cold packs were also placed. At all pharmacies where the author purchased the drugs, the shop staff neither checked if the author had a physician's prescription nor asked us to show it. At all of these pharmacies, a receipt indicating purchase details including but not limited to product name and quantity was issued. This document was printed from a computer in many cases but was handwritten in some cases.

Drug products sold at these pharmacies are primarily manufactured by large-scale companies (which are both Indian-capitalized and multinational). The customers are commuters and residents living near each station. At all eight pharmacies surveyed in Delhi City, drug products manufactured by large-scale pharmaceutical companies are sold. The interviewees strongly denied a possibility that counterfeit or substandard medicines may be distributed and answered that the quality of medicines they sell are reliable. Wholesalers of pharmaceutical products commented that generally speaking, pharmacies issuing a receipt indicating purchase details are trustworthy.

8.3.2   Survey Through Purchasing Drugs and Conducting Interviews in Uttar Pradesh State

At four pharmacies located in Uttar Pradesh State, which is adjacent to Delhi City and is about 70 km away from the city, the author purchased drug products and conducted the interview survey. As in Delhi City, the products purchased were sold at list prices according to the MRPs. It was also possible to purchase drug products manufactured by locally based minute pharmaceutical companies which are referred to a small scale industry (SSI).[2] Drug products sold at the pharmacies surveyed are primarily manufactured by both locally based and large-scale companies. At some of them, traditional medicines are also sold. The customers are residents in local communities.

---

[2]Locally based minute pharmaceutical companies, which are referred to as a SSI (Small Scale Industry) in India. The term SSI does not only apply to the pharmaceutical industry.

Table 8.1 Comparison of prices among the drug products purchased in the urban area

Nonproprietary name and specification	Brand name (company)	MRP/sheet and unit price per tablet (Rs = about 1.9 yen, in January 2015)	MRP ratio
Cetirizine Hydrochloride 10 mg	Cetcip (Cipla)	20.16/10TAB @2.02	1.00
	Cetzine (GSK)	20.16/10TAB @2.02	
Azithromycin	Azax-500 (Ranbaxy)	68.65/3TAB @22.88	1.00
	Aziwok 500 (Wockhardt)	114.25/5TAB @22.85	
Cefuroxime	Ceroxitum 250 (Intas)	175/4TAB @43.75	1.01
	Ceftum 250 (GSK)	174/4TAB @43.50	
Filgrastim injection 300 mg	Grafeel (Dr. Reddy's)	2249.9/injection (Discount 700Rs)	1.02
	Neupogen (Roche)	2200/injection	
Amoxycillin	Hipen P 250 (Zydus Cadila)	41.25/10CAP @4.13	1.05
	Mox Capsules 250 mg (Ranbaxy)	43.47/10CAP @4.35	
Sildenafil	Caverta 50 (Ranbaxy)	112/4TAB @28.0	1.08
	Penegra (Zydus Healthcare)	103.5/4TAB @25.88	
Chloroquine	Lariago (IPCA)	7.99/10TAB @0.80	1.14
	Resochin (Bayer)	6.95/10TAB @0.70	
Ibuprofen and Paracetamol	Flexon (Aristo)	14.08/15TAB @0.94	1.15
	Combiflam (Sanofi)	16.18/15TAB @1.08	
Ciprofloxacin	Ciplox 500 (Cipla)	93.36/10TAB @9.34	1.44
	Ciprodac (Cadila)	64.9/10TAB @6.49	
Amlodipine	Amloz 2.5 mg (Shreya Life Sciences)	19.95/10TAB @2.0	1.58
	Ampedin (Cadila)	47.39/15TAB @3.16	

(continued)

Table 8.1 (continued)

Nonproprietary name and specification	Brand name (company)	MRP/sheet and unit price per tablet (Rs = about 1.9 yen, in January 2015)	MRP ratio
Salbutamol and Theophylline	Bronkolin (Omni)	2.18/10TAB @0.22	1.64
	Theo-Asthalin (Cipla)	10.73/30TAB @0.36	

Source This table was prepared by the author

A pharmacy owner interviewed commented that 60–80% of products manufactured by locally based pharmaceutical companies are distributed through government procurement to public clinics (or what is referred to as "Dispensaries" in India) and the remaining, to local communities and the states in the east part of India that are poorer. He continued to say that although local people do not trust the products manufactured by locally based pharmaceutical companies, they buy these products when they have physicians' prescriptions. Substandard medicines are also distributed. These drugs are inferior in clinical efficacy because they contain less active ingredients. This fact is apparently well known among pharmacies, whereas patients and physicians do not know it, indicating the existence of information asymmetry.

8.3.3   Survey Results from Interviewing a Distributor of Pharmaceutical Products

The opinions of a distributor obtained through interview are summarized below.

8.3.3.1   Manufacturing by Locally Based Pharmaceutical Companies and Complicated Distribution

The distribution of generic drugs manufactured by locally based pharmaceutical companies in India is characterized by government procurement intended to provide these drugs through public clinics called Dispensaries. These companies aim to be successful in running a government procurement business and for them, the government is the largest customer. They have been well familiar with and complied with the Good Manufacturing Practice (GMP, which corresponds to the Japanese "Ministerial Ordinance on Standards for Manufacturing Control and Quality Control for Drugs and Quasi-drugs") and have manufactured good quality products. The interviewees also pointed out that for the purpose of securing profits, the content of an active ingredient is made closer to the lower limit of the specification. For example, when a specification for a certain active ingredient ranges from 90 to 110%, the actual content of the active ingredient would be between 92 and 93%, which might lead to deviations from the specification due to random errors during manufacturing, problems related to distribution control, or any other relevant causes.

As described above, the drug products manufactured by locally based companies are mostly subject to government procurement. The remainder is distributed to rural agricultural areas by an extremely large number of distributors located throughout India, via complicated channels. The number of wholesalers is about 5,000 in entire India and is more than 500 even in Delhi City. Local retailers procure drug products not from official dealers but from locally based wholesalers.

8.3.3.2 Limited Availability of Counterfeit Drugs and Informal Sector

The quality of India-made medicines has dramatically changed over the past decade. It has been said that the growing rate of Internet access has partly contributed to quality improvement. Although it varies depending on how counterfeit medicines are defined, the availability of counterfeits is currently limited. Even substandard medicines are not extremely bad in quality. If a counterfeit medicine is defined as a product containing an active ingredient between 50 and 60% of the specification, such a product should not be generally available in the market. If there are some such products, they would likely be counterfeited by criminals in the informal sector in local communities and would contain chalk powder but no active ingredients. The informal sector produces large scale of business, although illegally, and locally based minute companies, i.e., both manufacturers and distributors, are engaged in the illegal business.

8.3.3.3 Pricing and Quality of Pharmaceutical Products

Across the world, generic medicines are usually less expensive than brand name drugs (which are not always originators). In India, there is an additional factor that further leads to the price difference between the two, and the factor is the difference in taxes imposed (including but not limited to the commodity tax, the sales tax paid to the central government, the sales tax paid to the state government, and the tariff imposed when transporting a product from a state to another state). Only two of these taxes are imposed on generics, making them less expensive. The MRP varies depending on whether a drug is branded or generic and therefore, the price difference in MRP does not represent a difference in quality. Generic drugs may be equally as good as brand name ones in quality because generics are manufactured in compliance with the GMP and any other relevant standards.

8.3.3.4   Limits of the Central Government's Regulations and Problems with Distribution Infrastructure

The central government has endeavored to secure the quality of pharmaceutical products commercially available in the market, by placing various regulations and conducting sampling inspections. The endeavors have proven to be effective. At the same time, however, the country is too large to be kept under adequate vigilance. The Good Distribution Practice (GDP) needs to be observed for the purpose of securing the quality of pharmaceutical products during distribution.

In rural areas, however, facilities used for distribution of drugs are not adequately air-conditioned and thus, the distribution infrastructure does not satisfy the requirements of GDP. The quality of drugs may deteriorate under high-temperature and high-humidity environments. In addition, inadequate quality of packaging may cause drugs to fail to meet their specifications.

8.3.4   Survey Results from Interviewing a Pharmacy Owner

Opinions of a pharmacy owner obtained through interview are summarized below.

8.3.4.1   Drugs Distributed to Public Dispensaries and Price-Reducing Pressure in Negotiation for Government Procurement

Almost all drugs distributed to public dispensaries through government procurement can be regarded as substandard medicines that have a lot of quality-related problems. This is partly because the pressure for price reduction occurs during the process of negotiation for government procurement. Flour may be blended and the quality of a product becomes extremely poor. When compressed, tablets are easily broken into pieces. Substandard medicines are the consequences of human errors in some cases but are intentionally produced in other cases. Blending flour or charcoal to reduce the content of an active ingredient is an intentional production of substandard medicines. Even pharmaceutical companies officially licensed by the government intentionally produce substandard medicines. When procuring drugs, the government negotiates with the pharmaceutical companies about prices, which forces the companies to accept profit cuts.

8.3.4.2   Bribery Demands Constituting a Hotbed of Poor Quality

Bribery demands during government procurement are well-known acts. Bribes sometimes make rejected products be accepted. Furthermore, sales prices are set in accordance with the MRP, which causes locally based companies to sacrifice quality so as to secure profits because profit margins are small for these companies. The government sets specifications, which is meaningless if bribery is a common practice. When the business of a company does not go well, the company finds drugs which are selling well in the market and produces duplicates of these drugs. Even an officially licensed company has begun to have connections with gangsters when it has failed to achieve desirable sales because they have to continue to run a business anyway.

8.3.4.3 Asymmetry of Information About Medicines and the Internet

Patients know the names of large-scale pharmaceutical companies but have an extremely limited knowledge about quality. In contrast, physicians may prescribe drugs of inadequate quality if they receive entertainments from the companies engaged in the marketing of these drugs, and in this way, create demands for drugs of inadequate quality. This type of asymmetry of information about medicines is common to every country. However, in India in which public procurement accounts for a large proportion of drug distribution, whether or not a function to check quality is actually effective is an issue of particular significance.

The interviewee engaged in the distribution of pharmaceutical products told us that the improvement of drug quality noted in the last decade is largely attributable to the spread of the Internet. People have become able to compare products on the Internet and exchange information among consumers. The Internet has remarkably reduced transaction costs consumers need to bear. Consumers try to smash down the wall of information asymmetry and this behavior definitely has an impact on individuals involved in the market. Who accesses the market and in which way produces interactions and pressures are related to the supply and demand balance in the market, and affects quality from medium- to long-perspectives.

8.4 Discussion

8.4.1 Structure of the Indian Pharmaceutical Industry and the Roles of GMP

There are three influential associations in the Indian pharmaceutical industry. One of them is the Organization of Pharmaceutical Producers of India (OPPI) that primarily consists of large-scale foreign-capitalized enterprises such as European, American, and Japanese pharmaceutical companies. The remaining two have Indian-funded companies as members, i.e., the Indian Pharmaceutical Alliance (IPA) in which only invited 20 or so leading firms participate, and the Indian Drug Manufacturers' Association (IDMA) that represents 700 small- to large-scale pharmaceutical companies throughout the country (Institute for Health Economics and Policy 2015).

The government of India reports that there are more than 5,000 Indian-capitalized pharmaceutical companies (MHWFW Government of India 2003). This means that there exist many minute pharmaceutical companies that do not participate in industrial associations. The member firms of the IPA account for 75% of the total value of exports to the United States (Institute for Health Economics and Policy 2015). The structure of the Indian pharmaceutical industry can be divided into two segments of business: one is to export pharmaceutical products to developed countries, which is a business run by some Indian-capitalized pharmaceutical companies, and the other is to meet domestic demands, which is a business run by a group of Indian-funded pharmaceutical companies including many minute ones.

It has been pointed out that the spread of GMP is one of the major reasons why pharmaceutical products made in India for export to developed countries are high in quality. In India, it was decided in 2001 to upgrade the Indian GMP to the level of WHO-GMP and after a period of transition, the upgraded GMP was enforced in 2003 (Kamiike et al. 2011). This history is consistent with the comment given by the distributor interviewed in our survey that the quality of pharmaceutical products has improved over the last decade. In addition to the full-scale introduction of GMP in India, strict audits conducted by the regulatory authorities of developed countries are considered to function as a big deterrent for poor quality assurance.

However, there is a case which attracts our attention. Daiichi Sankyo Company, Limited, one of the Japanese leading pharmaceutical companies, acquired Ranbaxy Laboratories Limited, an Indian-based pharmaceutical company. After the acquisition, the US FDA conducted audits on manufacturing plants in India and issued warnings, but the quality management-related problems were not resolved. In the end, Daiichi Sankyo sold Ranbaxy to another company (Tsutsui 2014). This case may serve to indicate that even for a large-scale pharmaceutical company having excellent resources, the introduction of GMP would not be a perfect solution to foster a company-wide organizational culture that is highly sensitive to quality norms.

Regarding how to evaluate medicines distributed in the Indian domestic market, our interview has revealed differences in opinions about some aspects of the evaluation between the distributor and the pharmacy owner. The distributor commented that counterfeit medicines were distributed in India in the past, but as of today, counterfeits of extremely bad quality are no longer available in the market. A group of locally based minute pharmaceutical companies, which are outnumbered, underpin the domestic pharmaceutical industry because they manufacture relevant chemicals under contract for and supply drug substances or active ingredients to large-scale companies (Kamiike 2007). For the purpose of developing the pharmaceutical industry as a national policy, it was essential to encourage the entire pharmaceutical industry including locally based companies to introduce GMP, and the spread of GMP has greatly contributed to the improvement in general quality of medicines manufactured in India. On the other hand, the introduction of GMP required a substantial amount of investment, and locally based pharmaceutical companies faced difficult situations (Kamiike 2007).

Under these circumstances, together with the limitation of pharmacovigilance capability of the Indian drug regulatory authorities, we have to hold our judgment on the uniformity of quality of products manufactured by locally based pharmaceutical companies. Figure 8.3 illustrates the schematic structure of the Indian pharmaceutical industry and distribution.

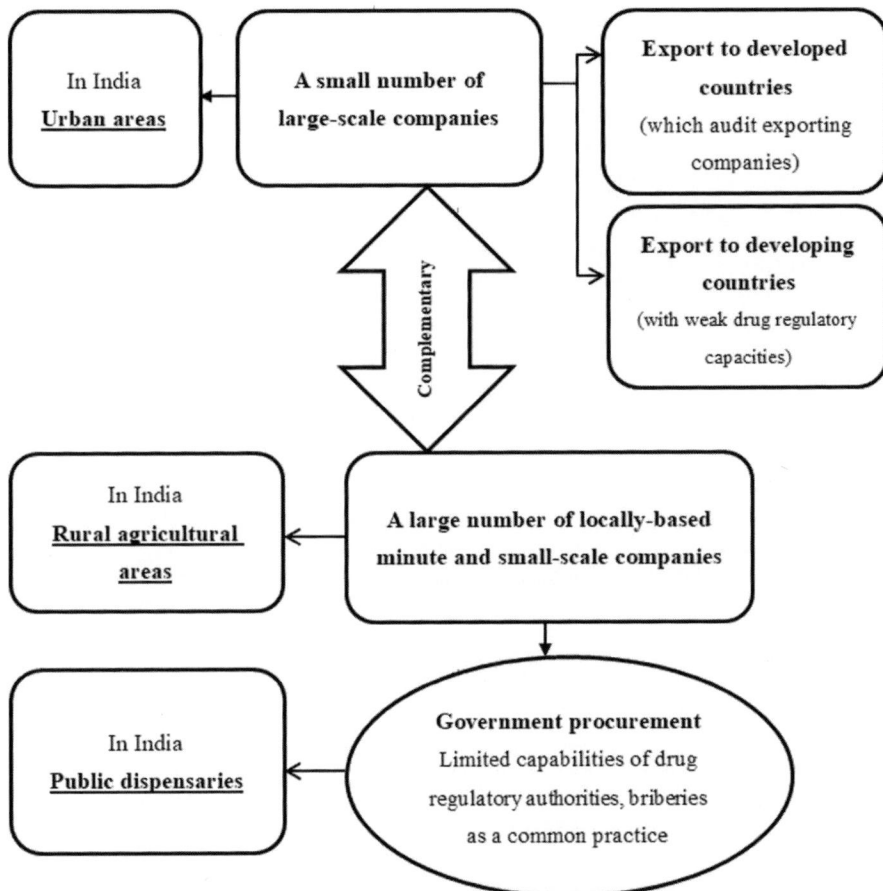

Fig. 8.3 Schematic structure of Indian pharmaceutical industry and distribution. *Source* This scheme was prepared by the authors

8.4.2 Challenges Related to the Structure of Locally Based Pharmaceutical Companies

The survey has demonstrated that structural problems related to quality still exist in the group of locally based pharmaceutical companies. The interviewed pharmacy owner pointed out that bribery is a common practice during government procurement.

In India, people living below the poverty line (<32 Rupees per day) account for about 22% (270 million people) of the total population (Institute for Health Economics and Policy 2015). The government provides special supports and preferential policies with SSIs (Kamiike 2007) and procures medicines from locally based pharmaceutical companies, i.e., SSIs, so as to supply medicines to public dispensaries. The wholesalers of medicines in Delhi City pointed out that one of the reasons why drug products manufactured by these minute locally based companies are accepted despite the existence of quality problems is explained by employment-related issues at these companies. They commented as described below.

> In India, counterfeit medicines may still exist but are actually very small in numbers. There are many substandard medicines. Brand name drugs are good in quality. Generic drugs are divided in two: generics manufactured by top-ranking companies (Ranbaxy, Sandoz, Glaxo, etc.) that are good in quality and those manufactured by other companies that are poor in quality.

> The government promotes GMP. However, generics manufactured by minute companies have quality problems. These products are less expensive by 30%. Our wholesaler does not handle these generics. They are handled by others in our district. These products may include counterfeit medicines.

> The number of minute pharmaceutical companies is significantly higher than 5,000. The government of India indicates in the official report that about 5,000 manufacturing sites are licensed. However, in realty, there are many more sites than this. Why are these minute companies not integrated? Because there is an employment issue. As long as there is a demand for their products, they continue to manufacture even if the products have quality problems. As long as they manufacture and sell their products, employees can be salaried.

For locally based pharmaceutical companies, supply to public dispensaries is a business incorporated in the social infrastructure. However, our survey has suggested that price-reducing pressure given in the process of negotiation for government procurement is combined with bribery practices. The government of India issued the guidelines that instruct the government officials not to conduct acts of injustice in relation to the dispensary management (Government of India). This means that the Indian government admits that bribery is a common practice. In India, corruption and briberies occur in many areas, including, among others, the administration of justice, police, public services, and public procurement (GAN 2017).

In the bidding arrangements for government procurement, wholesalers (or stockists) of medicines have negotiating rights (Institute for Health Economics and Policy 2015). The commission for the negotiation equals 10%–40% of a bidding price and in addition, the following vested-interest structure has been reported: the agent acts as a go-between for bribery (Singh and Rajiv 2013). This structure could cause manufacturers to sacrifice quality to secure profits.

Another factor which makes the situation even more complicated is suggested by the comment given by the interviewee: "the quality of drug products manufactured by locally-based companies are good, although they make the content of an active ingredient at only a little bit higher than the lower limit of the specification." This may serve to indicate a possibility that the following belief may be accepted: if active ingredients are within the range of specifications, then there are no problems in terms of quality control. This belief takes advantages of the concept of setting specification ranges for the sake of themselves. When controlling the content of an active ingredient, it is essential to determine it using a relevant device and the reference standard as a comparator. If the purity of a bulk drug is assumed to be 95% and only 92% of the bulk drug is combined so as to achieve economic savings, then the theoretical content in the finished product could be as low as 87%. No one believes that the content of active ingredients in commercially available medicines is 50% or 60%. However, in reality, the content of active ingredients is in many cases slightly below the lower limit of the specification. This suggests that even though the GMP is introduced, there exists the temptation to use an as narrow as possible safety margin for quality control at the manufacturing site.

Pharmaceutical products are affected by environmental factors such as heat, humidity, and light, resulting in deterioration of active ingredients and degeneration of pharmaceutical formulations (Yoshioka 1995). What is important for the quality of tablets, in particular, is not only the content of an active ingredient but also pharmaceutical stability which determines dissolution rates. For these reasons, even if a drug product satisfies the specification when manufactured, it may become deviated from the specification during distribution as the interviewed distributor pointed out.

The report on a nationwide survey performed by the government of India in 2009 revealed that out of 24,136 samples of drugs purchased from pharmacies and examined for the content of active ingredients and labeling, only 11 samples accounting for 0.046% (11/24,136) turned out to be counterfeit medicines (CDSCO 2009). On the basis of these results, this survey report argued against the media report that India is a supply source of counterfeit medicines. However, a survey conducted by the government of India in 2010 through 2012 revealed that the detection rates for substandard medicines were 4.8% (2,372/49,682) and 4.5% (2,186/48,082) (Edney 2014).

Regarding these circumstances, the organization Médecins Sans Frontières (MSF) that has experienced procurement of medicines from everywhere across the world for humanitarian aid commented as follows: "The availability of counterfeit medicines is definitely a problem, but substandard medicines constitute a greater problem. In the tropical zones in which countries like India are located, even high-quality drugs may become substandard if managed inadequately at pharmacies."[3] This suggests that pharmaceutical products manufactured to contain active ingredients at around the lower limit of the specification may frequently be deteriorated under a certain environment. In regions with a severe environment, it is considered that pharmaceutical stability and robust infrastructure for distribution may determine post-manufacturing maintenance of quality. This consideration should not be only discussed as a theoretical possibility but instead be demonstrated, which is one of the issues to be addressed in order to probe the true nature of the problem with counterfeit medicines. More specifically, what is important is not only to use rates of conformity with specifications (i.e., deviation rates) to analyze the quality of medicines but also to monitor mean values and variances for deviations from specifications both in a time-course manner and in a fixed-point observation way.

It was considered that the government of India implicitly accepts the presence of out-of-specification drugs firstly because a huge number of people in the underclass do not have adequate access to medicines in the transitional and development period in which the national standard of economy has not yet been sufficiently developed, and secondly because the capability of pharmacovigilance by the Indian drug regulatory authorities is still limited.

8.4.3 Sales Prices and Branding as Quality Indicators

In India, the MRP is set as a rule for all commodities including medicines, and is interpreted as a certain type of list price. As of 2013, the Drug Pricing Control Order controls the upper limit of pricing for 348 pharmaceutical products listed in the National List of Essential Medicines.

India has adopted a system that separates prescribing from dispensing drugs. Dispensing antibiotics requires physicians' prescriptions. However, at the pharmacies in which the author purchased drugs in this survey, the author was not asked at all to show physicians' prescriptions nor was allowed by the shop staff to confirm their existence. The drug products purchased were sold at list prices in accordance with the MRPs. The MRPs themselves vary depending on products, but a discount from the MRP was an exception. The distributor interviewed commented that the difference in MRPs does not represent a difference in quality, and sales prices do not function as an indicator of quality.

A study conducted to investigate a correlation between sales prices and drug quality demonstrated that the sale prices of drug products which failed to pass at least one quality test were lower significantly, i.e., by 13.6–18.7%, than those of conforming drug products although the differences were relatively small. It was

---

[3] A Bangladeshi medical doctor working for the Médecins Sans Frontières (MSF) who agreed to our interview told us that the MSF uses rigorous processes and strict criteria for acceptance when procuring medicines. If a drug fails to be clinically effective, they suspect that the quality of the drug might have deteriorated due to inadequate storage and management of the drug (Interview conducted by the author on December 1, 2014 in Tokyo).

concluded that the difference in selling prices may not be a proper indicator of quality (Bate et al. 2011). In other industries, the presence of information asymmetry may not provide an incentive for companies to supply high-quality products.

The interviewee commented that the growing rate of Internet access has contributed to quality improvement for medicines. This comment implies that the information asymmetry has gradually diminished, which affects suppliers. A Japanese study has demonstrated that when the value of a brand has been well established through long-term transactions between a company and consumers, the company may provide high-quality products to consumers if the consumers put their faith in the company's products using sales prices as a yardstick (Fukuda 2008). Although our study included a limited number of pharmacies, our interview survey revealed that at our surveyed pharmacies and other officially licensed pharmacies, drug products manufactured by large-scale pharmaceutical companies are predominantly those sold.

In light of this finding, coupled with comments obtained from the pharmacy employees during our interview, it might be presumed that the quality of pharmaceutical products distributed to pharmacies in Delhi City is not at such a level subject to international criticism. In the state adjacent to Delhi City, products manufactured by locally based pharmaceutical companies do not gain high trust from residents, and substandard medicines are distributed. On the basis of above-stated findings, it might be judged that apart from the distribution route to public dispensaries, the quality of drugs available in urban areas may differ from those distributed to local rural areas. However, this judgement is only based on the observation through our survey, not supported by chemical analysis for drug samples.

The Indian-capitalized pharmaceutical industry consists of a small number of large-scale companies and a lot of minute and small-scale companies. The latter group is a source of generics supplied to public dispensaries through government procurement. In the bidding arrangements for government procurement, pricing is prioritized during the negotiation and at the same time, the demanding for bribes by government officials is a common practice. Under these circumstances, minute and small-scale companies are forced to reduce costs, resulting in possibilities that they may deviate from specifications or may bring about drug products that are more easily affected by the environment.

In addition to the existence of an extremely large number of minute and small-scale pharmaceutical companies and the limited capability of the government to properly monitor and regulate the pharmaceutical affairs, there are many structure-related problems that discourage minute and small-scale companies from focusing on the improvement of the quality of products they manufacture.

On the other hand, the medicines manufactured by Indian-capitalized companies for exporting to developed countries are higher in quality than those distributed in the domestic market because these products are audited by the regulatory agencies of developed countries. In developing countries, however, the pharmacovigilance system of drug regulatory authorities is usually not sufficient, and it might therefore be assumed that even low-quality products may be imported as they are. These discrepancies between inside and outside India have brought about the two-sided observations about the quality of medicines made in India.

References

Bate, Roger, Ginger Zhe, Jin, and Aparna, Mathur. 2011. Does Price Reveal Poor-Quality Drugs? Evidence from 17 Countries. https://www.nber.org/papers/w16854.pdf. Accessed 1 September 2018.

Caudron, J.M., N. Ford, M. Henkens, et al. 2008. Substandard medicines in resource-poor settings: a problem that can be no longer be ignored. *Tropical Medicine and International Health* 13(8): 1062–1072. https://doi.org/10.1111/j.1365-3156.2008.02106.x. https://www.ncbi.nlm.nih.gov/pubmed/18631318. Accessed 1 September 2018.

CDSCO. 2009. Report on countrywide survey for spurious drugs. http://apps.who.int/medicinedocs/documents/s19288en/s19288en.pdf. Accessed 25 November 2014.

Delhi Metro Rail Corporation Ltd. https://www.researchgate.net/figure/Delhi-Metro-Rail-Network-Phase-I-and-II-Source-DMRC_fig1_280310604. Accessed 2 February 2019.

Edney, A. 2014. India's Poor Quality Drugs End Up in Africa, Study Finds. http://www.bloomberg.com/news/articles/2014-09-17/india-s-poor-quality-drugs-end-up-in-africa-study-finds. Accessed 16 February 2015.

Fukuda, Tsubasa. 2008. Hitaisho Jyohoka de Meka ga Kohinshitsu Seihin wo Kyokyusuru Insenteibu ni tuiteno Gemu Riron teki Kosatsu -Gijutsu Shinpo wo Koryoshite- [Game-theoretic discussion about incentives given to manufacturers to supply high quality products under information asymmetry—with technical progress into account -]. Hosei University. http://www.hosei.ac.jp/documents/campuslife/katsudo/kensho/2008/kensho31_02.pdf. Accessed 10 April 2016.

GAN. 2017. India Corruption Report. https://www.business-anti-corruption.com/country-profiles/india/. Accessed 22 September 2019.

Government of India. Dispensary management. http://deity.gov.in/content/dispensary-management. Accessed 27 November 2015.

Institute for Health Economics and Policy. 2015. *Shin Keizai Seicho no Iryo Hosho Seido ni kansuru Chosa Kenkyu -Indo no Iryo Hosho Seido- Hokokusho* [Survey Research on Medical Security Systems – the Medical Security System in India - Report]. Tokyo, Japan: Institute for Health Economics and Policy, Association for Health Economics Research and Social Insurance and Welfare, a General Incorporated Foundation. (In Japanese).

Kamiike, Atsuko, and Sato, Takahiro. 2006. WTO no Boeki Kanren Chitekishoyuken (TRIPS) Kyotei to Indo Iyakuhin Sangyo [The Agreement on Trade-Related Aspects of Intellectual Property Rights (TRIPS) of the World Trade Organization (WTO) and the Pharmaceutical Industry of India]. *Chiiki Kenkyu (Japanese Journal of Area Studies)* 7(2): 149–167. (In Japanese).

Kamiike, Atsuko. 2007. Indo Iyakuhin Sangyo ga Kakaeru Kadai [Challenges to be Addressed by the Pharmaceutical Industry of India], ed. Kubo, Kensuke. 55–79. Chiba: *Nihon no Jenerikku Iyakuhin Sangyo to Indo, Chugoku no Seiyaku Sangyo* [Generic Medicine Industry in Japan and Pharmaceutical Industry in India and China]. IDE-JETRO. (In Japanese).

Kamiike, Takahiro, Fujimori, and Aradhna, Aggarwal. 2011. Indo Seiyaku Sangyo ni okeru Seisansei Dainamikusu 'Nenji Kogyo Chosa' no Kohyo wo Riyoshite [Productivity Dynamics in the Indian Pharmaceutical Industry: Evidence from Plant-Level Panel Data]. Kobe, Japan: Research Institute for Economics and Business Administration, Kobe University. (In Japanese).

Khan, A.N., and R.K. Khar. 2015. Current scenario of spurious and substandard medicines in India. A systemic review. *Indian Journal of Pharmaceutical Sciences* 77(1): 2–7. https://www.ncbi.nlm.nih.gov/pmc/articles/PMC4355878/. Accessed 1 September 2018.

MHWFW Government of India. 2003. Report of the expert committee on A comprehensive examination of drug regulatory issues, including the problem of spurious drugs. http://planningcommission.nic.in/reports/genrep/health/Final_Report_mashelkar.pdf#search='Report+of+the+expert+committee+on+A+comprehensive. Accessed 17 October 2016.

Singh, A., and J. Rajiv. 2013. Bribery and corruption in public procurement: a unique approach. Express Pharma. http://archivepharma.financialexpress.com/sections/management/3111-bribery-and-corruption-in-public-procurement-in-india-a-unique-approach. Accessed 3 November 2015.

Tsutsui, Mikio. 2014. DaiichiSankyo ga Mondai no Indo Kogaisha wo Baikyaku, Baisyu kara 5 Nen no Kuhi, Kyogaku Sonshitsu Keijo demo Inseki Nasi [Daiichi Sankyo Sells Out an Indian Subsidiary 5 Years After Acquisition. No One Takes Responsibility for the Huge Loss]. Toyo Keizai. http://toyokeizai.net/articles/-/34803?page=2. Accessed 28 October 2014.

Ueda, Takaho. 1999. Hinshitu Barometa tosite no Kakaku [Price as a Barometer of Quality]. Gakushuin Economic Papers 36(1): 27–48. http://www.gakushuin.ac.jp/univ/eco/gakkai/pdf_files/keizai_ronsyuu/index2.html. (In Japanese) Accessed 1 September 2018.

Yoshioka, Sumie. 1995. *Iyakuhin no Anteisei* [Stability of Pharmaceutical Products]. Tokyo: Nankodo.

Chapter 9
An Example of Healthcare Service Market in Japan

9.1 Distribution of Poor Quality Medicines in Japan

The WHO reported data indicating that substandard and falsified medical products have been discovered in Japan (WHO 2017). This is true in some sense and is misleading in another sense. It is true in the following two meanings: (1) these products have been very rarely discovered in legitimate distribution channels; and (2) they have been continuously discovered in illegal trading on the Internet. It is misleading because the data of WHO may bring about a misunderstanding that poor quality medicines are a chronic problem in the official market of healthcare services to which the people of Japan have access.[1]

The above-stated two actual situations need to be carefully understood. First of all, the legitimate distribution channels are inseparable from the healthcare service market based on the universal health insurance system of Japan that is publically operated. In this market, even now, falsified medical products are discovered only extremely rarely. In the most recent case that occurred in January 2017, falsified products for Harvoni® Combination Tablets indicated for the treatment of hepatitis C were smuggled into the legitimate distribution channels. The National Health Insurance (NHI) drug price for Harvoni® is 54,700 Japanese Yen (JPY) per tablet. Selling falsified products is a profitable crime. The falsified Harvoni products were put into the officially approved bottles, but they contained vitamins or Chinese herbal medicines. In this case, no health damage was found and in only 1 prefecture out of the total of 47 prefectures in Japan, the fake 15 bottles were discovered. Spread of the fake products was minimized. The reason why the falsified products were smuggled into the legitimate distribution channels was because cash-and-carry wholesalers did not check the source of these products when they received them. This scandal was reported in the media throughout Japan and the Japanese Ministry of Health, Labour, and Welfare (MHLW) amended the law so as to obligate wholesalers or

---

[1]Interview conducted by the author on August 26, 2014 in Osaka.

© Springer Nature Singapore Pte Ltd. 2020
S. Kimura and Y. Nakamura, *Poor Quality Pharmaceuticals in Global Public Health*, Trust 5, https://doi.org/10.1007/978-981-15-2089-1_9

other relevant organizations involved in distribution channels to confirm the source of pharmaceutical products.

As described above, in Japan, counterfeit drugs are extremely rarely distributed through legitimate distribution channels and when they are found, the pharmaceutical industry and those engaged in the legitimate distribution channels all collaborate with one another in taking necessary responsive actions to eliminate such drugs from the market. The ordinary people of Japan do not consider that they happen to buy fake drugs insofar as they purchase medicines in the official market of healthcare services. Even a limited number of persons can understand what the term "counterfeit drugs" means.

On the other hand, we cannot ignore the distribution of counterfeit drugs within the Internet market, which includes, among others, medicines for erectile dysfunction (ED) treatment, slimming drugs, hair growth drugs, and health foods. The vast majority of the people in Japan access the market of publicly provided medical services; they neither have deep concern about problems related to the Internet market nor feel imminent dangers attributable to these problems.

Box 15: Nonofficial Distribution in Japan

In Japan, import of pharmaceuticals by a private individual is legally allowed. When an ordinary person imports privately a medicine from overseas (or purchases it overseas and brings it into Japan) for personal use, the person as a rule needs to submit prescribed documents to the relevant Regional Bureau of Health and Welfare (that is a regional branch office of the Ministry of Health, Labour, and Welfare (MHLW)) and obtain a certificate indicating that such import is not for sale.

It has been confirmed, however, that private importation via illegal traders through the Internet handles counterfeit drugs and causes health damage. The transaction volume of counterfeits has increased. The number of import injunctions for pharmaceuticals by the customs authorities due to infringement of intellectual property rights has been on the rise. In 2016, import injunctions were issued for a total of 622,655 product items (65.7% and 29.8% of which infringed trademark and patent rights, respectively), 91.9% of which came from China. Drugs accounted for 6.3% of the suspended items (Ministry of Financeto Japan).

In 2014, sales of nonprescription medicines through the Internet became lawful, although in a limited manner. The MHLW strongly opposed the lifting of the ban on online sales of medicines. In a lawsuit filed by online sales companies against the national government, arguing that banning online sales was in breach of the Constitution, the online traders won the lawsuit. The MHLW argued that the safety of pharmaceuticals had to be secured by face-to-face sales between consumers and pharmacists, which implied their real thought that they feared an increase in access to illegal distribution channels available on the Internet after removal of the ban.[2]

9.2 Article 25 of the Constitution of Japan

Before discussing the healthcare service market and healthcare systems in Japan, the authors would like to emphasize that the will of Japan as a state is endorsed by the legal rationale. Japan lost World War II in 1945 and came under the allied military occupation. The Constitution of Japan was drafted under the occupation, which is the strong basis for some advocates of constitutional reform because they argue that the US imposed the constitution on Japan. Apart from the argument on constitutional reform, the Constitution of Japan forms the highest legal grounds on which the social security for the people of Japan can substantially be achieved. Although whether the Constitution of Japan is a rigid constitution or not is controversial, the absence of constitutional reform from the end of World War II until today has contributed to long-term improvement of social security systems. Article 25 of the Constitution prescribes the right to life, one of the social rights, and the social mission of the state, as introduced below.

CHAPTER III RIGHTS AND DUTIES OF THE PEOPLE
Article 25

1. All people shall have the right to maintain the minimum standards of wholesome and cultured living.
2. In all spheres of life, the state shall use its endeavors for the promotion and extension of social welfare and security, and of public health.

This article clearly defines that public health is a measure to protect the right of life of the people and that the state is responsible for promoting public health.

---

[2]The online sales companies won a lawsuit in which the issue was whether the ban on online sales of medicines was unconstitutional or not. The MHLW argued that sales of pharmaceuticals should as a rule be face-to-face sales between consumers and pharmacists for the purpose of securing proper use. This argument has been interpreted to imply their concern that lifting the ban on online sales of medicines would increase access to illegal distribution channels available on the Internet. Online selling allows traders to sell medicines without checking if such medicines or their packages are genuine or fake, whereas face-to-face selling at pharmacies does not allow this. (An extract from an interview conducted by the author on a specialist on pharmaceutical products on July 13, 2015 in Tokyo).

Box 16: Article 25 of The Constitution of Japan

Article 25 of the Constitution of Japan is special because two paragraphs of the article explicitly specify the dual responsibilities that the state must take for the people.

Paragraph 1 was drafted primarily by Tatsuo Morito, an economist, and Yoshio Suzuki who were lawmakers from the old Social Democratic Party of Japan, by reference to Paragraph 1 of Article 151 of the Weimer Constitution that governed Germany during the Weimer Republic era.

Paragraph 2 was drafted by Brigadier General Crawford F. Sams belonging to the Legislative Division of the Government Section, the General Headquarters/Supreme Commander for the Allied Power (GHQ/SCAP), under the order of General Douglas MacArthur.

The GHQ/SCAP drafted Article 25 of the Constitution of Japan did not have the phrase "the minimum standards of wholesome and cultured living." Wording that expressed this intention was first incorporated into the revised draft of the Constitution by the "Constitution Study Group" that was a private organization established immediately after the end of World War II. As described above, Japan did not abandon its unyielding spirit for building a new Japan, even under the allied military occupation.

9.3   Two Insurance Acts and the Public Assistance Act

As the Constitution of Japan stipulates, the healthcare service market of Japan is formed by a combination of public and private sectors, for the purpose of promoting public health. The formation of this market is legally based on the Health Insurance Act and the National Health Insurance Act. Japan has adopted a universal health insurance coverage scheme, according to which every resident in Japan must belong to public insurance as an enrollee in a unit of the household as a rule.

The Health Insurance Act was first enacted in 1922. This Japanese Act prescribes the provision of insurance benefits for sickness, injury or death due to causes unrelated to employment or childbirth of a worker or a dependent of the worker. For the purpose of achieving the universal health insurance coverage scheme, in addition to the Health Insurance Act, the National Health Insurance Act was enacted in 1938 with an aim of securing provision of health care in rural areas and covers people who are not covered by the Health Insurance Act.[3]

---

[3]The National Health Insurance Act covers self-employed persons, retired persons under employees' health insurance, and other eligible persons. All individuals will reach the situation in which they are not able to work, and in this sense, the National Health Insurance Act provides the final safety net.

Health Insurance Act

Article 1: The purpose of this Act is to provide insurance benefits for sickness, injury or death due to causes unrelated to employment or childbirth of a worker or a dependent thereof, thereby contributing to the stability of lives and the improvement of welfare of the people.

Article 2: Health Insurance System, in view of the fact that it is the basis for the Medical Insurance System, must be implemented, in response to progress in aging, changes in disease structure, changes in socioeconomic situation, and the like, by constantly examining the concept of System in conjunction with other medical insurance systems and elderly insurance systems as well as systems closely related thereto, and by making integrated efforts to streamline medical insurance operation, optimize details of benefits and sharing of costs, and improve the quality of medical treatment that citizens undergo based on a result thereof.

National Health Insurance Act

Article 1: The purpose of this Act is to ensure the sound administration of national health insurance services, thereby contributing to the improvement of social security and the health of the people.

Article 2: National health insurance programs shall pay the necessary insurance benefits in relation to an insured person's illness, injury, childbirth or death.

Article 3: (1) Prefectural governments and municipalities (including special wards; the same shall apply in this article) in the prefectural governments concerned shall provide National Health Insurance programs pursuant to the provisions of this Act. (2) National health insurance societies may provide a national health insurance program pursuant to the provisions of this Act.

Article 4: (1) The national government must take necessary relevant actions to ensure the sound administration of national health insurance services, and shall proactively promote measures related to healthcare, medical care, and welfare as well as other associated measures for the purpose of contributing to the achievement of the purpose of this Act set forth in Article 1.

(Note: Paragraphs (2) through (5) of Article 4 are omitted.)

Every insured person has to pay premiums as an individual enrollee or as a household enrollee irrespective of the type of public insurance program they belong to. Needy persons who cannot maintain the minimum standards of living and cannot afford insurance premiums are withdrawn from national health insurance programs. These persons are protected by the Public Assistance Act, which is the third law providing the basis for the Japanese healthcare service market, as public livelihood assistance recipients.

Public Assistance Act

Article 1: The purpose of this Act is for the State to guarantee a minimum standard of living as well as to promote self-support for all citizens who are living in poverty by providing the necessary public assistance according to the level of poverty, based on the principles prescribed in Article 25 of the Constitution of Japan. (Enacted in 1950)

Persons to whom the Public Assistance Act applies[4] are also entitled to receive healthcare services which are as a rule equivalent to those provided to the insured persons, without bearing co-payments (with free of charge, provided that several conditions are met) under this Act. The core concept of the universal health insurance coverage scheme of Japan is to ensure provision of healthcare services under the health insurance programs to persons who can pay insurance premiums and under the public livelihood assistance program to persons who cannot afford premiums.

Box 17: Oral Evidence Regarding the Social Security System in Japan

The framework for social security system in Japan was built soon after the end of World War II. In addition to the health insurance system that attracts substantial attention because of its universal coverage scheme, the systems and programs for pension, public livelihood assistance, and long-term nursing care cover all citizens of Japan. They work altogether to provide a comprehensive safety net. It is worthy to note that the universal pension system and the universal health insurance system were both enacted in the same year, i.e., 1961.

A government official engaged in designing the universal pension scheme stated the reasons why this scheme actually began to function as follows: the political party in power worked seriously to fulfill their election campaign promise; and this ruling party and the administrative authorities ideally cooperated with each other in deciding individual responsibilities and carrying out their allocated duties (Suganuma 2018). The Beveridge Report[5] was a model for the design for Japan's universal health insurance scheme. A government official engaged in designing the universal health insurance coverage scheme stated that the three points listed below were the keys to success: (Suganuma 2018)

- Prior to improvement and integration of the existing programs, a measure was taken to expand the coverage of the national health insurance.
- Self-employed persons and very small-scale companies (with five or smaller number of employees) were incorporated into the system.
- At that time, Japanese people were consistently poor.

The third point above needs explanation. The government official mentioned above commented, *"When we observed the American situation, we considered that if 70% to 80% of the people had been satisfied to some extent with their lives, universal health insurance coverage system could not have been established, resulting in abandon of the vulnerable."*

---

[4]The number of public livelihood assistance recipients is 2.13 million individuals and 1.64 million households (in the fiscal year 2017).

[5]The *Beveridge Report*, officially entitled *Social Insurance and Allied Services*, is authored by William H. Beveridge to recommend widening of social security system. It served the basis for the post-World War II social security system in the United Kingdom.

> The comments of the government officials may serve to indicate that when they established the universal health insurance coverage scheme in Japan, they focused more on an inhibiting force generated by division of society than on economic factors of the state.

9.4   Outline of Japan's Healthcare Scheme

Japan's healthcare scheme is the universal health insurance system that is characterized by the following:

- All residents in Japan are covered by public health insurance programs (in which residents participate in a unit of household).
- Insured persons can freely choose medical institutions to receive healthcare services.
- Advanced medical care is provided at less-expensive medical costs.
- While the social insurance methodology is the basis, public funds are used to maintain universal health insurance coverage.

The universal health insurance coverage scheme is not composed of a single program but is an aggregate of multiple programs (Table 9.1). This is attributable to historical development. What is important is that the universal health insurance system consists of multiple programs and that even though there exist different insurers, the healthcare service market is a single market. Although insurance premiums vary depending on insurance programs, the same service is provided at the same fee and with the same rate of co-payment.

Tables 9.2 and 9.3 show healthcare resources supporting the healthcare service market. Matching between healthcare needs and healthcare resources has continuously been an extremely important and challenging policy, which is directly linked to the effectiveness of the system.

Table 9.1 Major health insurance programs comprising the universal health insurance system

Major health insurance programs	No. of insurers	No. of subscribers (unit: million)
National Health Insurance (NHI)	1,880	36
Public-Corporation Run Health Insurance	1	36
Health insurance managed by association	1,409	29
Mutual aid associations	85	9
Medical care program for the elderly in the latter stage of life	47	16

Source MHLW Japan 2018a

Table 9.2 Medical care facilities (As of October 1, 2015)

Category of medical care facility	No. of facilities
Hospital	8,480 (No. of beds: 1,565,968)
Clinic	100,995 (No. of beds: 1,007,626)
Dental clinic	68,737
Pharmacy	58,326

Source MHLW Japan 2018a

Table 9.3 No. of healthcare professionals (As of December 31, 2014)

Category of healthcare professionals	No. of professionals
Medical doctors	311,205
Dentists	103,972
Pharmacists	288,151
Nurses*	1,176,859
Public health nurses*	60,472
Midwives*	38,486

Note The numbers for job categories marked with * are those as of 2015

Source MHLW Japan 2018a

9.5 Characteristics of the Public Healthcare Service Market of Japan from the Perspective of Patients

The characteristics of the Japanese healthcare service market are discussed from the perspective of patients (consumers).

First of all, fair access to health care is worthy to note. As described in the previous section, individuals who can afford insurance premiums and co-payments for treatment expenses can freely choose medical institutions to receive healthcare services, with only a single health insurance certificate, from practitioners to university hospitals, anywhere throughout Japan.[6] Public livelihood assistance recipients who cannot pay insurance premiums can receive healthcare services free of charge at designated medical institutions.

Secondly, services provided under the health insurance system are benefits in kind, i.e., healthcare services. It is not a system according to which patients pay the total amount of medical expenses at medical institutions and later, part of the paid expenses

---

[6]In recent years, an increasing number of patients visited large-scale hospitals for the treatment of even mild disorders, which can be treated by practitioners, and this adverse effect was intensified. It was therefore decided to ask patients without having letters of reference from practitioners to pay, for example, 5,000 JPY (3,000 JPY for dental clinics) as an out-of-insurance coverage fee when they visit the hospital for the first time (note that in the case of emergency, there are exceptional rules).

Table 9.4 Rates of patients' co-payment

Category	Rate of a patient's co-payment
People aged ≥75 years	10% (although 30% for persons with more than a certain level of income)
People aged 70–74 years	20% (although 30% for persons with more than a certain level of income)
After reaching compulsory school age to 69 years of age	30%
Before reaching compulsory school age[a]	20%

Source MHLW Japan 2018a
[a]The Japanese educational system consists as a rule of elementary school for 6 years, middle school for 3 years, and 3 years for high school. The compulsory education is composed of elementary and middle school systems. Children at the age of 6 or 7 years enter elementary school

is refunded to the patients by the relevant health insurance providers. Strictly speaking, whenever benefits in kind, i.e., health care, are provided to patients, they pay co-payments according to the designated rate (Table 9.4) at reception desks (accounting departments) of medical institutions.[7] For prescription medicines patients take at home, they purchase the medicines at pharmacies by making co-payments for drug costs. The lack of necessity to pay the total expenses in advance accelerates access to healthcare services.

Thirdly, the high-cost medical care benefit system sets the maximum co-payment for individuals and therefore, the incentive to receive public healthcare services is spread all over the people. The recent hot topic was that the NHI Drug Price for Opdivo® (nivolumab, a human monoclonal antibody) indicated for the treatment of malignant melanoma was approximately 730,000 JPY for 100 mg at the time of official approval granted.

The use of Opdivo® amounted to 35 million JPY per patient per year. This medicine is included in the NHI Drug Price List, which means that the use of this medicine is covered by the health insurance programs, and the high-cost medical care benefit system reduces the monthly expenses patients need to pay out of their own pocket.

Table 9.5 shows the maximum monthly co-payment for the elderly (aged ≥75 years; applicable starting from July 2018) under the high-cost medical care benefit system. Lower income households are exempted from residence tax. The definition of the level of low income varies depending on municipal governments. Examples in Tokyo include a household consisting of a husband, a wife, and a child (and the spouse and the child are dependents) with less than 2.057 million JPY exempted from residence tax.

---

[7]When benefits in kind, i.e., healthcare services, are provided, co-payments out of the expenses are made at accounting departments of medical institutions.

Table 9.5 Maximum co-payment under the high-cost medical care benefit system of the National Health Insurance Scheme

Annual income	Co-payment at reception	Maximum for outpatient (per person)	Maximum for outpatient + inpatient (per household)
>3.7 million JPY	30%	57,600 JPY	80,100 JPY + (medical expenses-267,00 JPY) x1% *Note* 44,400 JPY for the case of multiple high-cost care*
1.65 million–3.7 million JPY		14,000 JPY (with 144,000 JPY as a limit)	57,600 JPY
Household exempted from residence tax 1	20% or 10%	8,000 JPY	24,600 JPY
Household exempted from residence tax 2		8,000 JPY	15,000 JPY

Note The term "multiple high-cost care" means that for persons who have received high-cost care three times within a 12-month period, the maximum co-payment of the fourth time and onward will be reduced to 44,400 JPY
Source MHLW Japan 2018a

There is another program under which an insured person who receives healthcare services overseas is refunded the cash corresponding to the amount of money calculated by deducting the co-payment from the expenses that are expected to be charged for the same medical care services provided in Japan.

9.6 Characteristics of the Public Healthcare Service Market of Japan from the Perspective of Healthcare Providers

The characteristics of the Japanese healthcare service market are discussed from the perspective of healthcare providers (i.e., healthcare professionals and medical institutions).

Firstly, in Japan, medical doctors, pharmacists, and medical institutions must be registered (authorized) as insurance doctors, pharmacists, and medical institutions by the Japanese Minister for Health, Labour, and Welfare before they can provide healthcare services to patients covered by health insurance programs. If a registered medical institution is deprived of its authorization by the central government due to a scandal or misconduct, such revocation is a lethal penalty for the institution, because the vast majority of the people in Japan have an incentive to receive public healthcare services.

Secondly, the treatment methods, methods of diagnosis, and pharmaceutical products covered by the health insurance programs are decided and managed by the central government. This coverage is determined by the Reimbursement of Medical Fees System[8] and the National Health Insurance (NHI) Drug Price List. This coverage is reviewed regularly and as appropriate, noninsured advanced medical treatments for which patients have to pay total expenses out of their own pocket are reviewed where it may be decided to be covered by the health insurance scheme.

Thirdly, clinical supplies necessary for the provision of healthcare services are procured from the market. If there is a difference between the price at which clinical supplies are purchased from the market and the price determined in the NHI Drug Price List, then this price gap yields margins for medical institutions. In the times during which price gaps were great and excessive sales incentives (such as cash back or gifts) by pharmaceutical companies prevailed, drug price margins were regarded as unfair profits. At the same time, it was true that these margins contributed to management of medical institutions.

9.7 Characteristics of the Public Healthcare Service Market of Japan from the Perspective of Pharmaceuticals Suppliers

The market for pharmaceutical products is as a rule freely competitive within the NHI Drug Prices. Newly developed originator products and their counterpart generics can, as a rule, be used under the health insurance coverage. When a new drug is officially approved, a company holding its license, i.e., the license holder, immediately starts to negotiate with the administrative authorities regarding the price of the new drug to be listed, and the agreed drug price is then included in the NHI Drug Price List. After an originator product has been available in the market for a certain period of time,[9] its generics can be manufactured and marketed by third-party companies. This means that originator products will be competitive with their generics in the same market of public healthcare services. When originator products and their generics coexist in the market, the quality of originators is the quality standard for generics.

The administrative authorities intervene in the quality of pharmaceuticals available on the market, as demonstrated in the three occasions described below. Firstly, they do so when they grant official approval for generic medicines because they review submitted data by a generic manufacturer, that is, an applicant, which compares the quality between the generic and its counterpart originator and audit the applicant. Secondly, they perform quality tests on sampled products from the market and give feedback

---

[8]When a patient is hospitalized and undergoes surgery, the first visit fee, the hospitalization fee for the length of stay (in days), the surgery fee, the test fee, and the drug fee are combined, and a medical institution providing insured services will receive the monetary amount obtained by deducting the patient's co-payment from the combined fees, from the medical fee claims review, and payment agency concerned.

[9]In Japan, "a certain period of time" means a longer period of the following two: a reexamination period imposed on a newly developed medicine (originator) or a valid term of the patent concerned.

on test results to the company concerned. Thirdly, they audit companies that procure raw materials for pharmaceuticals from overseas. Regarding the above-stated points, persons involved in the generics industry in Japan state as follows.[10]

> When we consider quality improvement on a decade-basis, we notice that in Japan, both local and central governments regularly sample generic products from the market to determine if they are equivalent to their counterpart originators or not. In the past, a dissolution test was not required for originators nor for generics. As an administrative attempt, "re-evaluation of quality" was integrated into the review process, which requires generic manufacturers to satisfy the dissolution specifications of counterpart originators.

> There is the Council for Investigation of Information on Quality of Generic Products consisting of members from Academia, Industry, and Government. It holds regular meetings at which they decide, for example, to sample anti-inflammatory agents from the market for this year. According to the decision, the local and central governments cooperate in testing anti-inflammatory generics marketed by all generic manufacturers and comparing dissolution profiles. Most of the tested generics conform to the specifications. If non-conformity is found, then the manufacturer concerned is informed of such result and receives administrative guidance, including the improvement targets set for the manufacture to achieve and the deadline set for the achievement. Feedback from the market is an extremely great regulatory power.

> From the viewpoint of patients, they first receive treatment with a new drug on the basis of disease model, and after the patent term for the new drug expires, their treatment may be switched to that with generics. However, patients may not want to receive generics if generics were different from their counterpart originators in terms of quality and quality control policy. What should be achieved is to establish a quality system for generics which is as rigorous as that for newly developed medicines so as to manufacture generics equivalent in quality to their counterpart originators. Generic manufacturers should of course be able to adequately respond to requests or inquiries from the drug regulatory authorities and should have equivalent facilities and equipment to those used for manufacture of originators, which enables generic manufactures to communicate with originator manufacturers on an equal footing. Otherwise, generics may not be spread.

> The GMP does not set the final goal regarding how to administer quality control programs, which therefore must be continuously innovated. The most important key in the process are human beings. Every country depends on manpower. Although there exists a variety of quality control tools, quality ultimately relies on human resources. Human resource capability will deteriorate and that's why training and education must be conducted to uninterruptedly upgrade their capabilities. Capital investment is necessary for facilities and equipment. All quality-related matters including those described above are adequately controlled and managed by quality system as comprehensively described in ICH Q10 (Pharmaceutical Quality System). For the purpose of improving quality control, management review is performed on managers and their equivalent persons in plants and results are evaluated by the top management. This whole process constitutes a quality system. Individual human resources are important because they drive the system.

---

[10]Interview conducted by the author on October 28, 2015 in Tokyo.

9.8 Characteristics of the Public Healthcare Service Market of Japan from the Viewpoint of Financial Resources

The total national health expenditure of the fiscal year 2016 was 42 trillion and 364.4 billion JPY, which was increased by 1 trillion and 557.3 billion JPY or by 3.8% when compared with that of the previous fiscal year, that is, 40 trillion and 807.1 billion JPY. Ninety-eight percent of the total national health expenditure is covered by the national health insurance programs. The national health expenditure per capita was 333,300 JPY. The national health expenditure accounted for 7.96% of the gross domestic product (GDP) and 10.91% of the national income (NI).

Evaluation of financial resources used for health spending in the fiscal year 2016 revealed that public funding accounted for 38.9% of the total health spending and insurance premiums, 48.8%, which was composed of 20.6% paid by business operators (employers), and 28.2% born by insured persons. In addition, the others accounted for 12.3% of the total health spending, and 11.6% of the others were co-payments born by patients at reception desks of medical institutions.

When the expenses paid by insured persons and the co-payments paid at reception desks of medical institutions are combined, 39.8% of the total national health expenditure came from the household budget of the people, whereas the co-payments at reception desks accounted for only 11.6%. This fact, together with the fact that patients do not need to pay the total medical costs in advance when they visit medical institutions, gives the people a strong economic incentive to utilize the public health insurance programs. In addition, co-payments by elderly patients are set at an extremely low level. Assuming that a 75-year-old patient with an annual income of 2 million JPY spends 1 million JPY of medical expenses for one month, as shown in Fig. 9.1; this patient has to pay only 44,400 JPY out of his/her pocket. This highlights how great the public burden is and the presence of a gap between generations because greater care is available for elderly patients.

Box 18: The Japanese Social Security Scheme Being Challenged by Aging Society

The social security scheme in Japan is supported by the health insurance programs, national pension system, and long-term care insurance system in all of which all residents of Japan as a rule must participate, and by the public livelihood assistance system. Japan is one of the countries in which society is facing the most rapid aging. Maintaining the social security scheme to cover the entire population of Japan is a huge financial challenge, in particular, expansion of the total national health expenditure is an urgent issue to be addressed (Owada 2018).

Although the economy remained stagnant and tax revenue remained sluggish, the total national health expenditure reached 34 trillion and 800 billion JPY in 2008. The health spending for the elderly (those aged ≥65 years old)

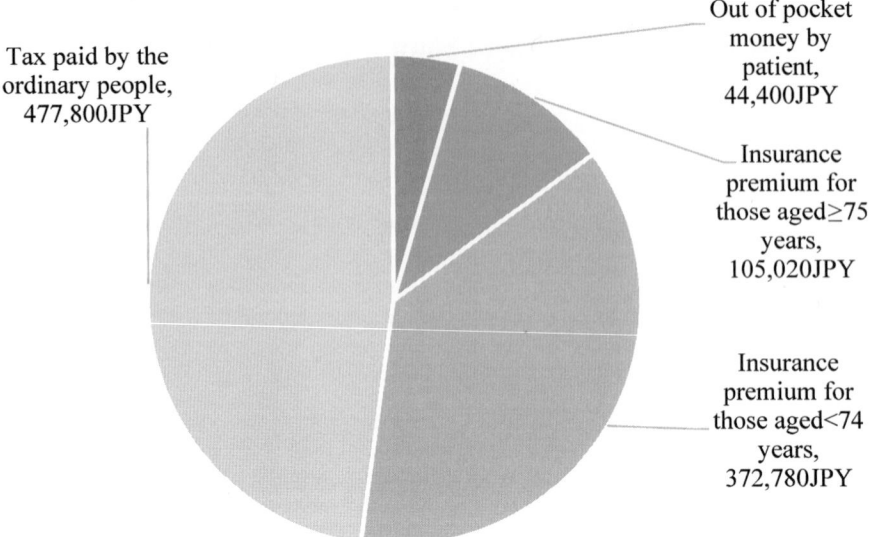

Tax paid by the
ordinary people,
477,800JPY

Out of pocket
money by
patient,
44,400JPY

Insurance
premium for
those aged≥75
years,
105,020JPY

Insurance
premium for
those aged<74
years,
372,780JPY

Fig. 9.1 Financial resources used for the late-stage medical care system for the elderly (aged ≥75 years). *Source* MHLW Japan, Public Relation Office of the Central Government/MHLW Japan, July 2017. Illustration changed by the author

accounted for 54.6% of this expenditure. The national health spending per person aged <65 years old was 158,900 JPY, whereas that for the elderly was 673,400 JPY which was four times greater (MHLW Japan 2018b). The problem is that health expenditure spent during the terminal phase, and in particular, for intensified treatment for 1 week prior to death, is very high.

Medicine has contributed to prolongation of life. We face the irony that aging society forces us to alter the existing medical care system. Formulating a governmental policy to achieve a balance between the financial burden imposed on the public sector and benefits from the healthcare system is a social experiment in Japan.

9.9 Discussion

The universal health insurance system in Japan has achieved equal and efficient access to health care. The WHO appraises this Japanese unique system as introduced below (WHO 2018).

Since the 1960s, the universal health insurance system in Japan has provided comprehensive coverage to all Japanese citizens. Associating with economic growth, Japan has achieved numerous successes in health such as control and eradication of common infectious diseases, substantial decrease of transport accident death, and most famously, achieving the world's highest life expectancy.

The health care in Japan is characterized by the universal health insurance system. The presence of a system does not always assure the good performance of a market. The healthcare system in Japan and the good performance of the healthcare service market are summarized in the points described below.

Firstly, the universal health insurance system in Japan is based on the Constitution of Japan that is the highest will of political governance. What makes the system effective stems from the political will.

Secondly, for the purpose of achieving a fair distribution of healthcare services, which are scarce resources, Japan does not choose to leave the provision of healthcare services in the market of completely free economy. Public funding is necessary to secure the universal health insurance coverage, under which public livelihood assistance recipients who cannot afford insurance premiums are given healthcare services equivalent to those available to persons who can pay premiums. One of the reasons why this universal coverage has become practical is, as the WHO points out, the good fortune that Japan enjoyed during post-war economic growth. There are some countries experiencing economic prosperity which are unlikely to be proactive in financing public funds.

Thirdly, multiple bodies implement healthcare insurance programs. This is attributable to the historical background before and after the establishment of universal health insurance coverage. Even though the implementing bodies and insurance premiums are different, the basic healthcare services provided under the universal health insurance system are identical. This is extremely important. Regarding the safety net, Japan does not intend to impose social division. In the past, Japan has adopted a self-deprecating image by ridiculing herself as a society of all 100 million people in the middle class. The universal health insurance system has functioned to unify the post-war Japanese society.

Fourthly, the core of the Japanese healthcare service market consists of incentives for the three stakeholders, i.e., patients, healthcare professionals (medical institutions), and pharmaceutical (healthcare) industry. The individual incentives have complemented one another and have maintained a good balance between the quality of healthcare services and access to healthcare services. In particular, those on the supply side of generic medicines have a strong incentive to aim at good quality and this incentive has been fostered in a single market of healthcare services in which generics can coexist with their counterpart originators. Substantial portions of the Japanese healthcare service market are open to the private sector. This openness has been favorably balanced with the regulatory intervention by the administrative authorities, which has created incentives for the private sector and their compliance with the code of conduct. Attention should be focused on the fact that various policies on quality, which have been formulated by the pharmaceutical regulatory authorities, have intensified the incentives of suppliers.

Individuals engaged in on-site manufacturing have indicated an important point that the essential matters for GMP-based quality control are human resource development and investment. Merely introducing the articles of GMP or facilities indicated in GMP does not assure quality. Quality control requires short-term costs and at the same time, long-term investment. The persons engaged in the generics industry commented in our interview that they consider quality improvement on a decade basis. This comment indicates that the following two actions are necessary: to design a healthcare service market which gives incentives over a long period of time; and to perform long-term and strategic management system.

References

MHLW Japan 2017. Relation Office of the Central Government.
MHLW Japan. 2018a. https://www.mhlw.go.jp/file/06-Seisakujouhou-12400000-Hokenkyoku/0000172pdf#search=%27%E5%9B%BD%E6%B0%91%E7%9A%86%E4%BF%9D%E9%99%BA%E5%88%B6%E5%BA%A6%E3%81%A8%E3%81%AF%27. (In Japanese) Accessed 13 May 2018.
MHLW Japan. 2018b. Sei, Nenrei Kaiyubetsu Kokumin Iryohi [National Health-Care Expenditure By Sex and Age]. http://www.mhlw.go.jp/toukei/saikin/hw/k-iryohi/08/kekka5.html. (In Japanese) Accessed 13 May 2018.
Ministry of Finance Japan. 2018. Heisei 28 Nen no Zeikan ni okeru Chiteki Zaisanken Singaibuppin no Sashitome Jokyo [Banning status in 2016 of IPR Violating Goods at Customs]. https://www.mof.go.jp/customs_tariff/trade/safe_society/chiteki/cy2016/20170303b.htm. (In Japanese) Accessed 17 August 2018.
Owada, Masahide. 2018. Cho-Koreika Shakai ni okeru Iryo Seido -Kateii Seido to Jintobarai Hoshu ni yoru Taio [Health Care System in a Super-Aged Society -Countermeasure with Family Doctor System and Remuneration by Capitation-]. CIPPS No.122. http://cipps.org/essay/pdf/info122.pdf. (In Japanese) Accessed 13 May 2018.
Suganuma, Takashi, et al. 2018. *An Oral History of Social Policy Development in Post-War Japan-120 Hours of Testimony from the Governmental Officials*. Tokyo: Yuhikaku. (In Japanese)
WHO. 2017. WHO Global Surveillance and Monitoring System for substandard and falsified medical products Reports and Executive summary. http://www.who.int/medicines/regulation/ssffc/publications/gsms-report-sf/en/. Accessed 3 June 2018.
WHO. 2018. Japan Health System Review. http://apps.who.int/iris/bitstream/handle/10665/259941/9789290226260-eng.pdf;jsessionid=A3E4F4161FA77B56D837EAA71DAF2222?sequence=1. Accessed 18 August 2018.

Chapter 10
Aiming for Global Safety
Net—An Interpretation and Lessons

10.1 Direction of the Observations and Discussions Described in the Previous Chapters

The WHO raised questions about the quality of medicines while initially focusing on counterfeiting. The observations and discussions described in Chaps. 1–9 demonstrate the following: the problem of substandard medicines exists in the opposite end of criminal cases; discontinuity does not exist between the two but instead, a variable continuity exists between the two in a situation-dependent manner; and this continuity complicates awareness of the problem.

First of all, we have to determine the direction of discussions after taking into account the magnitude of the two problems and the priority given to the responsive actions required. Speaking of extremes, which one of the following two should be regarded as a problem: the case of counterfeited ED-treating drugs that have been used as propaganda by pharmaceutical industries in the Japan–US–EU trilateral world, or affordable but non-quality-assured medicines that people living in poverty can access. Here is a question: Who would gain and benefit from an intentional act of mixing up the two problems to complicate the situation further? If this question is too aggressive, then we need to go back to the starting point and identify the reason why the two problems must be distinguished from each other. The WHO raised questions about the quality of medicines because the Organization recognized the importance of protecting global public health. We do not disregard the magnitude of the impact of counterfeit medicines on the pharmaceutical industry.

When discussing the quality problem of pharmaceuticals, however, we must prioritize the problem of quality of generics which the poor of the world can barely afford. In accordance with the structure of this book, the authors discuss firstly the international environment, secondly the internal environment inside emerging countries, and thirdly the challenges the WHO faces.

© Springer Nature Singapore Pte Ltd. 2020
S. Kimura and Y. Nakamura, *Poor Quality Pharmaceuticals in Global Public Health*, Trust 5, https://doi.org/10.1007/978-981-15-2089-1_10

10.2   International Environment Surrounding Pharmaceutical Products

10.2.1   Generation of Conflicts of Interests Among Emerging, Developed, and Developing Countries

During the times of globalization, some emerging countries, in particular India and China, have grown to be supply sources of generics to the rest of the world. They have adopted the policy of achieving import substitution industrialization so as to export raw materials and finished products, and have received advanced technologies from developed countries through the utilization of technology transfer (Kamiike and Sato 2006). As emerging countries have gained power, two international relationships of interest have been generated. Firstly, a complementary relationship with the developed world has been created. At present, emerging countries play an important role in the supply system of generics across the world and have formed such a complementary relationship with the developed world (Minato 2007). Therefore, the quality of pharmaceutical products imported from emerging countries is a priority matter for developed countries.

As demonstrated by the interview survey described in Chap. 8, developed countries including Japan perform stringent audits on exporting companies in the emerging world and as appropriate, issue warnings and enforce export embargos (FDA 2013) so as to assure at least the minimal necessary level of quality. This is because the quality of medicines imported from emerging countries is not totally reliable.

Secondly, the capacity of developing countries, which import medicines from emerging countries, to regulate and supervise pharmaceutical affairs has attracted attention. As discussed in Chap. 4, developing countries, in particular several African countries, do not possess adequate and sufficient drug regulatory capacities and infrastructure to control drug quality. With regard to the quality of medicines, emerging countries which export medicines are in opposition to developing countries, which rely on imported medicines.

10.2.2   Conflicts of Interests Over Intellectual Property Rights Between the Developed and the Emerging Worlds

Developed countries have moved toward intensification of intellectual property rights along with the flow of globalization that occurred in the US in the 1980s (Mori 1994). Research-based pharmaceutical companies in the developed world have positioned monopolizing control of their originator products through the use of intellectual property rights, at the core of their business model (IFPMA 2016). This monopolizing control with intellectual property rights has produced some extremely popular drug products, referred to as blockbuster drugs, that yield enormous sales and profits.

Development of new medicines has increasingly required huge investment, know-how, and long time periods (Yamane 2008). This is why strategies utilizing intellectual property rights have been considered the driving force for developed countries to gain profits and to grow. After the period of monopolizing control of newly developed medicines when intellectual property rights expire, these new medicines face competition with generics, which exposes global pharmaceutical companies to international competition. India finally completed the introduction of an internationally accepted patent system (i.e., substance patents) in 2004 (Minato 2007).

India did not introduce the substance patent system by making the best use of the internationally accepted principle whereby administration of a patent system is left to the discretion of the State. Until the introduction of substance patents, India had attempted to produce generic copies of their counterpart originators medicine, newly developed in the developed world, by using different manufacturing methods. This could be interpreted as a learning period for emerging countries. However, beyond that, these countries set their own rules for novelty, a requirement for a patent, even after the introduction of substance patents, and have continued to cause friction with developed countries regarding patent rights (Minato 2007).

10.2.3 Factors that Have Complicated Interests Over Intellectual Property Rights

At least two factors have complicated the issue of intellectual property rights: one is the HIV/AIDS pandemic and the other, the TRIPS Agreement.

HIV/AIDS emerged in around 1981 at which the move toward intensification of intellectual property rights began. For the subsequent 10 years, HIV/AIDS became disseminated across the world. In the beginning, AIDS was a lethal disease and its pandemic invaded countries whether they were developed, emerging, or developing. The debut of antiretroviral agents effective for HIV further augmented the complexity of the issue of intellectual property rights. Newly developed anti-HIV/AIDS drugs were protected by the relevant intellectual property rights and provided benefits within the developed world whereas these drugs were out of reach of public health in emerging and developing countries,[1] which did not look at this situation with their arms folded but appealed to international public opinion.

When former South African President Nelson Mandela tried to import more affordable medicines for the purpose of contributing to the treatment of the people, 40 pharmaceutical companies attempted to prevent their import; however, their attempt was a failure, which attracted a great deal of attention (MSF) from AIDS patients groups negotiating with the IFPMA at the WHO Headquarters regarding self-manufacture of anti-HIV/AIDS drugs in their mother countries (Yamane 2008).

---

[1] At present, 99% of major anti-HIV/AIDS drugs are manufactured by generic companies. An annual cost per patient was 10,000 US dollars at the beginning and currently has reduced to 300 US dollars.

The TRIPS Agreement and negotiation pertaining to the Agreement complicated the situations related to intellectual property rights. The TRIPS Agreement provided an opportunity of making a decision on the timing at which newly developed medicines under monopolizing control with intellectual property rights could be taken over by generics, i.e., benefits of new medicines could be more widely available at affordable prices (Yamane 2008). In other words, setting the conditions for maintenance of health and promotion of public health was put into the hands of international organizations engaged in trade. What this exactly means is that the profits and superiority of developed countries would be secured by artificially controlling the spread of knowledge, despite the fact that knowledge intrinsically tends to spread due to its nature.

The core issue at the WHO Ministerial Conference held in Doha in 2001 was on how to balance protection of pharmaceutical-related patent rights with protection of public health, that is, how to keep a balance between the profits of rights-holders and social benefits (Kato 2003). As a measure to keep this balance, the right to grant compulsory licenses was included in the Doha Declaration. Developed countries have accumulated dissatisfaction with the establishment of compulsory licensing rules. At this Ministerial Conference, the developed world insisted on intellectual property rights until the very end of the discussion. Japan was one of the developed countries that opposed the production of affordable anti-HIV/AIDS generics (Africa Japan Forum 2003). This attitude of Japan was a good example indicating what the developed world was interested in. Through the past 10-year trade negotiations, many developing countries were under pressure from the developed world to be forced to follow stricter rules[2] than the TRIPS Agreement (MSF).

10.3   Internal Environment of Emerging Countries

The vast majority of development and supply of pharmaceutical products is conducted by private companies, and because of this, these companies need to be motivated to find solutions to problems of the market. Resolving market problems will contribute to the development of society. The motivation is intensified by various forms of incentives. Market-related challenges mutually interact with motivation/incentives.

---

[2]After 1995 in which the TRIPS Agreement became effective, free trade agreements (FTAs), which require developing countries to observe more stringent rules regarding the protection of intellectual property rights than those of the TRIPS Agreement (i.e., TRIPS Plus), were concluded. The United States is a central player of the conclusion. The TRIPS Plus is characterized by its unilateral nature in that it does not impose any new obligation on the United States and transplant the US law system as they are into the other country of the Agreement. It has been reported that the negotiations on the TRIPS Plus have been successful because the conclusion is tied up with the access of agricultural products to the US market that is the desire of the developing countries concerned; the synergistic issue linkage strategy is effectively combined with the synergistic threat strategy based on Special 301 (Osawa 2008).

10.3.1 Gap Between Industrial Promotion and Norms in Emerging Countries

In this subsection, the authors discuss a gap between industrial promotion as an external framework of company activities and norms that embody the internal reality of these activities.

Pharmaceutical products have spread across the world through technology transfer, the technical basis of which includes "specification and standardization" as discussed in Chap. 3. This specification and standardization have made it possible to secure the quality of pharmaceutical products and in addition, ensure interchangeability between newly developed medicines and generics as well as those among drug regimens. In other words, this interchangeability is a significant driving force to contributing to the spread of pharmaceutical products across the world as mass-produced products and enabling emerging countries to promote their national pharmaceutical industries so as to participate in the world economy.

As shown in the case of the Indonesian National Institute of Health Research and Development (NIHRD) described in the interview in Chap. 7, manufacturing facilities of pharmaceutical products, specifications, and testing methods that specify quality, and relevant guidelines such as the GMP can be introduced through technology transfer, for the time being, as something that emerging and developing countries borrow from developed countries. Since pharmaceutical products can be manufactured and distributed in emerging and developing countries, there are greater opportunities to produce poor quality pharmaceuticals as well. Poor quality goods are found at a certain probability, which raises the two questions described below.

Firstly, are norms which encourage emerging and developing countries to observe quality specifications intensified in parallel with the degree of industrial promotion? Secondly, if not, what is the cause of such discrepancy? Technology transfer is not a mere transfer of know-how. In his book entitled "Technology Transfer-Discussion from history: USA and Japan," Kobayashi states, "Technology transfer is not only a concept of phenomenon but also a concept of norms; describing something from a single perspective on society means thinking an ideal state in that perspective, and within this thought, norms emerge" (Kobayashi 1981). Thus Kobayashi's statement agrees with the questions a Japanese specialist dispatched to Indonesia had, as introduced below.

Regarding the norms observed in the administration of the Indonesian Pharmacopeia, the Japanese specialist dispatched from the Japan International Cooperation Agency (JICA) to the NIHRD of Indonesia described as follows during our interview.[3]

> When testing pharmaceutical products, the authority to view the application dossiers for the medicine to be tested was limited on site. It seemed to me that staff tested the medicine without understanding the rationale for testing and the meaning of "approval of a drug." In other words, as a rationale for testing, the content of the application dossiers was not linked

---

[3]Interview conducted by the author on July 13, 2015 in Tokyo.

with relevant articles of the Pharmacopoeia. They did not recognize the pharmaceuticals officially approved in Indonesia.

I was told that the director of the Institute was entitled to view the application dossiers and advised repeatedly staff on site as follows; "You tell the director to view the dossiers because the information described there is necessary for testing and inspection." But none of them followed my advice. An individual responsible for onsite testing was a section manager, reporting to a general manager. Even the section manager did not understand the limited authority to view documents and the rationale for testing. I would assume that is why they had no questions about what they were doing.

The capacities of developing countries to adequately implement pharmaceutical administration and regulations have long been questionable, and it seemed to me that no improvement had been made. My successor was dispatched from the Japanese National Institute of Health Sciences and told me that the situation hardly changed. A failure to improve the administrative capacity might be related to a lack of consideration about the basics of regulating and guiding pharmaceutical affairs. The Indonesian Pharmacopoeia was established by Japan about 30 years ago and since then, no revision was made. I have heard that the Indonesian Pharmacopoeia will be revised by making an exact copy of the USP. I explained to the staff that it would be meaningless to list medicines not approved in Indonesia, in the Indonesian Pharmacopoeia, although it seemed to me that they did not understand my explanation. In the times in which poor quality pharmaceuticals are available, developing a pharmacopoeia by own efforts has a great significance.

The survey described in Chap. 7 sheds light on the actual state in which prescription-only drugs can be purchased in local pharmacies without having prescriptions. Regarding the gap between the laws/regulations and the reality, the pharmacists interviewed commented that, "Here no ideal pharmacies exist." Their term "ideal" could be interpreted to balance complying with laws/regulations and meeting the demands of people living in poverty. Pharmacists are aware that they have no choice but to sell prescription-only drugs even without prescriptions for the purpose of meeting the demands and needs of people living in poverty. When distribution of pharmaceutical products is considered part of technology transfer to developing countries, norms contributing to compliance with laws and quality specifications are in the relationship of a trade-off with how to treat the poor.

Our survey in India described in Chap. 8 has demonstrated that bribery and corruption involving government officials are deep-rooted problems. The local guide hired by the author for the survey commented that even the government intervenes in the site to guide those concerned, government officials given bribes overlook problems, which is commonly observed. It was also pointed out that man power engaged in the administration is insufficient for regulating and guiding lots of minute companies.

As in Indonesia, in India also laws and regulations are established but they are not effective in reality. The case studies in these two countries are common in that whether or not various rules including laws and regulations can keep norms at a required level is substantially determined by social conditions.

10.3.2 Challenges of Markets in Emerging Countries

In the previous subsection, the authors discussed that norms are deeply related to social conditions. Here, we need to discuss what those social conditions are. The private sector is responsible for the vast majority of the supply of pharmaceutical products. In this subsection, we discuss the private sector (pharmaceutical companies and distributors).

Ranbaxy Laboratories Limited has grown to be an Indian large-scale pharmaceutical company. The case on this company introduced in Chap. 8 demonstrates that it is not easy for a company to ensure compliance with technical requirements and legal regulations and in addition, to establish corporate governance according to which the company fulfills its responsibility to society. Apart from an argument on whether or not compliance and governance are transferred from developed to developing countries in the same manner as that for technology transfer, it is also demonstrated that there is no guarantee that corporate growth and the nature of norms will be automatically intensified in parallel.

During our survey in India described in Chap. 8, the interviewee commented that locally based minute pharmaceutical companies sometimes make the content of an active ingredient at around the lower limit of the specification. Active ingredients are expensive, and saving them yields profits. With regard to this phenomenon, a Japanese engineer pointed out that they are prone to making a compromise that "there would be no problem as far as the content is within the range of the specification." This means specification is inductively established through many case studies as well as trial and error; and conversely, the specification thus established is deductively applied so that it will not escape from the tendency toward inferiority. In emerging countries, if products are not sufficiently good enough to export to developed countries but meet specifications when sold and someone desires to buy them, then manufacturers of such products may sell them.

On the other hand, Japanese manufacturers of generic medicines determine the quantity of an active ingredient to be charged, while taking into account the specification ranges for that active ingredient. They say that when they can anticipate how much a generic medicine would deteriorate during its shelf life, they take appropriate actions to prevent the content of an active ingredient in the finished product from decreasing below the lower limit of the specification during the period of transportation, and then ship the product. Norms represent the attitude of being faithful to quality requirements even though no one can see the adherence. It is not sufficient, however, to conclude this issue using the diagnosis of the phenomenon, that is, lack or immaturity of quality concept. We need to discuss the market in which economic activities actually take place.

One of the typical challenges for the market is observed in India, in which a double standard exists as follows: good quality pharmaceutical products manufactured by large-scale pharmaceutical companies are primarily available in urban areas, whereas medicines of inferior quality manufactured by locally based pharmaceutical companies are distributed in rural areas. This market challenge is attributable to the following social structure and customs: the existence of many minute pharmaceutical companies and the structure of supply of their products to public dispensaries, and government procurement process and bribery.

The term "double standard" used above requires a special explanation: this "double standard" is not caused by two systems intentionally designed by a supplier. A specialist in quality control of pharmaceutical companies mentioned how difficult it is for a single company to have two systems and intentionally use either system depending on the situation. Assuming a medicine for which the specification range for its active ingredient is set at 90%–110%, the content at 95% before shipment meets the specification. However, if there is a possibility that the active ingredient may be deteriorated by 5% or more during distribution due to the climate[4] in regions where the medicine is to be distributed, then it is reasonable not to ship the medicine.

They can say that the medicine meets the specification because the content of its active ingredient is 95% when it is sold. In addition, if the medicine is sold at affordable prices, then there would be plenty of cases in which no one hesitates to sell the medicine as qualified goods. What the term "double standard" means here refers to the intentional use of either of the two ways depending on the situation, as described above.

In the national markets of Indonesia and India, if the governments would keep quiet about the difference in quality between pharmaceutical products available to the group of people having higher economic power and those used by the poor (i.e., the double standard), then the incentives companies see when conducting their activities might not be linked with the challenge of the market, that is, eradication of poor quality pharmaceuticals. Actually, there might be an incentive for companies to adapt themselves to the market in which the double standard for quality is accepted because such adaptation could ensure profits with less management efforts.

The world cannot be clearly divided into two types of economies, that is, the formal economy in which people having economic power reside and the informal economy in which people living in poverty reside. Active exchanges and interactions occur between the two (Neuwirth 2011). The same person sometimes resides in the formal economy and other times, in the informal one. The same thing occurs in international transactions. It is said that African countries always regard India and China with enmity. Our analysis of the IMPACT (see Chap. 6) revealed that at a meeting of the Executive Board of WHO, Niger criticized carefully without mentioning a name of exporting country, saying "Africa is the dumping ground for drugs such as counterfeit medicines." The individual who was transiently moved to the WHO pointed out during our interview that African countries treat India and China like enemies. This observation might be a stereotypical view in which the bureaucracy and politicians deny the informal society.

---

[4]The quality of pharmaceutical products is deteriorated by the environmental conditions including but not limited to temperature, humidity, and light. Climate zones are areas with distinct climates, and there are four major climate zones in the earth. In the area with high temperature and high humidity (e.g., Southeast Asia), the quality is most affected. The stability of pharmaceutical products must be based on the climate of areas in which they will be distributed.

Regarding the fact that the acceptance rate is 49.4% for medicines illegally sold in Africa and 67.8% in India, a mean acceptance rate of legitimate pharmaceutical products exceeds 90%. A possibility was pointed out that the dissemination of low-quality medicines across Africa may be attributable to Indian companies engaged in manufacture and distribution (Ginger 2014). Emerging countries represented by India and China supply high-quality medicines to developed countries on one hand and provide medicines of inferior quality to African countries on the other hand, which demonstrates a double standard of the exporting countries. Namely, companies by themselves cause problems in the international market. The capacity to exert adequate drug regulatory functions to control the challenges of the international market is markedly insufficient in African countries, and is limited for the governments of India and China.

Our case study of India demonstrated that pharmaceuticals are goods driven not by quality but by pressure of the government, and shed light on the fact that the incentive for lots of small-scale pharmaceutical companies is to meet the government's requirements. These findings may serve to indicate that the national market might lack an incentive for companies to develop and conform to norms.

10.3.3 Constraints Due to Social/Cultural Conditions and Trade-off in Emerging Countries

In this subsection, the authors discuss the political/policy-related trade-off which occurs under the constraints due to social/cultural conditions. The greatest social constraint is a "household budget," that is, the magnitude of the poor population.

Pharmaceuticals are products of highly advanced technology and are different in characteristics from gigantic engineering such as nuclear power and space development. Pharmaceutical products are used by ordinary people in society. This means that completion and development of technology related to pharmaceuticals would require the following two: one is the availability of technology to develop and manufacture pharmaceutical products and the legislation to regulate the pharmaceutical affairs, and secondly, unlike the other types of advanced engineering, the technology needs to be complemented by the social conditions including, but not limited to, economic standard of the people, social systems and infrastructure, awareness of the people, and culture. A set of processes from the development to use of a medicine is much longer than that in any other field and is deeply embedded in society. As such, the process is substantially exposed to both direct and indirect influence of society. The social status determines the level of technology and infrastructure involving the whole life cycle of a medicine and even the level of its quality.

The journalist interviewed during our survey in Indonesia commented that in Indonesia, the problems with counterfeit medicines are a very sensitive matter, and pointed out that there are things which people are ashamed of in Indonesia, such as corruption, insufficient education, and crime, and these lurk behind the problems. She emphasized that the Indonesian society has to overcome many challenges. Importantly, she highlighted the dynamism and quality of the aspect of Indonesian society that is invisible, and also pointed out that the people's level of education and knowledge is not always linked directly with the norms of society. Our survey revealed no correlation between educational background and selection of self-medication.

Kobayashi mentioned above continues to comment, "Technology transfer to developing countries involves more serious problems; it has been more clearly recognized in recent years that the model of Westernized advancement for technology does not apply to many developing countries due to the situations of receiving countries. This recognition indicates that the value of indigenous culture in recipients needs to be given substantial consideration" (Kobayashi 1981). This comment functions as a warning against the determination based on the value of developed countries.

The specialist in pharmaceutical products described the impact of the diversity in actual situations of emerging and developing countries, in particular the social systems of Asian countries, on quality, as outlined below.[5]

> Individual states have their own systems, culture, and national characters. Thailand and Vietnam appear to do well for their capacities. Hong Kong is very good and is incompatible with China. Hong Kong fulfills its duties under the culture of UK. Hong Kong and Singapore are better than South Korea. These countries are relatively small countries. Indonesia is an extremely large country consisting of multiple ethnics, and therefore, it is difficult to implement governance. In China, nation-wide power games occur. In India, individual state governments have strong power, which substantially influences the quality; unacceptable quality products in a state may have no problems after they escape from the state and run into an adjacent state.

The pharmacists interviewed in Indonesia criticized the government for failing to make its pharmaceutical regulations effective in reality. This criticism is based on their adequate understanding that the state has to regulate and control pharmaceutical products. The pharmacists also suggested that the large size of the population who live in poverty and are not protected by the social insurance system has a great impact on the actual effectiveness of laws and regulations. We could conclude that self-medication which has become a normalized practice in emerging and developing countries is born from social conditions including poverty.

The specialist dispatched from the JICA also pointed out that the government of Indonesia is not unconcerned about the actual effectiveness of pharmaceutical regulations but instead cannot manage it because of the order of priority of their activities necessary for the state management. It would be assumed that in India, industrial development was given priority over the quality improvement for pharmaceuticals contributing to the enhancement of public health. This could be interpreted as a trade-off strategy which has to be chosen by countries without sufficient resources to attain both industrial development and enhancement of public health. In the process of building a new nation after decolonization, a lot of developing and emerging countries are forced to choose trade-off strategies.

The "quality" of pharmaceutical products and the "norms to observe the GMP" to secure the quality were the requirements set by the developed world, and were

---

[5]Interview conducted by the author on July 13, 2015 in Tokyo.

separated from the social and technological situations peculiar to emerging countries. It would be assumed that these requirements might have forced emerging countries to give priority to the development of their exporting businesses over the promotion of public health in their own countries.

Medicines manufactured by emerging countries were very rapidly incorporated into the global economy and as a result of this, they did not undergo adequate inter-mediate stages where they can develop their own technology, otherwise they should be more mature in quality. It could also be interpreted that the dissemination of poor quality pharmaceuticals would represent dissemination of different levels of quality depending on the situations of individual countries although such levels of quality should have remained within the countries in which they were generated. Emerging countries had no choice but to accept the logic of developed countries for the purpose of functioning as a supply source of medicines to the developed world. The result of this is a double standard.

10.3.4 Policy-Makers' Will to Address Market Challenges and Public Health

In this subsection, the authors discuss the "corporate" and "government" sectors, both of which are responsible for the market.

In his book entitled "Technology Development in Post War Japan—Imitation or Creation," Nakaoka states that, "Companies are directly responsible for industrial technology, and the technology is strongly linked with market challenges that may change at different times. In other words, fostering technology from which we learn how to find solutions to market challenges plays a substantial role" (Nakaoka 2002).

Our interview survey described in Chap. 9 demonstrated that generic manufacturers have become motivated to aim at achieving the quality that is equivalent to or more than that of their counterpart originators. In Japan, this motivation is attributable to the incentives generated by the two conditions: one is that under the universal health insurance system, patients' access to health care is assured, and the other is that newly developed medicines and generics are competitive in the same market. In addition, it would be assumed that the policies of the Japanese government to increase pen-etration rates of generics[6] offered an incentive to generic manufacturers to further improve the quality.

On the other hand, how the Japanese pharmaceutical administration and regula-tions function also needs to be evaluated. The Council for Investigation of Informa-tion on Quality of Generic Products established by the industry in collaboration with the government of Japan, the practice that the administrative authorities regularly sample products from the market and perform quality tests on the sampled products, and GMP audits conducted at the time of an official approval granted constitute the

---

[6]The volume-based penetration rate of generic medicines in Japan increased, as indicated by 48.7% in 2014 and 59.0% in 2016. The government of Japan aims at increasing this rate to 80% by 2020.

mechanism for maintaining the quality at adequate levels. The people of Japan gain benefits from the mechanism through the health insurance system, and feedback from consumers who are the beneficiaries and feedback involving pharmaceutical affairs would contribute to the maintenance and improvement of the Japanese systems on pharmaceutical products. These situations were not achieved in a single day but represent the social mechanism created by long-term interactions between the private sector that is responsible for the supply of pharmaceutical products, as described by Nakaoka, and the public sector. In these situations, private companies can ensure profits and at the same time, the government can be responsible for public health through its policies; both of the two are attained.

When turning our eyes to emerging and developing countries, we notice that meeting the demands of their own countries is a challenge for the national market. In both Indonesia and India, there are large gaps between urban and rural areas in terms of health care. For these countries, growing to aim at being a supply source of medicines for the world was a challenge of the national governments' policies to promote industrial development.

The sufficiency rate of essential medicines in Indonesian public medical institutions is 65.5% (Suwa 2014). Sixty-seven percent of the total population in India live in rural areas, and the sales of medicines in the rural areas only account for 17% of the total (Institute for Health Economics and Policy 2015). This imbalance is a great challenge for the national market and at the same time, is a challenge for public health. Our survey in Indonesia revealed that at officially qualified pharmacies, prescription-only drugs are sold without prescriptions and that prescription-only drugs are sold at drugstores and warung, both of which are illegal distribution channels. The greatest reason for these facts is because many people living in poverty are not protected by the public health insurance system.

When poor people buy medicines for self-medication in order to save the money necessary for visiting medical doctors, the underlying thought is that "It's better than using no drugs," which is supported by a previous study in Sudan (Alfadl et al. 2013). Poor quality pharmaceuticals vary depending on how poor the quality is. If the expiration dates for medicines are past but there is no problem with their use, in reality, such medicines could be distributed to meet the demands of people living in poverty. This phenomenon might represent the result of seeking a point of compromise to balance the market challenge for poor people and the challenge for public health.

Ginger states that the elimination of low-quality pharmaceuticals without accepting any exception is a sensitive issue because such elimination may take away the route of access to medicines from people living in poverty (Ginger 2014). This statement embodies the dilemma the poor face, that is, they have to accept the reality that they have no choice but to live under the poor and rich divide.

Nakaoka states "the quality of market needs is influenced by the quality of society in which the market needs are generated. Technology is also influenced by the quality of society while making dynamic responses to the market needs" (Nakaoka 2002). The expression "the quality of society" has a wide range of meanings and is ambiguous. In addition, this wording might imply not diversity but a more linear relation between superiority and inferiority. Consequently, for the sake of this book, the authors read what Nakaoka tries to communicate as the impact of the poor, which constitute large proportions of the population in emerging and developing countries.

People living in poverty have less purchasing power and are inferior in the capacity of proposing issues and needs. Private companies would rarely set the poor as a target of their business activities. The poor have a limited power to raise market challenges. Many people living in poverty should be the main players of public health and their limited power has an impact on what Nakaoka refers to as the expression "the quality of society." Our survey in Indonesia described in Chap. 7 demonstrated that local pharmacists paid a lot of attention to education for patients. This illustrates the attitude of local pharmacists who try to understand the social problems for people living in poverty and support them at the grassroots level.

It is reported that the government procurement process for medicines in India functions as the government's measures to rescue locally based pharmaceutical companies, rather than providing an opportunity in which these companies can learn how to find solutions to market-related challenges (Kamiike 2007). In other words, the "public health-related challenges for the poor" is not well balanced with the "market challenges." The situations of individual countries that force their governments to accept their own domestic disparities reflect on the policy-makers' will.

10.4 WHO's Policies on Pharmaceutical Products

The important target of the WHO is the poor called "Bottom Billion"; people comprising one billion people in low-income countries and one billion people in middle-income countries.[7] The supply of essential medicines and newly developed medicines to save lives at prices affordable by the poor and in adequate quality was an important challenge to the WHO.

10.4.1 WHO's Policies on Pharmaceutical Products (1): Enhancement of Essential Medicines

The WHO fell behind the United Nations with regard to implementing adequate measures to fight against AIDS and therefore, it would be assumed that the WHO took its policies on pharmaceutical products in two directions for the purpose of verifying the significance of its existence. The first policy was to enhance and spread the essential medicines the WHO developed as a measure to promote public health; the WHO has endeavored to effectively position these essential medicines. The second

---

[7]From the lecture by the ex-Deputy Secretary General of WHO at Osaka University Medical School on March 20, 2014.

policy was to make it easier to access new medicines which have already been approved and are expected to be developed in the future.

The first policy, i.e., "enhancement of essential medicines," had two issues to be addressed. The first issue was concerned with "quality," in which the "quality" conforming to specification is indispensable. The WHO endeavored to build systems to support developing and emerging countries, e.g., issuing various types of guidelines including the WHO-GMP and establishing the prequalification system. The concept of essential medicines is not adopted by many developed countries however. This is attributable to the prejudice that the concept of essential medicines was originally developed for developing countries and to the fact that pharmaceutical products exceeding the types of essential medicines have already been supplied in adequate quality and quantity. It would be assumed that because of these reasons, developed countries may not be so enthusiastic about the essential medicines.

At the Conference of Experts held in Nairobi in 1985, the WHO appealed to the international society that medicines with secured quality should be supplied, with the intention to focus the attention of developed countries to the essential medicines. It would, therefore, be considered that the IMPACT implemented the WHO's policies on pharmaceutical products although belatedly. The World Bank has pointed out two issues from the perspective of donors: it would not be possible to obtain the essential medicines for developing countries from developed countries or in case if it is possible, then their prices are not internationally reasonable.

The second issue of the first policy "enhancement of essential medicines" was "making newly developed medicines be essential medicines," which is represented by the addition of newly developed anti-HIV/AIDS drugs to the list of essential medicines. In other words, the issue was to increase the ease of access to new medicines. Specifically, the hurdle to access the existing new medicines was lowered. It was decided at the World Health Assembly that the WHO gives advice on the essential medicines (Yamane 2008). As newly developed drugs were added to the list of essential medicines, discussion about problems related to patents began within the WHO. Out of 311 medicines included in the list of 2005, 13 anti-retroviral agents and other 16 medicines including antimalarial drugs were protected by patents (Yamane 2008).

The lowered hurdle was contrary in nature to the second policy, i.e., "promotion of access to newly developed medicines," described in the next subsection, because the second issue of the second policy was to promote the enforcement of compulsory licensing, resulting in alleviation of the monopolizing control of newly developed medicines with intellectual property rights.

10.4.2 WHO's Policies on Pharmaceutical Products (2): Promotion of Access to Newly Developed Medicines

The second policy, i.e., "promotion of access to newly developed medicines," had two issues to be addressed. The first issue was "development of new medicines" to urge development of new medicines to treat infectious diseases. Specifically, its goal was to establish a mechanism or an international environment to promote the development of new medicines to treat neglected diseases endemic in developing and emerging countries (WHO 2006). The background behind this first issue set by the WHO was that the developed world had a monopoly on the capacity to develop new medicines and in addition, neglected diseases were regarded as endemic ones and were not considered to be an important issue for the developed world. Under these circumstances, the WHO had no choice but to be involved in the discussion about enforcement of intellectual property rights as an incentive to the pharmaceutical companies in developed countries, because the private sector of the developed world had a monopoly of the development of new medicines.

The WHO always prioritizes public health and therefore, it was difficult for the WHO to discuss how to treat profits of research-based pharmaceutical companies. The WHO had to pay attention to the argument by the pharmaceutical industry that profits yielded by the protection of newly developed medicines with intellectual property rights represent a return on investment for the purpose of developing next new medicines. Thus, the WHO became involved in the discussion about enforcement of intellectual property rights. It would be assumed that this involvement might make emerging countries consider that the WHO intervened in this issue by taking sides with the developed world. The WHO might have no intention to provoke this resentment of the emerging world, though. The resentment was clearly demonstrated by the following criticism made by Brazil at a meeting of the Executive Board of WHO held in 2009: "The WHO was the proper forum to discuss methodologies to protect public health and promote access to medicines but not to discuss the enforcement of intellectual property rights."

There existed another background situation behind the first issue "development of new medicines" of the second policy "promotion of access to newly developed medicines": in the developed world, classical types of infectious diseases were steadily controlled and the development of new medicines such as antibiotics slowed down (WHO 1996). In addition, both in the developed and the developing as well as emerging worlds, the area of noncommunicable diseases (or lifestyle-related diseases) became a more important marketing target for pharmaceutical companies, and consequently, their development resources were shifted to this area. From the perspective of public health, the WHO considered it necessary to fight against the two, i.e., infectious and noncommunicable diseases (WHO 1997). However, occurrences of reemerging infectious diseases and dissemination of drug-resistant bacteria have reduced the effectiveness of therapies which were previously effective, which has produced a strong sense of crisis. The pharmacists working in Indonesian pharmacies commented that they have deep concerns about the development of drug resistance due to self-treatment with antibiotics. They recognized that this is a great risk of losing therapeutic measures. They were concerned about people living in poverty who cannot purchase an adequate amount of antibiotics and have to stop taking them halfway through treatment. India, Russia, and China are problematic countries in terms of the development of multidrug-resistant tuberculosis (WHO 2016), which might not be unrelated to the problems emerging countries have in the quality and use of medicines.

The second issue of the second policy "promotion of access to newly developed medicines" was "promotion of the enforcement of compulsory licensing" to alleviate the monopolizing control of newly developed medicines with intellectual property rights because, although the TRIPS Agreement permits compulsory licensing, it became difficult in reality to grant compulsory licenses. The authors have already discussed the conflicts of interests related to compulsory licensing and here, would like to only state that the TRIPS Agreement might have a great impact on the WHO's policies on pharmaceutical products.

In light of the above-stated discussion, the authors consider that the difficulties the WHO faced with regard to its policies on pharmaceutical products could be summarized into the two points as described below.

a. Developed countries were not always enthusiastic about the enhancement of the essential medicines and expressed objection against the addition of newly developed medicines to the list of essential medicines. On the other hand, emerging and developing countries had limited resources they could utilize for the whole pharmaceutical administration.
b. Developed countries were dissatisfied with the enforcement of compulsory licensing because it inhibits the monopoly of intellectual property rights. Nevertheless, the WHO expected the development of new medicines by the developed world, using the enforcement of intellectual property rights as an incentive to do so. Unexpectedly, the WHO's expectation was inconsistent with the enforcement of compulsory licensing. In addition, the involvement of WHO in the discussion about intellectual property rights caused emerging and developing countries to have a sense of distrust against the WHO and developed countries.

The Sustainable Development Goals (SDGs) include the enforcement of compulsory licensing. This might serve to indicate that the United Nations understood the above-described situations and reflected the WHO's intention more strongly in the SDGs than in the Millennium Development Goals (MDGs).

10.5 Significance of Existence of WHO/IMPACT and Their Limitations

In this section, the authors discuss the association between the significance of the existence of the WHO and the failure of the IMPACT.

The WHO was established by the intergovernmental agreement among the countries concerned, and is an independent international agency with its own initiative under international law; the initiative is separate from that of the United Nations. The WHO is one of the agencies within the family of the United Nations and is entrusted with improving and controlling global public health as specified in the Constitution of WHO. As of May 2016, 194 countries participate in the WHO. Each Member State has the right to cast one vote. This means that at the World Health Assembly which is the supreme decision-making body for WHO, arguments made by developing and emerging countries are relatively stronger. In this respect, the World Health Assembly is different from the United Nations Security Council.

The WHO has substantially contributed to the advancement of policies on pharmaceutical products. In 1975, the WHO introduced the concept of essential medicines to identify the values of pharmaceutical products. In the Declaration of Alma-Ata in 1978, the WHO clearly positioned these essential medicines in public health. Consequently, the international problems with medicines are directly related to how significant the existence of WHO is, as specified in the Constitution. Under these circumstances, it was quite natural for the WHO to lead the IMPACT. Although the IMPACT reached a deadlock, it called the attention of international society to the problems related to the quality of medicines, which should be highly appreciated.

10.5.1 Problems Which Were not Made Visible and Hastiness of IMPACT

As described in our investigation of IMPACT in Chap. 6, at the Conference of Experts held in Nairobi in 1985, the WHO first mentioned poor quality pharmaceuticals primarily distributed in developing countries. It would be understood that at that time, the WHO had concerns about counterfeit medicines because the counterfeits might shake the foundation of the essential medicines the WHO continued to place importance upon. It would be assumed that at that time, there might be neither data that clearly visualized the whole picture of risks related to public health nor analyses of such data that could convince the Member States of the seriousness of problems related to counterfeit medicines. Only a few research reports regarding poor quality pharmaceuticals were published. At a meeting of the Executive Board of WHO held in 2009, Member States criticized that the data available were not sufficient enough to identify the magnitude of the problem.

In other words, the problem of poor quality pharmaceuticals had been left unaddressed for more than 20 years. Establishment of the IMPACT caused the problem of poor quality pharmaceuticals, which had been considered to affect only developing countries, to have an impact on developed countries, and as a result of this, the developed world had to take some action to address the problem.

Sporadic case studies reported until today used the content of an active pharmaceutical ingredient as an indicator to determine the quality of the medicine concerned.

Their results indicated one of the following: conforming or nonconforming to specifications. In many reports, drugs were determined counterfeit mostly when they did not contain active ingredients at all or contained highly toxic impurities at extremely high concentrations, resulting in serious health hazards such as death. The judgment as regards counterfeit or not was increasingly based on arbitrary conclusions, which might have fostered the foundation in which emerging and developing countries accumulated a feeling of resentment in an invisible manner. What made the situation even worse was the presence of only a few prospective studies using the definition of counterfeit medicines.

The WHO recommended that a "definition" was necessary as a tool for information exchange among Member States so as to combat counterfeit medicines. However, the "definition" proposed by the IMPACT had no practical value as a justifiable judgment on counterfeiting and merely complicated the discussion. Since data available did not visualize risks, the IMPACT employed a strategy to appeal to international society. The Taskforce regarded counterfeiting as a crime, and frequently used sensational words such as "threat," "combat," and "eradicate." This attitude represented a failure to visualize risks objectively. These words were frequently quoted by scientific papers and the media, and thus, widely disseminated.

The basic stance of IMPACT was based on the Concept Paper that had been prepared in advance. The gist of the Concept Paper was the same as the idea underlying the Nairobi Meeting, and was taken over by the IMPACT. Under the circumstances in which data were insufficient, the WHO focused on "counterfeit medicines" and treated substandard medicines as something like an afterthought. The person dispatched to the WHO clarified during our interview that this afterthought was based on an emotional desire to terminate the wandering discussion. It would be assumed that the abbreviation SSFFC into which substandard and counterfeit medicines were integrated with the same row might cause further confusion and turbulence.

In the Concept Paper that provided the base for the establishment of the IMPACT, it is clearly stated that the IMPACT was established without forming an adequate level of international consensus for its establishment. This represented the frustration the WHO had with the fact that the WHO should have addressed the issue but actually left it unaddressed for over 20 years. In addition, the idea underlying the Nairobi Meeting held in 1985 was taken over by the IMPACT. This means that the WHO/IMPACT did not fully consider the changes noted in the world during this 20-year period, that is, the rise of emerging countries and the consequences of the rise.

In summary, the following facts all provoked the resentment from emerging and developing countries: the WHO failed to visualize the problem of poor quality medicines; the WHO had to be involved in the issue of intellectual property rights; many international organizations such as INTERPOL and customs were members of IMPACT; and the IMPACT was hastily established without obtaining an approval from the World Health Assembly of WHO. These factors interacted with one another in a complicated manner, making it difficult to make the international society understand the problem of poor quality pharmaceuticals and form an international consensus about the problem, which resulted in the subsequent failure of IMPACT.

10.5.2 Externalization of the Problem

Externalization of the problem involves perception. Recognizing the problem of poor quality pharmaceuticals as a result of crime implied the presence of criminals outside the system for pharmaceutical products that has been built up by the WHO and its Member States.

One specialist who once worked for the WHO and was therefore engaged in the IMPACT commented during our interview that the countries such as India and China that most strongly protested against the IMPACT were deeply troubled by the problem of counterfeit medicines, and were afraid that if the problem might be uncovered by a third party because such a divulgence would make their situation really difficult. This comment would make us understand that behind the scenes of diplomacy, emerging and developing countries mutually criticized one another, from which it would be assumed that these countries might be aware that the quality-related problem existed inside their own countries. However, we could not totally rule out a possibility that in emerging and developing countries, there might be no move to externalize the problem, although the WHO did so, because it was said that even among the administrative authorities of Member States, the issues of responsibility and of saving or losing face were always the focus of their concern. This was assumed to be especially true between the authorities responsible for pharmaceutical administration and regulations and the law enforcement authorities such as the police.

Meadows points out a tendency "to blame someone because individuals are apt to think that a cause of a problem exists not here but there" (Meadows 2008). The WHO considered that the problem of counterfeit medicines was caused by individuals outside the system and has been built up by the international society and Member States. This consideration might be advantageous to emerging countries as well.

It would be assumed that the externalization of the problem by the WHO might enable the administrative authorities of each country to blame other countries, rather than admitting their responsibilities. The problem of counterfeit medicines that have been claimed strongly by the developed world has a great deal of political significance on whether or not the emerging and developing world will lose or save face; specifically speaking, if an emerging or developing country was named for counterfeiting, then that country would lose face; conversely, if "criminals" were determined to be responsible for counterfeiting, the magnitude of losing face would be lowered and they might be able to blame other countries for such criminals. Consequently, emerging and developing countries mutually criticized one another and expressed their dissatisfaction with the developed world. Namely, the problem was externalized both internationally and inside each Member State, and this would be a cause to accelerate the confusion.

The externalization of the problem was also greatly advantageous for the WHO because the Organization did not need to name a particular Member State. It is the culture of WHO as a consultant to give consideration, which may be excessive, to Member States. The element "consideration" is indispensable in the real world but works to blur the contour and nature of an event. In his book entitled "The Geopolitics of Emotion," Moisi explains that the sinuous emotions by emerging countries toward developed countries make the world go around[8] (Moisi 2009). Interactions of emotions are more complicated in the international organizations consisting of many member states than in bilateral relations. Administration of the IMPACT became difficult because many countries and international organizations participated in the Taskforce. In addition, the emotions toward the developed world that the emerging and developing world commonly had in their fundamental thoughts made things more complicated.

10.5.3   Mistakes and Limitations of WHO/IMPACT

In this subsection, the authors undertake an in-depth discussion about the reasons why the IMPACT reached the deadlock.

In this book, the authors have so far focused on the changes in the international society and emerging countries for about 20 years from the 1980s in which the Nairobi Meeting was held to the time at which the IMPACT was established. The IMPACT formulated the following strategies: a communication strategy which targeted patients, healthcare professionals, and the media; a law enforcement strategy in collaboration with INTERPOL and police; a regulatory implementation strategy to promote the GMP and quality control; and a technology-related strategy to assess technologies to combat counterfeit medicines and promote exchange of information about these technologies.

The Concept Paper that provided the base for the establishment of the IMPACT was extremely optimistic about how to address the problem. This would mean that the Paper fail to design and administer the IMPACT. Although the IMPACT reached a deadlock, the expenses required until the deadlock were as small as about 200 million Japanese Yen, which remained within the scope of awareness-raising campaign for Member States. Cracking down activities involving INTERPOL caused emerging countries to have antipathy toward the WHO/IMPACT and developed world.

It is not reasonable, however, to conclude that the limitations of WHO would only be attributable to its failure in strategies and operation. The strategies of IMPACT did not incorporate the factors that have been discussed in this book, i.e., changes in global supply–demand structure, social situations in emerging and developing countries, issues to be addressed in relation to technology transfer, and issues associated with intellectual property rights. Their strategies were all symptomatic, which would result from the mistakes in the awareness of WHO/IMPACT; or the lack of awareness. However, the mission of WHO and its scope cannot exceed what is prescribed by the Constitution of WHO. The WHO works as a consultant for all Member States

---

[8]In his book entitled "The Geopolitics of Emotion," Dominique Moisi states that feelings of humiliation which have sunk in the deep thoughts of emerging and developing countries cannot be ignored.

including developed to developing countries and at the same time, its recommendations have no binding force. The difficult issue for the WHO to address was that India and China have grown as supply sources for generic medicines to the world but were not mature enough to ensure that their national entities concerned all complied with laws and regulations without fail.

One thing clarified through our discussion in this book is the negative issues generated by international conflicts of interests over intellectual property rights. These rights separate newly developed medicines from generics and in addition, make it difficult for emerging and developing countries to balance industrial promotion and public health. In other words, intellectual property rights divide the globe into two worlds, i.e., developed and emerging/developing. Throughout the period during which these two worlds confronted each other regarding how an international consensus can be reached regarding the enforcement of intellectual property rights and how monopolizing control of these rights can be managed, the developed world has made concessions one after another. Nonetheless, the framework for intellectual property rights apparently has not changed at heart and so far, has been incorporated into the global system and has induced conflicts of interests.

The conflicts of interests generated by global systems regarding intellectual property rights underlie the limitations of WHO/IMPACT.

10.6   Challenges of International Cooperation for Technology Transfer

The WHO provides technical guidance to emerging and developing countries, and developed countries also give their cooperation in achieving technology transfer. The authors discuss this international cooperation while referring to the cases of the Japan International Cooperation Agency (JICA). Specifically, we look back on the episodes described during our interview by the three specialists who were dispatched at a request of the JICA to Indonesia so as to provide technical guidance regarding pharmaceutical products (see Chap. 7).

The first two interviews may serve to shed light on the gaps between the international cooperation provided by the JICA and the actual situations. The first gap exists among three stages of a hierarchical structure, i.e., a sponsor, a planning/management unit, and individuals responsible for on-site training. The second gap exists between the assistance providing countries and the receiving countries. When a sponsor is Japan, a planning/management unit is the JICA, and individuals dispatched are responsible for providing guidance on-site. Essential questions raised by on-site trainers suggest the challenges of bureaucracy-driven international assistance that need to be addressed, and this does not only apply to the JICA.

The third interview highlights the challenges assistance-receiving countries face. More importantly, it suggests that in Indonesia, the conditions for the rescue that were proposed by the IMF weakened the power of the government to control the state. It would be assumed that donors might tend to put recipients together only by looking at similar situations noted in the recipients although recipients are different from one another in many things. Negative aspects resulting from institutionalized assistance, given by international organizations, warrant further critical discussion. The episodes described in Chap. 7 strike to the heart of this matter, but because of their nature, they are hardly documented on official records to be utilized as feedback.

The dissatisfaction with international assistance that was expressed by developing countries at a meeting of the Executive Board of WHO (see Chap. 6.6) was toward the developed world and at the same time, might represent their irritation about the challenges inherent in their own countries.

10.7 Lessons

Firstly, the problem of poor quality pharmaceuticals cannot be understood from the viewpoints of intensifying pharmaceutical regulations and improving undeveloped technologies. Secondly, the WHO's policies on pharmaceutical products have two aspects which are contradictory to each other, and modern medicine is inconsistent. This can be expressed as dilemma. Thirdly, it is difficult for emerging and developing countries to intensify norms and find solutions to market challenges. Fourthly, some interactions of the international environment contributed to the failure of WHO/IMPACT. These four factors are complicated within themselves and mutually interact with one another to form a structure producing conflicts of interests.

The WHO has the greatest concern about the quality of generic medicines. The WHO by itself has positioned generics as the essential medicines for public health. The private sector is responsible for the vast majority of the supply of pharmaceutical products. New medicines developed by the private sector of the developed world yield enormous economic benefits by monopolizing control of them with intellectual property rights. These new medicines are widely available as generics after the period of monopolizing control expires.

Generics are affordable and are resources for global public health. However, access to generics by people living in poverty is still not secured. The private sector is also responsible for the vast majority of the supply of generic medicines, and private companies do not run a business without ignoring the economic principles. There is no doubt about the idea that pharmaceutical products are essential resources for public health, although in reality, the economic principles overweigh this idea.

In light of the above, the authors summarize the lessons from the theme of this book as described below.

10.7.1 Locality and Globalization of the Problem

Poor quality pharmaceuticals have two sources: one which exists within a country and the other which is inflow from other countries. Policies on pharmaceutical products are put into the hands of the state sovereignty. Each country has its own local situations regarding the priority of policies, availability of resources, limitations of their own capacities, and the international and national face the state has to keep. This can be collectively referred to as "locality." Pharmaceuticals easily cross borders. When an issue originally confined to a single state begins to spread beyond the region and across the world, the issue is incorporated into the move of globalization. We remember the following fact that is nothing special: behind the phenomenon that is collectively referred to as the "problem of poor quality pharmaceuticals," processes which complicate a phenomenon generated locally are embedded in the move of globalization.

Does simplifying a phenomenon having a complicated background identify a true issue or make us consider that there might be a true issue? We need to think about the answer to this question. The WHO emphasized criminality when the Organization raised the question about quality and it could be interpreted that this emphasis might fail to make all stakeholders stand at the same starting point. It could also be interpreted that the global-scale conflicts of interests might forcefully alter the significance of the WHO's questioning.

10.7.2 Conflicts of Interests Over Intellectual Property Rights

Intellectual property rights regarding pharmaceutical products substantially contributed to the phenomenon of complicating the problem. Intensification of and inclination to intellectual property rights began in the US. These rights are strongly effective particularly in the field of pharmaceutical products.

The battle for intellectual property rights between the developed and the emerging/developing worlds symbolizes globalization. This is also an issue of determining how an outcome resulting from knowledge is allocated to whom as a benefit. More accurately speaking, this is an issue of determining who would gain "1" or "0" as a result of "monopoly." The field of pharmaceutical products represents a typical case of this issue, and the allocation of the outcome under globalization is in many cases similar to the case noted in the field of pharmaceuticals. The trickle-down theory is expected to provide benefits of globalization, and now, we need to make a clear judgment on whether or not this expectation is adequate.

10.7.3 Significance of Political Commitment

People living in poverty have difficulties in accessing pharmaceutical products and substantially influence the incentive to improve quality. Pharmaceuticals are products supplied by the private sector to gain profits and in the supply, pricing is given priority over quality. For the promotion of public health, governments of emerging and developing countries have the policy to supply medicines while prioritizing affordable prices. The WHO claims that the governments of Member States have an insufficient commitment to address the problem of counterfeit medicines, and here, that commitment means strengthening penalties for counterfeiting and seriously cracking down on counterfeits.

Distribution of pharmaceutical products represents an infrastructure that does not function until it is embedded in society. Simply intensifying pharmaceutical and law-enforcing regulations cannot resolve the problem of counterfeit medicines. Political will to equally cover the demands of informal and formal sectors is necessary. This political will has to be embodied in systems which must be effective.

10.7.4 Responsibilities of International Organizations and Member States

The WHO/IMPACT lacked the social perspective with which they should have tried to find solutions to the challenges of public health emerging and developing countries faced, in relation to the change noted in the nature of pharmaceuticals along with globalization, that is, they were more strongly characterized by products yielding profits. This lack, together with the lack of data visualizing risks, resulted in the externalization of the problem, and consequently, obscured the location and contour of the problem. Externalization of the problem results in two challenges: one is the inconsistency that exists within own policies on pharmaceutical products, and the other is the awareness by Member States of their responsibilities and roles for the essential medicines.

The limitations of WHO/IMPACT are related to two reasons that mutually interact with each other. One reason is because the Constitution of WHO specifies that the WHO is not entitled to force Member States to do what the Organization recommends. The other reason is because Member States do not achieve their roles in and contribution to the promotion of public health in both their own countries and the world to an extent commensurate with their economic positioning. Member States by themselves are responsible for the change in the nature of the WHO and its limitations.

10.8 What This Book Suggests

In this book, the authors wonder why the IMPACT initiative established under the auspices of WHO reached a deadlock, and attempted to reach the heart of the problem of quality of pharmaceutical products by investigating the strategies formulated by the IMPACT, e.g., those concerned with pharmaceutical regulations and cracking down, and in addition, by analyzing the technological and social aspects relevant to the quality problem. The authors would like to summarize this chaotic problem of poor quality pharmaceuticals as described below.

Social situations are not uniform among countries. The magnitude of this nonuniformity is small among developed countries and great in emerging and developing countries. Rich and poor people seem to live together in the same society, and the poor is greater in number. The healthcare service market the poor can access is virtually separated from that the rich access. Quality is cost and is reflected in pricing. To people who cannot afford medicines sold at reasonable prices, such medicines are supplied even with quality sacrificed (and this means, in this way, the market functions). Why does this work? The answer is because pharmaceutical products are the goods essential for saving lives and QOL. Many people who cannot receive legitimate health care live in the circumstances in which they have to accept anything that is "better than nothing."

At the international level, the gap, confrontation, and mutual dependence between the developed and the emerging/developing worlds have intensified. The key words here include technology transfer, emerging countries which have become supply sources for the world, the HIV/AIDS pandemic which incidentally occurred, monopolizing control with intellectual property rights, and the WHO's policies on pharmaceutical products. Namely, the international environmental factors and the national factors inside emerging countries were combined, which contributed to the emergence of poor quality pharmaceuticals and their distribution across the world. We should not consider if this is a good effect resulting from globalization or not, but instead, we need to understand that globalization not only connects goods, capital, human resources, and information beyond borders but also complicates and alters the relationships of interests among stakeholders.

We should not overlook what underlies the conflicts of interests, that is, the change of pharmaceutical products; pharmaceuticals are no more an ethic or ideal but have changed to become goods that are dependent on monopoly and economic principles. Well, this expression may not be accurate. What has altered is our awareness, behavior, and values that have been influenced by globalization. The method of entrusting individual countries with the spread of the essential medicines so that they were expected to individually take their own actions independently was insufficient to make the essential medicines widely available for the purpose of promoting "Health for All." Globalization has accelerated the increasing gap between developed countries and the other ones. This acceleration is more remarkably noted in people living in poverty who are socially vulnerable. Countries which were exploited under colonization and after the end of World War II, were tossed about by international organizations are also vulnerable in the international society. It would be assumed that this might be the reason why these countries expressed fierce opposition against the IMPACT.

The discussion in this book starts with the perspective on separation of the quality and ends up with the separation of the market. When the separation of the market advances to an unacceptable level, such advancement represents serious division in society. In other words, the problem of quality of pharmaceutical products could be an indicator for separation and division in society. Both inside each country and on a global level, division in society and community is observed everywhere. Inclination to economic competition through the use of monopolizing control overwhelms activities which try to repair the divided situation. We need to initiate discussion with the aim of establishing a system to ensure development, supply, and quality assurance of pharmaceutical products which is under the joint administration and management of the international society. This means that we need to answer the question: Can we incorporate a new incentive which can replace the monopolizing control including the concept of intellectual property rights, into the global system?

The pharmaceutical industry strongly claims that development of new medicines is associated with risks, and requires huge amounts of investment and long periods of time. However, the industry scarcely mentions the voluntary contribution made by many patients that is necessary to verify the efficacy and safety of pharmaceutical products, and hardly talks about victims during the development process. No one argues loudly that the verification in human subjects is "human experimentation" under the name of "clinical study". Patients are medical resources necessary for the development of new medicines and at the same time, constitute the market.

This is true despite the fact that the Declaration of Helsinki formally states the ethical principles for medical research involving human subjects. This might be equivalent to sealing off the discussion about who should possess knowledge obtained from information on ten thousands to dozens of ten thousands of patients subsequent to the launch of a medicine in the market. The most difficult issue regarding the problem of intellectual property rights is not the protection of the rights but "monopolizing control" with the rights. Is this peculiar to the pharmaceutical industry? In other words, is the pharmaceutical industry the only industry which cannot obtain financial resources for long-term development without depending on the "monopolizing control?" Why should pharmaceutical products be treated as exceptions when compared with other industries or other inventions? In-depth discussions about these questions have not been made at a satisfactorily level.

In inverse proportion to improved performance of computers due to technical innovation, their prices have reduced. Conversely, prices of pharmaceutical products have risen in proportion to improved performance. What causes this difference? No one has answered this question. We should not keep the ideal in name only but step forward to make primary healthcare services available with the essential medicines be a common social capital and to substantiate the concept of global public goods (Kaul et al. 1999). We can no more rely on benefits from the free economy, which has been accelerated by globalization and left to take its own course. We have to devise political goals and methods with which we can give high priority to the establishment of a global safety net.

References

Africa Japan Forum. 2003. Koeizuyaku he no Akusesu [Access to Anti-HIV Drugs]. https://www.
google.com/search?hl=ja&hq=inurl%3Awww.ajf.gr.jp&ie=Shift_JIS&oe=Shift_JIS&filter=0&
q=TRIPs&submit.x=8&submit.y=9. (In Japanese). Accessed 22 March 2014.

Alfadl, A.A., M.A. Hassali, and M.I. Ibrahim. 2013. Counterfeit drug demand: perceptions of
policy makers and community pharmacists in Sudan. *Research in Social and Administrative
Pharmacy* 9(3): 302–310. https://doi.org/10.1016/j.sapharm.2012.05.002. https://www.ncbi.nlm.
nih.gov/pubmed/22835708. Accessed 1 September 2018.

FDA. 2013. FDA prohibits manufacture of FDA-regulated drugs from Ranbaxy's Mohali, India,
plant and issues import alert. http://www.fda.gov/NewsEvents/Newsroom/PressAnnouncements/
ucm368445.htm. Accessed 13 December 2016.

Ginger, Z.J. 2014. Poor quality drugs in global health. Maryland Center for Economics and Policy.
http://mcep.umd.edu/project/poor-quality-drugs-global-health. Accessed 16 September 2015.

IFPMA. 2016. Intanetto Hanbai to Anzenna Iyakuhin Akusesu ni Kansuru
IFPMA/PhRMA/EFPIA/JPMA no Kyodo Seimei ni Tsuite [Joint Announcement by
IFPMA/PhRMA/EFPIA/JPMA on Internet Sales and Safe Access to Medicines]. http://www.
jpma.or.jp/event_media/release/pdf/120724_01_j.pdf. (In Japanese) Accessed 8 September
2016.

Institute for Health Economics and Policy. 2015. Shin Keizai Seicho no Iryo Hosho Seido ni kansuru
Chosa Kenkyu -Indo no Iryo Hosho Seido- Hokokusho [Survey Research on Medical Security
Systems—the Medical Security System in India—Report]. Institute for Health Economics and
Policy, Association for Health Economics Research and Social Insurance and Welfare, a General
Incorporated Foundation: Tokyo, Japan. (In Japanese).

Kamiike, Atsuko, and Takahiro, Sato. 2006. WTO no Boeki Kanren Chiteki Shoyuken
(TRIPS) Kyotei to Indo Iyakuhin Sangyo [WTO trade-related intellectual property
rights (TRIPS) agreement and pharmaceutical industry in India]. *JCAS* 7(2): 149–
167. http://www.cias.kyoto-u.ac.jp/files/img/publish/alpub/jcas_review/JCAS_Review_07_02/
JCAS_Review_07_02_009.pdf (In Japanese). Accessed 26 August 2018.

Kamiike, Atsuko. 2007. Indo Iyakuhin Sangyo ga Kakaeru Kadai [Challenges to be Addressed by
the Pharmaceutical Industry of India], ed. Kubo, Kensuke, 55–79. Chiba: Nihon no Jenerikku
Iyakuhin Sangyo to Indo, Chugoku no Seiyaku Sangyo [Generic Medicine Industry in Japan and
Pharmaceutical Industry in India and China]. IDE-JETRO. (In Japanese).

Kato, Akiko. 2003 Progressive development of protection framework for pharmaceutical invention
under the TRIPs agreement: focusing on patent rights. *Bulletin of Institute of Intellectual Property*.
http://www.iip.or.jp/summary/pdf/detail02j/14_19.pdf. Accessed 4 September 2016.

Kaul, Inge., Grunberg, Isabelle., and Stern, Marc A. 1999. *Global Public Goods—International
Cooperation in the 21st Century*. Trans. United Nations Development Programme.

Kobayashi, Tatsuya. 1981. *Gijutsu Iten -Rekishi kara no Kosatsu: Amerika to Nihon* [Technology
Transfer—Discussion from History: USA and Japan]. Tokyo: Bunshindo. (In Japanese).

Meadows, Donella H. 2008. *Thinking in Systems: A Primer*. Trans. USA: Sustainability Institute.

Minato, Kazuki. 2007. *Indo Seiyaku Sangyo—Hatten no Seidoteki Haikei to TRIPS Kyoteigo no
Henka* [Pharmaceutical Industry in India: The Institutional Background of Development and
Changes after TRIPS Agreement]. ed. Kubo Keisuke, 21–54. In Nihon no Jenerikku Iyakuhin
Shijo to Indo, Chugoku no Seiyakusangyo [Generic drug market in Japan and Pharmaceutical
industry in India and China]. Chiba: IDE-JETRO. (In Japanese).

Moisi, Dominique. 2009. *The Geopolitics of Emotion*. Trans: Doubleday.

Mori, Makoto. 1994. *Tokkyo no Bunmeishi [History of patents from the perspective of civilization]*.
Tokyo: Shinchosya. (In Japanese).

MSF. *Kusuri no Nyushu wo Habamu Kabe no Kokufuku [Challenges to the Wall that
Blocks Access to Medicines]*. http://www.msf.or.jp/about/access_campaign/overcome.html. (In
Japanese) Accessed 9 October 2016.

Nakaoka, Tetsuro. 2002. *Sengo Nihon no Gijutsukeisei [Technology Development in Post War Japan -Imitation or Creation-]*. Tokyo: Nihonkeizai Hyoronsya. (In Japanese).

Neuwirth, Robert. 2011. *Stealth nations: the global rise of the informal economy*. Trans. New York: Pantheon Books.

Osawa, Toshihiko. 2008. TRIPS-PLUS strategy of the US, *Journal of Intellectual Property Association of Japan* 5(1): 55–56.

Suwa, Yoshihiro. 2014. *Kokumin Kaihoken heto Ugokidashita Indonesia HerusuKea Sangyo no Miryoku to Otoshiana [Attractive Points and Pitfalls of Healthcare Industry in Indonesia Moving Towards Universal Health Insurance Coverage]*. ITmedia Executive. http://mag.executive. itmedia.co.jp/executive/articles/1406/02/news014_4.html. (In Japanese) Accessed 1 September 2018.

WHO. 1996. *World health report 1996—fighting disease, fostering development*. http://www.who. int/whr/1996/en/. Accessed 26 August 2018.

WHO. 1997. *World health report 1997—conquering suffering, enriching humanity*. http://www. who.int/whr/1997/en/. Accessed 26 August 2018.

WHO. 2006. *WHA59.24. Public health, innovation, essential health research and intellectual property rights: towards a global strategy and plan of action*. http://apps.who.int/medicinedocs/ documents/s21428en/s21428en.pdf#search=%27WHO.+2006.+WHA59.24%. Accessed 27 October 2014.

WHO. 2016. Global tuberculosis report 2016. http://apps.who.int/iris/bitstream/10665/250441/1/ 9789241565394-eng.pdf?ua=1. Accessed 13 December 2016.

Yamane, Hiroko. 2008. *Chiteki Zaisanken no Gurobaruka -Iyakuhin Akusesu to TRIPS Kyotei-* [Globalization of Intellectual Property Rights -Access to Medicines and TRIPS Agreement-]. Tokyo: Iwanamishoten. (In Japanese).

Chapter 11
Epilog

This book discusses the status regarding the quality of pharmaceutical products; the logics of developed countries intersect with the actual situations of emerging and developing countries in a complicated manner. Not only in the theme of this book but also in many other fields, it is universally observed that the logic of the developed world is given priority. In the past, Japan was an underdeveloped country in terms of technology and society and was also a least developed country. The path of the current-day emerging and developing countries overlaps that of Japan.

In his book entitled "GENERIC," J.A. Greene presents a good picture of the sudden rise, bitter struggles, and defamation of the generic pharmaceutical industry in the US. He describes the US situation in the 1960s (Greene 2014) as outlined below.

> Regarding generic medicines, the belief in their promising future and value conflicted with the situation supported by the laws stating that only branded medicines prescribed by medical doctors can be dispensed by pharmacists.
>
> An attorney at law, a member of the Subcommittee on Antitrust Policy, warned the other members, saying, "Large-scale pharmaceutical companies try to make the government agencies conduct surveillance to determine if their trademarks are unlawfully used, by utilizing the euphemistic expression of 'counterfeiting.'"
>
> In addition to this conflict, fear of counterfeit medicines was not eradicated over a period from early in the 19th century to the end of the 1960s in the US. There was no doubt that the Mafia was engaged in counterfeiting medicines.

His descriptions notify us that the contemporary theme the authors discussed in this book already occurred many decades ago in the US; it is like déjà vu all over again. In the US, at that time, large-scale pharmaceutical companies attacked generic medicines by claiming that generics were related to crime and of poor quality, whereas there existed a group believing that generics would be useful for public health. The above-described situation in the US experienced in the past is generally the same as the current attitude of research-based pharmaceutical companies in developed countries toward the generic medicines manufactured and distributed by developing and emerging countries. The difference is that the current-day developed world makes

© Springer Nature Singapore Pte Ltd. 2020   213
S. Kimura and Y. Nakamura, *Poor Quality Pharmaceuticals in Global Public Health*, Trust 5, https://doi.org/10.1007/978-981-15-2089-1_11

the best use of the slogan of WHO to promote public health, as a cover for their attacks against generics.

Greene describes how a category of generic medicines was established and the history of entanglements involving generics. The described course was a process whereby knowledge was placed in the public domain. During the process, there existed a conflict between the profit of private companies and the public benefit insofar as a balance between the two, whether or not those concerned were aware of this conflict. Private companies were most concerned with the maximization of economic profits. As opposed to this, people were dissatisfied with the long period of time they had to wait until they received the benefits available from knowledge that should have been in the public domain.

Will this conflict be resolved in the near future? Probably not. Until the present, low-molecular compounds have constituted the mainstream of pharmaceutical products. Manufacture of these compounds is relatively easy and because of this, it is not so difficult to produce generics of their low-molecular counterpart originators. These generics are not identical to their counterpart originators but it is practical to produce clinically equivalent generics. At present, antibody agents are located at the forefront of pharmaceutical products. What corresponds to generics of low-molecular compounds is now referred to as "biosimilars" for antibody agents. The difficulty in manufacturing biosimilars is due to the essence of biologics. Biological medicinal products are characterized by the complexity and heterogeneity of their structure which is regarded as the "essence of biologics." Development of biosimilar requires thorough clarification of the quality characteristics of originators. The conventional concept of specification does not work, and verification of equivalence in clinical trials is required. This is not required for generics of low-molecular weight compounds. As of today, many pharmaceutical companies in emerging and developing countries lack both financial and development capacities to satisfy these requirements.

From middle- and long-term perspectives, however, the pharmaceutical industry in developing and emerging countries and their capacities to develop medicines will catch up with those in the developed world.[1] When emerging countries manufacture pharmaceutical products which are useful for developed countries also and are protected by patents, how will the developed world that has had the overwhelming advantage over the emerging/developing world, change their strategy to have a monopolizing control of newly developed medicines with patents?

The private sector has so far been primarily responsible for the development of new medicines, which is one of the causes provoking confrontation between the private and the public sectors. A venture company developed medicine to treat meningitis, but there was no incentive for pharmaceutical companies in developed countries to develop such medicines. Under these circumstances, the Bill & Melinda Gates Foundation provided funds with which the US National Institutes of Health (NIH)

---

[1]The Nihon Keizai Shimbun (Japan Economic Newspaper) reported on December 5, 2017 that Sun Pharmaceutical Industries Limited, an Indian company, makes an application for approval for a medicine to treat dermatologic disease to the Japanese Ministry of Health, Labour, and Welfare (MHLW), and that Luye Pharma Group Ltd., a Chinese company, submits a clinical trial plan notification regarding a medicine to treat psychiatric disease to the MHLW.

and a research laboratory in the Netherlands developed the medicine. No patent fees were charged and a manufacturing company was selected through public invitation. The profit is only 50 cents. Historians of the future may evaluate this case highly as a good model from the outset, and one which contributes to opening a door toward the possibility of altering the existing global pharmaceutical development framework.

The contribution by "*Oyaitoi-gaikokujin*" (foreign advisors hired by the Japanese government for their specialized knowledge) that Japan experienced in the Meiji Era represented the transfer of intellectual property. It is said that Japan's development was a miracle, but the assistance and support Japan received from many foreign countries during that era was uncommon and should, therefore, be regarded as a miracle.

We generally tend to consider that judgments or decisions made by individuals having authority are justifiable and accept them as they are. We are tainted by the belief that even complicated problems can be resolved by direct management or intervention. When a problem is set, one assumption underlying this setting is that the problem will promptly be resolved. In other words, the problem which is the theme of this book was combined with the idea of management, and was framed by the WHO to be a problem that can easily be resolved.[2] This book has demonstrated that the awareness of WHO, government agencies of countries, and policy-makers representing the pharmaceutical industry lacked social and technological perspectives and also that these entities failed to objectify themselves. Consequently, "WHO and international organizations led by the developed world tried to put the whole matter of poor quality outside the globalized system which they have driven and accelerated. This attitude can be a kind of denial for the sake of developed world."

The present-day globalization is primarily driven by the ideology of developed countries.[3] This is common to the intervention of the developed world in the developing world that is suggested by Miichi (Miichi et al. 2001). The difference between the two is that emerging countries proactively try to integrate globalization into their own policies on both public health and industrial promotion so as to catch up with the developed world. This is the challenge for countries who desire to reach developed countries. Knowledgeable individuals observe that, "people in developing countries are apt to talk about the state-of-the-art things of the world." This comment depicts that high-income countries have been a model for the rest of the world to observe. A total of 194 Member States of the WHO entrust the Organization with the authority to lead public health, which means that the healthcare systems of wealthy countries function as a model for middle- and low-income countries.

The Constitution of WHO states that to make modern medicine and drug regimens using the modern medicine widely available across the world is the mission of WHO,

---

[2]D. Kahneman designates the phenomenon in which the way of presenting a problem has an unreasonable impact on thinking or preference, as "framing effect." He demonstrates that acceptance of such framing as it is requires enormous amounts of cost and results in political failure of significance (Kahneman 2012).

[3]Hirofumi Uzawa, a Japanese economist, points out that the theory of neoclassical economics was incorporated into politics by US President Donald Regan, UK Prime Minister Margaret Thatcher, and Japan Prime Minister Yasuhiro Nakasone (Uzawa 2000).

in much the same way as genetic code is written, one outcome of which was the establishment and failure of IMPACT. The interactions and conflicts of interests between the developed and the emerging/developing worlds represent the essential aspect of present-day globalization. Apart from the incidental involvement of the pandemic of HIV/AIDS in the confrontation, the interactions and conflicts of interests do not randomly occur, but greatly depend on the initial conditions that specify the world. This characteristic is noted in the Constitution of WHO and in the framework for intellectual property rights.

Official development assistance (ODA) is the transfer of incomes from high- to low-/middle-income countries. This improves cash flow in receiving countries but social stocks do not automatically improve. When Japan struggled to become a modern nation, the good fortune for Japan was the contributions by "*Oyaitoi-gaikokujin*" (see Box 2) in developing human resources with many talents and in-depth expertise, which remained in Japan to revolutionize the nation to the Meiji era. The human resources are the source of development to be triggered from the inside. The essence of technology transfer is transfer of knowledge. If you are successful in acquiring intellectual properties and incorporating them into a cycle of development, then you can have the power to improve the driving forces forward.

Meadows states: "When we face problems, we blame other persons and something else because we are not responsible for the problems; we try to resolve them by focusing on measures outside ourselves. For example, starvation, poverty, environmental deterioration, economic instability, unemployment, chronic diseases, drug addiction, war, and similar problems have not disappeared, despite analyses and splendid technology. This is because these are essentially system-related problems." Thus, she emphasizes that rebuilding the existing system is the only way to resolve the problems (Meadows 2015). This means that there are no immediate ways to find resolutions. The international assistance needs to focus on the accumulation of human resources in emerging and developing countries, and these countries need to have a robust political will not to leave the division of society.

References

Greene, J.A. 2014. Trans. *GENERIC The unbranding of modern medicine*. John Hopkins University Press.

Kahneman, Daniel. 2011. *Thinking, Fast and Slow*. USA: Farrar, Straus and Giroux.

Meadows, H. Donella 2015. *Thinking in Systems A primer*. White River Junction, VT, USA: Chelsea Green Publishing Co.

Miichi, Masatoshi, Saito Osamu, and Wakimura Kohei. 2001. *Shippei, Kaihatsu, Teikokuiryo—Ajia ni okeru Byoki to Iryo no Rekishigaku* [Diseases, Development and Imperial Medication—History on Diseases and Medication in Asia]. Tokyo: Tokyo University Press. (In Japanese).

Uzawa, Hirofumi. 2000. *Shyakaiteki Kyotsu Shihon* [Social Common Capital]. Tokyo: Iwanami Shinsho. (In Japanese).

Printed in Great Britain
by Amazon